Tyndale Old Testament Commentaries

Volume 4

TOTC

Numbers

To my father John
and the memory of my mother Grace (1916–1980)

TYNDALE OLD TESTAMENT COMMENTARIES

VOLUME 4

GENERAL EDITOR: DONALD J. WISEMAN

NUMBERS
AN INTRODUCTION AND COMMENTARY

GORDON J. WENHAM

Inter-Varsity Press

IVP Academic
Evangelically Rooted. Critically Engaged.

InterVarsity Press, USA
P.O. Box 1400
Downers Grove, IL 60515-1426, USA
World Wide Web: www.ivpress.com
Email: email@ivpress.com

Inter-Varsity Press, England
Norton Street
Nottingham NG7 3HR, England
Website: www.ivpbooks.com
Email: ivp@ivpbooks.com

©1981 by Gordon J. Wenham

First published 1981
Reprinted in this format 2008

InterVarsity Press®, USA, is the book-publishing division of InterVarsity Christian Fellowship/USA® <www. intervarsity.org> and a member movement of the International Fellowship of Evangelical Students.

Inter-Varsity Press, England, is closely linked with the Universities and Colleges Christian Fellowship, a student movement connecting Christian Unions in universities and colleges throughout Great Britain, and a member movement of the International Fellowship of Evangelical Students. Website: www.uccf.org.uk.

USA ISBN 978-0-8308-4204-9
UK ISBN 978-1-84474-259-2

Set in Garamond 11/13 pt
Typeset in Great Britain by Avocet Typeset, Aylsebury, Bucks
Printed in the United States of America ∞

InterVarsity Press is committed to protecting the environment and to the responsible use of natural resources. As a member of Green Press Initiative we use recycled paper whenever possible. To learn more about the Green Press Initiative, visit <www.greenpressinitiative.org>.

Library of Congress Cataloging-in-Publication Data

Wenham, Gordon J.
  Numbers: an introduction and commentary / Gordon J. Wenham.
    p. cm.—(Tyndale Old Testament commentaries; v. 4)
  Originally published: 1981.
  Includes bibliographical references and index.
  ISBN 978-0-8308-4204-9 (pbk.: alk. paper)
  1. Bible. O.T. Numbers—Commentaries.   I. Title.
  BS1265.53.W46 2008
  222'.1407—dc22

                                                    2008031507

British Library Cataloguing in Publication Data

A catalogue record for this book is available from the British Library.

P	19	18	17	16	15	14	13	12	11	10	9
Y	27	26	25	24	23	22	21	20	19		

CONTENTS

Maps

GENERAL PREFACE

The aim of this series of Tyndale Old Testament Commentaries, as it was in the companion volumes on the New Testament, is to provide the student of the Bible with a handy, up-to-date commentary on each book, with the primary emphasis on exegesis. Major critical questions are discussed in the introductions and additional notes, while undue technicalities have been avoided.

In this series individual authors are, of course, free to make their own distinct contributions and express their own point of view on all controversial issues. Within the necessary limits of space they frequently draw attention to interpretations which they themselves do not hold but which represent the stated conclusions of sincere fellow Christians.

In the Old Testament in particular no single English translation is adequate to reflect the original text. The authors of these commentaries freely quote various versions, therefore, or give their own translation, in the endeavour to make the more difficult passages or words meaningful today. Where necessary, words from the Hebrew (and Aramaic) Text underlying their studies are transliterated. This will help the reader who may be unfamiliar with the Semitic languages to identify the word under discussion and thus to follow the argument. It is assumed throughout that the reader will have ready access to one, or more, reliable rendering of the Bible in English.

This commentary on Numbers from Dr Wenham provides a thorough, scholarly exegesis, readily understandable by any reader. He faces up to critical questions such as those of date and

authorship, and stresses the difference in theological emphasis
between this book and the rest of the Pentateuch. Prominent topics well covered include the character of God, the land, and the people of God; nor does he neglect the Christian use of this book. His
study should do much to rescue the book of Numbers from being
a little-read, rarely-quoted source of Old Testament texts, and help
us to appreciate it as an integral part of Scripture worthy of detailed
study in its own right.

Interest in the meaning and message of the Old Testament con-
tinues undiminished and it is hoped that this series will thus further
the systematic study of the revelation of God and his will and ways
as seen in these records. It is the prayer of the editor and publisher,
as of the authors, that these books will help many to understand, and
to respond to, the Word of God today.

D. J. Wiseman

AUTHOR'S PREFACE

If 'Guide me, O Thou great Jehovah' is one of the best known hymns in the world, the book of Numbers, whose story that hymn summarizes, is much less familiar. Its very title puts the modern reader off. In ancient times numbers were seen as mysterious and symbolic, a key to reality and the mind of God himself. Today they are associated with computers and the depersonalization that threatens our society. Furthermore the pervasive influence of the romantic movement with its stress on spontaneity and individual freedom has made it yet more difficult for us to appreciate Numbers' insistence on organization, ritual and hierarchy. In time and ethos there is a great gulf between the book and our age, which it is the commentator's task to try to bridge.

Bridge-building demands that first and foremost the commentator should expound the plain historical meaning of the text, what it meant to the original author and his readers. Exegesis is therefore the main concern of this, as indeed of most biblical commentaries. Critical discussions of the sources, their date and the editorial processes by which they were combined to form the book tend to subjectivity, and anyway are of minor importance in recovering the original meaning of the text. For these reasons I have restricted discussion of such issues to the introduction and additional notes. More vital to the Christian reader is guidance on the abiding significance of the text. Speaking about the stories in Numbers, the apostle Paul remarked that 'they were written down for our instruction' (1 Cor. 10:11). Again limitations of space preclude a thorough treatment of this theme, but in the introduction and at the end of each section of commentary I have very briefly indicated how the New Testament uses the material in Numbers. This I hope will be of value to those who have the task of applying the teaching of Scripture to the modern church.

Most of this commentary has been written during a year's sabbatical leave spent at the Hebrew University in Jerusalem and at the Oxford Centre for Postgraduate Hebrew Studies. I am most grateful to these institutions for their support. I should also like to thank the Queen's University of Belfast for allowing me leave of absence, and particularly my colleagues in the department of Semitic Studies and in the faculty of theology who undertook my teaching and other university duties while I was away. Most of my scholarly debts are acknowledged in the footnotes. Professors Jacob Milgrom and Calum Carmichael, however, deserve special mention. Their friendly willingness to share their insights into the interpretation of the biblical text enriched my understanding of Numbers at many points. Finally, I must also thank Professor D. J. Wiseman for inviting me to write this commentary and for his personal encouragement throughout my academic career, Miss Lesley Townsend and Miss Gretta Totten for typing it, and David Payne, Desmond Alexander and my wife for help with proof-reading.

Originally I had dedicated this commentary to my parents. The present dedication reflects the sad circumstance that after the manuscript was complete my mother was killed in a car crash. Her family and friends miss her greatly. Her sons in particular owe her an incalculable debt. We thank God for all she taught us and did for us, and rejoice that she is now one with the church triumphant enjoying for ever the presence of her Lord and Saviour.

Gordon Wenham

CHIEF ABBREVIATIONS

ANET	*Ancient Near Eastern Texts*[2]
BASOR	*Bulletin of the American Schools of Oriental Research*
BZAW	*Beihefte zum Zeitschrift für die alttestamentliche Wissenschaft*
CBQ	*Catholic Biblical Quarterly*
DJD	*Discoveries in the Judaean Desert*
E	Elohistic source
HTR	*Harvard Theological Review*
HUCA	*Hebrew Union College Annual*
IBD	*The Illustrated Bible Dictionary*
IDB	*The Interpreter's Dictionary of the Bible*
IDBS	*The Interpreter's Dictionary of the Bible*, Supplementary volume, 1976
IEJ	*Israel Exploration Journal*
J	Yahwistic source
JAOS	*Journal of the American Oriental Society*
JBL	*Journal of Biblical Literature*
JJS	*Journal of Jewish Studies*
JQR	*Jewish Quarterly Review*
JSS	*Journal of Semitic Studies*
P	Priestly source
PEQ	*Palestine Exploration Quarterly*
RB	*Revue Biblique*
TB	*Tyndale Bulletin*

VT	*Vetus Testamentum*
VTS	*Supplements to Vetus Testamentum*
ZAW	*Zeitschrift für die alttestamentliche Wissenschaft*

Commentaries

Baentsch	*Exodus, Leviticus, Numeri* by B. Baentsch (Hand-Kommentar zum Alten Testament), 1903.
Binns	*The Book of Numbers* by L. E. Binns (Westminster Commentaries), 1927.
Calvin	*Commentaries on the Four Last Books of Moses* by J. Calvin, 1563 (ET, 1852).
Cazelles	*Les Nombres*[3] by H. Cazelles (Bible de Jérusalem) 1971.
Dillmann	*Die Bücher Numeri, Deuteronomium und Josua*[2] by A. Dillmann (Kurzgefasstes exegetisches Handbuch zum Alten Testament), 1886.
Gispen	*Het boek Numeri I–II* by W. H. Gispen (Commentaar op het Oude Testament), 1959, 1964.
Gray	*A Critical and Exegetical Commentary on Numbers* by G. B. Gray (International Critical Commentary), 1903.
Greenstone	*Numbers with Commentary* by J. H. Greenstone (The Holy Scriptures), 1939.
Heinisch	*Das Buch Numeri übersetzt und erklärt* by P. Heinisch (Die heilige Schrift des Alten Testaments), 1936.
Keil	*The Pentateuch* III by C. F. Keil (Biblical Commentary on the Old Testament).
Noordtzij	*Het boek Numeri* by A. Noordtzij (Korte Verklaring der Heilige Schrift), 1941.
Noth	*Numbers: A Commentary* by M. Noth (Old Testament Library), 1968.
Rashi	*Pentateuch with Rashi's Commentary: Numbers* (ET by M. Rosenbaum and A. M. Silbermann).
Saalschütz	*Das Mosaische Recht*[2] by J. L. Saalschütz, 1853.
Snaith	*Leviticus and Numbers* by N. H. Snaith (New Century Bible), 1967.
Sturdy	*Numbers* by J. Sturdy (Cambridge Bible Commentary), 1976.

| de Vaulx | *Les Nombres* by J. de Vaulx (Sources Bibliques), 1972. |
| Wenham | *The Book of Leviticus* by G. J. Wenham (New International Commentary on the Old Testament), 1979. |

Texts and versions

AV	Authorized Version (King James)
BHS	Biblia Hebraica Stuttgartensia
LXX	The Septuagint (pre-Christian Greek version of OT)
MT	Massoretic Text
NEB	New English Bible
NIV	New International Version
RSV	Revised Standard Version
TEV	Today's English Version

INTRODUCTION

1. Title and contents

Numbers is the English translation of the Greek title of the book *Arithmoi*, a title no doubt given to it because of the census returns found in chapters 1 – 4 and 26. The fifth word of the book, *bĕmidbar* 'in the wilderness', constitutes its Hebrew title. This more aptly describes its contents, for it is wholly concerned with the forty years the tribes of Israel spent wandering in the wilderness between Mount Sinai and the plains of Moab.

Numbers begins with a series of directions organizing the people to march from Sinai to the promised land. The tribes are counted, their arrangement in the camp and on the march is specified, the unclean are expelled from the community, the altar and the Levites are dedicated to the service of God, and a second passover is celebrated. The nation is now ready to begin the advance towards Canaan (1:1 – 10:10). Twenty days later the journey begins, difficulties are encountered on the way, but Kadesh on the borders of

Canaan is safely reached (10:11 – 12:16). From Kadesh twelve spies
are sent out to inspect the land. Their report is so discouraging that
the people propose returning to Egypt (13:1 – 14:4). God then threatens to annihilate the nation, but is persuaded by Moses' intercession
to commute the sentence to forty years' wandering in the wilderness.

Chapter 15 contains laws about cereal offerings, libations, high-
handed sins, and tassels on garments. Chapters 16 – 17 relate
several rebellions against the prerogatives of the priests and Levites.
Chapter 18 sets out the offerings they are to receive and chapter 19
the rules about purification after death.

In chapters 20 – 21, after an interval of nearly forty years, the
movement towards the land resumes with conquests over Canaanites in the Negeb and Amorites in Transjordan.

The rest of the book (chapters 22 – 36) relates what happened to
Israel as they waited to cross the Jordan opposite the city of Jericho.
These chapters include Balaam's prophecies about Israel's future (22
– 24), idolatry at Baal Peor (25), another census (26), laws about land,
festivals and vows (27 – 30). The defeat of the Midianites and the
request of the tribes of Gad, Reuben and Manasseh to settle in
Transjordan are the subject of 31 – 32. Finally there is the list of
places at which Israel camped (33) and a group of laws dealing with
the distribution of the promised land (34 – 36).

2. Structure

This brief summary of the contents of Numbers highlights one of
the gravest problems it poses for commentators: how is the order,
or disorder, of the material to be explained? Is there any reason for
the apparently random juxtaposition of law and narrative, which
makes Numbers look like 'the junk room of the priestly code'? Most
commentators offer no explanation except a source-critical one, suggesting that the laws come from a priestly source (P) whereas the narratives are for the most part derived from the epic JE traditions. That
Numbers contains various sources is obvious, but this does not solve
the mystery of the editor's method. Why should he have arranged
his source material as he did, when the material itself shows he was
a person deeply concerned with order and organization?

De Vaulx suggests that the mixture of law and narrative enables the editor to put over the idea that 'the saving history and the law are not simply past events, but that they are always contemporary. The successive redactors of stories and laws all remind their contemporaries that the saving history concerns everyone and that it is today that they must do the will of God.'[1] In his commentary he endeavours to show that there is a coherence between the theme of the laws and the narratives: both are concerned with the nation's journey towards Canaan. The laws prescribe how Israel is to travel organized as the holy army of God to the land of promise, and what they are to do when they arrive there (cf. 1 – 10, 28 – 30, 34 – 36), while the narratives describe the twists and turns in the journey (11 – 14, 20 – 21). This analysis is basically correct, though it does leave certain features in the centre of the book (e.g. chapter 15 and the Balaam episode) unexplained. More detailed study suggests a motive for the inclusion and position of much of this other material.

Throughout the Pentateuch chronological notices divide the material into large cycles of narrative or blocks of law. Shorter units are indicated by inclusion, that is, by the repetition at the end of a section of a sentence or phrase with which it began, and by the threefold groupings of laws and narratives. All these devices are used in Numbers.[2]

Another principle explains the position of certain laws at apparently inappropriate points in the narrative. The promulgation of a law carries with it the implication that God will put Israel into a situation where she can fulfil the law. Thus laws can function as promises. The clearest example of this is to be found in chapter 15, where the demand to offer grain, oil and wine along with animal sacrifice is an implicit pledge that one day Israel will enter Canaan despite the events described in the previous chapters 13 – 14. The six laws about the land (33:50 to the end) similarly remind the reader that the promise is on the verge of fulfilment.

Much the most important principle in the arrangement of the

1. de Vaulx, p. 29.
2. Chronological notes 1:1; 10:11; 20:1; inclusion 4:24, 28; 6:2, 13, 21; 7:1/9:15; threefold groups of laws 5:5 – 6:21; ch. 15; 33:50 – 36:12; of narratives 11:1 – 12:16; 16:1 – 17:12; 22:2 – 24:25.

book of Numbers is its use of rondo form, or perhaps more exactly
variation form. It is cast in large cycles in which three important eras
of revelation, at Sinai, Kadesh, and in the plains of Moab, are separated by two bridge passages describing the journeys from Sinai to
Kadesh, and from Kadesh to the plains of Moab. Theologically these
cycles exemplify the principle of typology: history repeats itself, with
variation of course, because it is based on two factors which do not
change: God's character and man's sinfulness. Though Numbers like
other parts of the Bible[3] does present history as cyclical, there is a
development within each cycle, and it is by comparing each cycle
with the preceding one that the full significance of the later phase
becomes apparent. If typology determines the overall structure of
the book, we should also note that it also underlines the threefold
grouping of the murmuring stories in chapters 11 – 12, 16 – 17 and
the Balaam narrative in chapters 22 – 24, as well as the sixfold pattern of encampments in chapter 33.

The material in Numbers cannot be understood apart from what
precedes it in Exodus and Leviticus. The three middle books of the
Pentateuch hang closely together, with Genesis forming the pro-
logue, and Deuteronomy the epilogue to the collection. Diagrammatically the material in Exodus to Numbers may be represented as
follows:

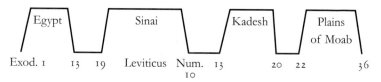

Egypt   Sinai   Kadesh   Plains
                                        of Moab

Exod. 1   13   19   Leviticus Num. 13   20 22   36
                                  10

Exodus to Numbers thus falls into three cycles, of which the second and third belong entirely to Numbers. The material in the later
cycles does not repeat that found in the first in any mechanical way.
In particular the episodes in Exodus 1 – 13 are of a markedly different character from the later periods of dramatic revelation associated with Sinai, Kadesh and the plains of Moab. But from Exodus
13:17 the recurrence of similar topics and motifs at the same point

---

3. E.g. Judges, Kings.

in the cycle seems more than coincidental. This impression is confirmed by explicit allusions to the previous occasions in the stories themselves (e.g. Num. 28:6; 32:8ff.). The synopses below bring out the parallels between the three journeys, and between the three occasions of law-giving, at Sinai, Kadesh and the plains of Moab. By definition it overlooks the differences between the three cycles, which are exegetically at least as important as the similarities. The reader is expected to compare and contrast the nation's behaviour on the different occasions.

Journeys

Red Sea to Sinai		Sinai to Kadesh	Kadesh to Moa
Led by cloud	*Exod. 13:21*	= *Num. 10:11ff.*	
Victory over Egypt	*14*		cf. *21:21–35*
Victory song	*15:1–18*	cf. *10:35f.*	*21:14–15*
Miriam	*15:20–21*	= *12*	= *20:1*
People complain	*15:23–24*	= *11:1*	= *21:5*
Moses' intercession	*15:25*	= *11:2*	= *21:7*
Well	*15:27*		= *21:16*
Manna and quails	*16*	= *11:4–35*	
Water from rock	*17:1–17*		= *20:2–13*
Victory over Amalek	*17:8–16*		cf. *21:1–3*
Jethro	*18:1–12*	cf. *10:29–32*	

Stops

Topic	Sinai	Kadesh	Moab
Divine promises	*Exod. 19:5-6; 23:23ff.*	*Num. 13:2*	*22–24*
40 days	*24:18*	*13:25*	—
Rebellion	*32:1–8*	*14:1ff.*	*25:1–3*
Moses' intercession	*32:11–13*	*14:13–19*	—
Judgment	*32:34*	*14:20–35*	*25:4*
Plague	*32:35*	*14:37*	*25:8–9*
Laws of sacrifice	*34:18ff.; Lev. 1–7.* etc.	*15:1–31*	*28–29*
Trial	*Lev. 24:10–23*	*15:32–36*	*27:1–11*
Rebellion against priests	*Lev. 10:1–3*	*16:1–35*	—
Atonement through priests or Levites	*Exod. 32:26–29*	*16:36–50*	*25:7–13*
Priestly prerogatives	*Lev. 6–7; 22*	*17–18*	*31:28–30 35:1–8*
Impurity rules	*Lev. 11–16; Num. 9:6–14*	*19*	*31; 35:9ff.*
Census	*Num. 1–4*	—	*26*

Some of the correspondences between the cycles have long been recognized by commentators, e.g. the two stories about water from the rock (Exod. 17:1–7 // Num. 20:2–13); but the overall arrangement of the material in three extended cycles has not been noted hitherto. It is not however unique. Deuteronomy is based on three long speeches by Moses (1 – 4, 5 – 28, 29 – 30). An even closer parallel is provided by the book of Genesis. The three major cycles about the patriarchs, Abraham, Jacob and Joseph, are each introduced by the formula 'These are the generations of Terah, (Isaac, Jacob)' (Gen. 11:27; 25:19; 37:2), and interrupted by shorter blocks of material introduced by the same formula (25:12; 36:1). The primeval history (Gen. 2 – 11) follows a similar pattern; narrative (2:4 – 4:26), genealogy (5:1 – 6:8), narrative (6:9 – 9:28), genealogy (10:1–32), narrative (11:1–9), genealogy (11:10–26). Except in 11:1, each section again begins with the formula 'These are the generations of'.

These parallels with Numbers suggest that casting material in triadic form was an established literary device for the biblical writers. It does not mean that they have distorted the record by using what seems to us a rather contrived form. All history writing involves selection (cf. John 20:30–31; 21:25) if any sense is to be made of the past. The Bible focuses our attention on events of theological significance, first by recording them, and second by setting them in a context which conveys their meaning. Though its methods may not be those of modern critical historians, neither ancient nor modern methods of history writing necessarily involve creating facts or being untruthful. The honesty of the biblical records is attested by their inclusion of much material that does not fit the cyclical scheme exactly: the traditions they inherited had to be handed on faithfully even where they were inconvenient from a purely literary standpoint.

3. Sources

The ultimate source of most of the material in Numbers is divine. Nearly every section begins 'The LORD spoke to Moses' or with some similar remark. But to determine how the inspired words were preserved and passed on prior to their incorporation in the Pentateuch is much more difficult and has occasioned warm controversy. This is partly because there are so few statements within the Pentateuch about the sources which its editor or editors used in compiling the book, and partly because much of the material it contains supposedly reflects conditions a long time after the Mosaic period.

Explicit indications of sources are rare in Numbers. 33:2 states that 'Moses wrote down their starting places', evidently implying that a Mosaic document was used to compile the list of Israelite encampments found in this chapter. 21:14–15 contains a quotation from the Book of the Wars of the LORD, an otherwise unknown document, usually supposed to consist of poetry.

Especially striking is the inclusion in Numbers of material that is expressly attributed to non-Israelites. There is the Amorite song recounting their victory over the Moabites (21:27–30), and the oracles of Balaam, the Mesopotamian seer hired by the Moabites and Midianites to curse Israel (23 – 24). How such material came into Israelite hands must remain conjectural. It is possible that captured Amorites or Moabites reported these sayings to their conquerors, but this is only surmise.

According to the most widely received critical theory, there are four major sources in Numbers: J the Yahwistic source, E the Elohistic source, P the Priestly source and P$_s$, a supplement to the Priestly source. In many passages scholars who believe in these sources confess themselves uncertain whether the material is to be assigned to J or E. A similar uncertainty surrounds the differentiation of P and P$_s$; but there is a wide measure of agreement on the distinction between the epic JE material on the one hand and the priestly (P and P$_s$) material on the other. The legal material and narratives illustrating legal points are assigned to P, whereas pure narratives are ascribed to JE.

According to Gray, who presents the arguments for this type of analysis most judiciously, the following passages belong to J or E:

10:29 – 12:15; 13:17b–20, 22–24, 26–33; 14:1b, 3–4, 8–9, 11–25, 39–45; 16:1b, 2b, 12–15, 25–26, 27b–34; 20:1b, 5, 14–21; 21:1–9, 11b–32; 22:2 – 25:5; 32(?); 33(?).

In chapters 32 and 33 Gray believes both JE and P are present, but he does not think they can be disentangled convincingly. The rest of the material Gray assigns to P, P$_s$ or editors.

Three main arguments are put forward in favour of this documentary analysis. First, it is argued that the diversity of the material in Numbers is best explained by the presence of several sources.

Secondly, the existence of the documents JE and P in Genesis and
Exodus makes it probable that they continue in Numbers. Thirdly,
the laws and traditions show evidence of having originated in different periods. This last argument will be considered in more detail
in the next section 'Date and authorship'. Here I shall concentrate
on the other two arguments.

The argument from diversity of subject-matter proves little about
sources. Indeed once the plan of Numbers is grasped, the mixture
of law and narrative is less suggestive of multiple sources. Nor does
the diversity of style necessarily prove the book had several authors.
If I had to draft a law, I should adopt a very different style and vocabulary from that used in commentary writing. Poets can also write
prose, but again their syntax, style and vocabulary will vary as the form
of their writing dictates. The style and vocabulary of the narrative sections of Numbers will therefore inevitably differ from the cultic laws
in the book: such differences are a function of the subject-matter.

To prove the existence of different sources it is necessary to compare like with like, cultic laws with cultic laws and narrative with narrative, and utilize the minutest points of morphology and syntax to
demonstrate diversity or homogeneity of authorship.[4] The crude vocabulary counts used in traditional source criticism do not demonstrate diversity of source, only diversity of subject-matter. Until such
refined techniques are used in pentateuchal studies one can still talk
of priestly (P) material or epic material (JE) in Numbers, as long as
it is not asserted that this material must necessarily derive from different sources or authors.

If it is accepted that Genesis is composed of J, E and P, it is natural to suppose that the same sources continue into Numbers.
However, it is universally admitted that the clearest criteria for distinguishing sources in Genesis do not apply in Numbers. For example the divine name criterion (Yahweh = J, Elohim = P or E) does
not serve to distinguish between the sources after Exodus 6. And real

---

4. See the studies of Y. T. Radday, *The Unity of Isaiah in the Light of Statistical
Linguistics* (Gerstenberg, 1973), 'The Unity of Zechariah in the Light of
Statistical Linguistics', *ZAW*, 87, 1975, pp. 30–35, 'The Book of Judges
Examined by Statistical Linguistics', *Biblica*, 58, 1977, pp. 469–499.

doublets, that is duplicate narratives or laws, are rare in Numbers, and even some of the most plausible cases are not regarded as proof of diverse origin by source critics.[5]

The source analyses of those stories which are split between J and E (e.g. Balaam 22 – 24) or between JE and P (the spies (13–14), Korah, Dathan and Abiram (16) prove equally dubious. They are dealt with in more detail at the appropriate point in the commentary. There it is shown that the supposedly early version of the stories (JE) presupposes elements found only in later versions (P or P_s), and it is argued that division into sources spoils the literary design of these tales. Finally, the way chapter 33 brings together elements from the travelogues of JE and P speaks against assigning the travel notes to different sources, if the integrity and antiquity of Numbers 33 is admitted.[6]

Were it not assumed by commentators on Numbers that J, E and P had been shown to be continuous documents in Genesis, they would have looked for alternative critical hypotheses to explain the phenomena in Numbers more economically. Recently it has been argued that Genesis has been composed by bringing together large blocks of material, e.g. the stories of Abraham, the primeval history, and joining them end to end.[7] (The classical documentary theory sees the main sources as long strands, each containing a little bit about each topic, creation, flood, Abraham, etc., which have been knitted together to form the present narrative.) The structure of Numbers outlined above lends itself to the type of analysis proposed by Rendtorff for Genesis. Thus we may think of an editor bringing together a block of material dealing with Kadesh, a block dealing with the plains of Moab and linking them to the Sinai material using short travelogues. This would avoid splitting up well-constructed

---

5. For example Gray (p. 389) recognizes that the two censuses, Numbers 1 and 26, may both derive from P, while Noth (pp. 211, 257) argues that both stories about the daughters of Zelophehad are later additions to P.

6. On the originality and coherence of Numbers 33, see G. I. Davies, *The Way of the Wilderness* (Cambridge University Press, 1979), pp. 58ff.

7. By R. Rendtorff, *Das überlieferungsgeschichtliche Problem des Pentateuch* (de Gruyter, 1977).

units within these blocks (the spies, Balaam) into contradictory sources.

4. Date and authorship

Traditionally it was held that Moses was the author of the entire Pentateuch except for the account of his death in Deuteronomy 34. This would mean it was composed in either the middle of the thirteenth century BC or in the late fifteenth century BC.[8] The chief arguments in favour of this view are statements within the Pentateuch that Moses did write some of it down (Exod. 24:4; Num. 33:2; Deut. 31:9, 22), the constant claim that the laws were revealed to him (Exod. 25:1; Lev. 1:1; Num. 1:1, etc.), and the assumption by the New Testament of Mosaic authorship (Matt. 8:4; 19:7; Luke 24:44; John 1:45).

Towards the end of the last century an entirely different view of the composition of the Pentateuch came into vogue. The analysis of the material into the sources J, E, D and P was combined with dating them long after Moses. Nowadays J is customarily dated to the tenth century BC, E to the ninth, P to the sixth and P_s later still. There is thus an immense gap between these sources and the time of Moses. It is admitted that JE may contain some old traditions reaching back to Mosaic times, but P is regarded very much as an idealization of the past, not a reliable historical record. Its laws and institutions are held to reflect the much later period in which it was written, not the Mosaic period. Numbers in particular is therefore considered a mixture of the relatively early J and E sources and the very much later P and P_s sources. These various sources were combined by a succession of editors, the last of whom worked in about the fifth century BC.

---

8. The dating of the Mosaic period is itself controversial. Till recently the scholarly consensus has favoured the thirteenth century for the exodus and conquest. J. J. Bimson, *Redating the Exodus and Conquest* (University of Sheffield, 1978) has however recently argued that the archaeological evidence fits an Israelite invasion of Canaan at the end of the Middle Bronze Age (15th century) better than at the end of the Late Bronze Age.

Full discussion of the various theories will be found in Introductions to the Old Testament.[9] Here it must suffice to indicate some of the chief objections to the late dating of the P material in Numbers. The case for a late date of P depends on a hypothetical reconstruction of the history of Israelite religion, that is at odds with what the Bible itself asserts about that history. Were it not for our age's philosophical romanticism, which views the supposed unfettered freedom of JE as a primary early and positive manifestation of the human spirit, and the law-bound rituals of P as a later and less desirable development, it is doubtful whether an exilic or post-exilic date for P would have become so widely accepted, for such a dating raises major problems. For example, in post-exilic times the ratio of priests to Levities was 12:1 (Ezra 2:36ff.; cf. 8:15), whereas the tithe law in Numbers 18:26 implies a ratio of priests to Levites of 1:10. Other institutions such as the ark, the anointing of the high priest, the Urim and Thummim, so important in the P material, had also disappeared in the post-exilic.era.[10]

If this were the only evidence for the early origin of P, it might be put down to the reliability of its tradition. Other data cannot be so easily explained this way. For example, much of the technical terminology of P became obsolete after the seventh century BC: the books of Chronicles, Ezra and Nehemiah use different terms for the same concepts as P discusses, while the book of Ezekiel (7th/6th century) stands linguistically between P and Ezra in its usage.[11]

A comparison with Ezekiel is instructive in other ways. Ezekiel quotes from and alludes to the book of Leviticus a great deal,[12]

---

9. See, for example, G. Fohrer, *Introduction to the OT* (Abingdon, 1968) or R. K. Harrison, *Introduction to the OT* (Tyndale, 1970).

10. Y. Kaufmann, *The Religion of Israel* (Allen and Unwin, 1961), pp. 175ff.

11. A. Hurvitz, 'The Evidence of Language in Dating the Priestly Code', *RB*, 81, 1974, pp. 24–56. J. Milgrom, 'Priestly Terminology and the Political and Social Structure of Pre-Monarchic Israel', *JQR*, 69, 1978, pp. 65–81.

12. Wenham, pp. 9, 359. For fuller list of parallels see D. Hoffman, *Das Buch Leviticus* (Poppelauer, Berlin, 1905–6) I, p. 478; II, pp. 3f., 81f., 319f., 359–361, 384–386.

especially the laws in Leviticus 18 – 26. But he also uses Numbers 34 to describe the limits of the new promised land, and Numbers 35:1–8 is the basis of his conception of the priestly and levitical land around Jerusalem. But whereas Numbers 35 thinks of villages of Levites scattered throughout the land, Ezekiel envisages long strips of land adjacent to Jerusalem inhabited by priests or Levites. The programme of Numbers is a practical one, but Ezekiel's is that of an utopian visionary.[13]

Similarly Deuteronomy, dated by no-one much later than the 7th century, shows great familiarity with the contents of Numbers.[14] It is important to note that it is not merely to the JE parts of Numbers that Deuteronomy alludes, Miriam's leprosy (Num. 12; Deut. 24:9), the journeys of Israel (20:14 – 21:20; Deut. 2:1–25), the conquest of Transjordan (21:21–35; Deut. 2:26 – 3:10), Balaam (22 – 24; Deut. 23:4–5), but also to material found only in P, the laws on priestly dues (18; Deut. 18:2), the incident at Meribah Kadesh (20:12; Deut. 32:51–52), vows (30; Deut. 23:21–23) and the cities of refuge (35:9–34; Deut. 19:1–13). In episodes split between JE and P (e.g. the spy story, the settlement of the two and a half tribes in Transjordan), Deuteronomy is aware of details found in both P and JE (13 – 14; 31; Deut. 1:19–46; 3:12–29). This suggests that all of Numbers is prior to Deuteronomy. And if JE and P are no longer to be regarded as originating in widely different periods of history, a reformulation of the source analysis along the lines suggested in the previous section no longer presents great difficulties.

Comparison of Numbers with other Old Testament books permits only a relative not an absolute dating, as long as the date of these other books is disputed. Rendtorff has rightly underlined the uncertainty of most critical discussion of these issues. 'We possess hardly any reliable criteria for dating pentateuchal literature. Every

---

13. Cf. M. Greenberg, *JAOS*, 88, 1968, pp. 59–66; M. Haran, *Temples* and *Temple Service in Ancient Israel* (Clarendon, 1978), pp. 112ff.

14. See M. Weinfeld, *Deuteronomy and the Deuteronomic School* (Oxford University Press, 1972), pp. 179ff. J. Milgrom, 'Profane Slaughter and a Formulaic Key to the Composition of Deuteronomy', *HUCA*, 47, 1976, pp. 1–17.

dating of the pentateuchal "sources" rests on purely hypothetical assumptions, which only have any standing through the consensus of scholars."[15] Such candour from one of the most eminent scholars in the field of pentateuchal criticism is noteworthy. If he is right, one could date almost any part of the Pentateuch to any period between the time of Moses and the time of Ezekiel.

There are some pointers in Numbers that its contents should probably be dated early within this broad period. Parallels to the census lists (Num. 1 and 26) are found in the Mari texts (18th century BC) from Mesopotamia, in old kingdom Egyptian documents, and in classical sources. The names of the tribal leaders (1:5–15) are characteristically second millennium in form. So was their mode of encampment. The tribes of Israel camped in a square with the tent of their divine king at the centre (Num. 2). This arrangement was followed by Rameses II (13th century) on his campaigns, whereas first-millennium Assyrian royal tent enclosures were circular. The role of the priests and Levites guarding the tabernacle (Num. 4) finds parallels in Hittite texts.

The design of the lampstand (Num. 8) shows it comes from the Late Bronze Age (15th to 13th centuries). Trumpets were used in the Egyptian new kingdom to summon to war and worship (Num. 10). Tasselled garments (Num. 15) are attested among Israel's neighbours from the mid-second millennium onwards. In style and form the letter to Edom (Num. 20) resembles second-millennium diplomatic notes. A bronze serpent (Num. 21) and a tent shrine used by Midianites in the 12th century have been found at Timna. The content and language of the Balaam oracles and the other poems in Numbers suggest an early date of composition and their committal to writing no later than the early monarchy period. The laws on sacrifice in Num. 28 – 29 resemble a 14th-century ritual calendar from Ugarit. Finally, the boundaries of Canaan as defined in Numbers 34 correspond to those of the Egyptian province of Canaan in texts of the 15th to 13th centuries BC.

This evidence lends weight to the book's own testimony that the traditions on which it is based originated in the Mosaic period. How much expansion, revision and rewriting they underwent in the

---

15. R. Rendtorff, *Das überlieferungsgeschichtliche Problem des Pentateuch*, p. 169.

centuries before they reached their final form, possibly in the early days of the monarchy, is hard to determine by critical methods. It is perhaps fairer to give the tradition the benefit of the doubt, than to assume everything must be late unless there is evidence to the contrary. But precise dating of the material is largely irrelevant to exegesis, for it is the final form of the text that has canonical authority for the church, and that is the focus of interest in the chapters that follow.

5. The Hebrew text of Numbers

All modern English translations of Numbers are based on the Massoretic Text (MT), that is Hebrew manuscripts of the Old Testament produced in the 10th century AD. Fragments of Numbers from caves by the Dead Sea (6 from Qumran and 2 from Murabaat) show that the Hebrew text of the book was preserved very carefully in the thousand years preceding the production of the MT.

The Dead Sea Scrolls have yet to be fully published, but preliminary study has shown that sometimes they contain readings attested only in the Samaritan Pentateuch or presupposed in the Septuagint, the third-century BC Greek translation.[16] Rarely are these readings superior to the traditional Massoretic Text, and as Gray has shown even when the ancient versions differ from the MT, they do not usually presuppose the existence of a different Hebrew reading but are attempts to interpret the MT.[17]

Only in the old poems contained in Numbers 21 – 24 is there a noticeable degree of textual corruption. Here the versions offer very little assistance in improving the text, and conjectural emendation and philological reinterpretation are necessary to make sense of the text in a few passages.

---

16. The fragments of Numbers so far published are to be found in *DJD* I, p. 53; *DJD* II, p. 78. Brief comments on other unpublished manuscripts are to be found in P. W. Skehan, 'The Qumran Manuscripts and Textual Criticism', *VTS*, 4 (1957), pp. 148–160 and idem in *Jerome Bible Commentary* II (R. E. Brown editor) (London, 1968), p. 564.

17. Gray's commentary offers the fullest and best treatment of the textual problems.

This commentary is based directly on the Hebrew text, but I have generally quoted the RSV translation except where I disagree with its rendering. Differences between it and the NEB and TEV are noted where these involve emendation of the Hebrew or significant reinterpretation of problematic words.

6. Problems of interpreting Numbers

a. The importance of ritual

In the preface I alluded to the great gulf that separates the mentality of our age from that of Numbers, a gulf that makes it very hard for us to appreciate much of the book. We are moved by the tragedy of the spies and Moses' exclusion from the promised land, and we can enjoy the comedy of the Balaam story, but these narratives comprise a relatively small proportion of the whole book. Most of it concerns various rituals and organizational details that are dull to read, hard to understand, and apparently quite irrelevant to the church in the twentieth century. Of course, these problems are not confined to Numbers: the situation is similar in Exodus and Deuteronomy, and even less narrative is to be found in Leviticus.

Yet the sheer bulk of ritual law in the Pentateuch indicates its importance to the biblical writers. This judgment is confirmed by modern anthropologists; for them the key to understanding a society's fundamental values is its ritual system.

> Rituals reveal values at their deepest level ... men express in ritual what moves them most, and since the form of expression is conventionalized and obligatory, it is the values of the group that are revealed. I see in the study of rituals the key to an understanding of the essential constitution of human societies.[18]

In short, if we do not understand the ritual system of a people, we do not understand what makes their society tick. It is not without purpose, then, that more than half of the Pentateuch, always

---

18. M. Wilson, *American Anthropologist*, 56, 1954, p. 241, quoted by V. W.
Turner, *The Ritual Process* (Routledge and Kegan Paul, 1969), p. 6.

considered the most authoritative section of the Old Testament, consists of ritual regulations, instructions about building the tabernacle, laws on sacrifice and festivals and so on. If we can understand these arrangements we shall be near to grasping the very heart of ancient Israel's religion and its values, at least according to cultural anthropologists.

But it does not come easily to us. Moderns have a built-in antipathy to ritual and symbolic gestures. We prefer to do without it, and when others use ritual, to ignore it. Victor Turner, who has probably done most in recent times to open up the interpretation of ritual symbolism, candidly admits that when he first studied the Ndembu tribe in Zambia he ignored their rituals. But

> Eventually, I was forced to recognise that if I wanted to know what even
> a segment of Ndembu culture was really about, I would have to
> overcome my prejudice against ritual and start to investigate it.[19]

Most Old Testament scholars share a similar aversion to studying ritual. If rituals are really so vital to understanding a society and its values, one would expect books on Old Testament religion and theology to devote long sections to expounding the significance of Old Testament ritual, particularly the sacrificial system. But all the recent works I have consulted slip over this aspect of biblical religion very quickly, though the practice of sacrifice was the very heart of biblical worship.

In this respect modern writers are displaying the same prejudice as the founding father of modern critical study of the Old Testament, Julius Wellhausen. He never disguised which parts of the Bible he liked and which he found uncongenial. Two fundamental value-judgments run through his greatest work, *Prolegomena to the History of Israel* (1878). The first is that freedom and spontaneity are good, while organization and ritual are bad. The second is that spontaneity is early, but organization is late. These presuppositions of his work explain how he can argue with such conviction for the order of sources JEDP. JE, where worship is free and disorganized, was

---

19. V. W. Turner, *The Ritual Process*, p. 7.

written first; D, with its organizing tendencies, came next; the hide-bound ritualism of P must be latest of all.

While it is easy to guy Wellhausen's approach to the history of Is-raelite religion by saying that he saw the liberal Protestantism of JE gradually degenerating into the mediaeval Catholicism of P, it must be admitted that his basic value-judgments are shared by very many who would not subscribe to his critical position. This no doubt par-tially explains the continuing attraction of his views, however doubt-ful some of the intellectual arguments in their favour may be. It has been shown that Wellhausen's immediate intellectual precursors were de Wette and Herder, the great philosopher of history who wrote in the late 18th century.[20] More broadly still one could describe his basic outlook as common to post-enlightenment man.[21] Boschwitz aptly summed up Wellhausen's work by saying it en-shrined the essence of Protestant individualism.[22]

This gives a clue as to why we find ritual as such, and the Old Tes-tament law in particular, so dull and uncongenial. Not only do we not realize its significance, but we minimize the importance of form and organization in both our religious and secular callings. The evangelical Christian tends to regard extempore prayer as more spir-itual than liturgy. Casual modes of dress and speech, e.g. the wide-spread use of Christian names, bespeak a society that wants to re-move the markers of social stratification which characterized it in the past. Charismatic house groups spring up to replace the long-established churches. Though such attitudes are more obvious among Protestants, similar trends are discernible within Catholi-cism. Yet ultimately we cannot get away from both ritual and or-ganization. If hand-shaking is on the decline, kissing is on the increase. A university lecturer may no longer wear a gown and mortar-board, but he can still be distinguished from his students by

---

20. L. Perlitt, *Vatke und Wellhausen* (*BZAW*, 94, de Gruyter, 1965).

21. For a survey of the transformation of European thought in the eighteenth century see P. Hazard, *The European Mind 1680–1715* (Penguin, 1964) and *European Thought in the Eighteenth Century* (Penguin, 1965).

22. F. P. Boschwitz, *Julius Wellhausen: Motive und Massstäbe seiner Geschichts-schreibung* (Marburg, 1938), p. 42.

his tie and sports jacket. Students freed from the shackles of compulsory school uniform almost immediately adopt the unofficial uniform of their peers. House groups claiming to dispense with formal liturgy and professional ministers soon establish their own idiosyncratic way of conducting worship and a recognized leadership, for without organization they wither away. Thus, however much ritual and organization are anathema to modern man, they re-emerge despite the most strenuous attempts to eliminate or minimize them.

It is no good, then, ignoring rituals as if they were of no consequence. Every society has them, though the outsider is always more aware of them than the native. The latter has grown up with them and takes them for granted, while someone entering a foreign culture is immediately conscious of the differences between his own customs and those of the people he is now living among. He soon realizes that he must assimilate his habits to his neighbours', if he wishes to be accepted as part of their society. This outward assimilation of behaviour to the accepted norms of the society is taken at least to indicate conformity to local values and attitudes. It is thus essential to attempt to understand a society's rituals, if we are to understand its values; and if we are to understand its religion, we must pay very close attention to its manner of worship and the rituals associated with it.

b. The essence of ritual

What then is the essence of religious ritual in the Bible? It is a means of communication between God and man, a drama on a stage watched by human and divine spectators. Old Testament rituals express religious truths visually as opposed to verbally. They are the ancient equivalent of television; the ancient equivalent of radio was prophecy and prayer. These were the recognized modes of communication between the human and divine worlds in Bible times. Like words, rituals are a two-way channel of communication. On the one hand they are dramatized prayers, expressing men's deepest hopes and fears; on the other hand they are dramatized divine promises or warnings, declaring God's attitude towards man.

A clear example of the two-sided nature of ritual is found in the

ordeal prescribed for a woman suspected of adultery (Num. 5:11–
31). Basically this is a curse that if she is guilty, she will be childless.
The curse, however, is elaborated in several different ways: the
woman offers a sacrifice, her hair is untied, she drinks a potion containing dust from the tabernacle floor, and the very words of the
curse. These actions underline the seriousness of the suspected
fault. The ritual gives public expression to the national and the divine abhorrence of adultery. It is both a prayer to God for judgment
if she is guilty and a warning from him that she will not escape. This
double-sided nature of ritual is also evident in the New Testament
rites. Baptism declares both the forgiveness of sins by God to the
penitent and is also a confession of faith by the believer (Acts 2:38;
Rom. 6:1–9).

Though these rituals may be likened to television, the analogy is
rather weak. Television may be vivid, but it does not permit spectator participation, which is of the essence of Old Testament rituals.
Everyone involved had to play his own role on a public stage under
the eyes of man and God. No-one would fancy being put to the public ignominy of the adultery ordeal. Very few would care for the expense, let alone the messiness, of Old Testament sacrifice. It is easy
to sing,

> Just as I am, without one plea,
> But that Thy blood was shed for me;

but to bring a whole bull, kill it, skin it, chop it up and then watch
the whole lot burn on the altar, would be quite another matter. Yet
this was precisely what someone who offered a burnt offering (Lev.
1) was expected to do. Without doubt these Old Testament rituals
were a prodigiously powerful teaching medium; the most eloquent
modern preacher is dumb by comparison.

It is important to notice that the use of rituals and symbols was
not confined to crisis situations that would precipitate the need for
a public ordeal or the offering of sacrifice. The Pentateuch is concerned to create a total religious environment replete with reminders
of God's presence, his promises and his demands. The most striking of these is the tabernacle itself, described in much detail in Exodus 25 – 40. Like the rituals we have already discussed, there are two

aspects to the symbolism of the tabernacle. It served both as a pledge of God's presence with his people, and as a warning of his holiness and his demands. Similarly the food laws (Lev. 11; Deut. 14) and prohibitions against mixtures (Lev. 19:19; Deut. 22:9–11) acted as daily reminders that God had separated Israel from the nations to be a people of his own possession, and effectively served to segregate the holy people of God from their Gentile neighbours. Today people wear rings, badges and crosses as marks of status or convictions. The Old Testament also provides for such symbolic ornaments. Everyone had to wear tassels on their clothes as a reminder that they belonged to a kingdom of priests and a holy nation and therefore had to obey the commandments (Num. 15:38–41; Deut. 22:12). Deuteronomy prescribes that extracts from the law had to be bound in little boxes and carried on the forehead or wrist (*tĕpillîn*) or fastened to the doorposts (*mĕzuzôt*) as a means of teaching children the importance of the law (Deut. 6:7–9).

c. The interpretation of ritual and symbol

Though these rituals and symbols may have been highly effective teaching media in their own day, it is extraordinarily difficult to recover their original meaning today. This is demonstrated by the very different interpretations placed on the various sacrifices, or on the significance of the food laws. Often one feels that the commentators, sure that these ancient texts have a message both for Old Testament times and for today, are guessing wildly in an attempt to make the text relevant. Bonar, for example, held that sheep were clean because they remind the believer that the LORD is his shepherd, but that pigs were unclean because they are pictures of men wallowing in the mire of iniquity.[23]

Keil, still one of the most valuable nineteenth-century commentators, can be equally arbitrary when interpreting sacrificial ritual. For example, he states that sin offerings were instituted for putting an end to the separation between man and God created by sin. This is symbolized in the sin-offering ritual by the worshipper placing his

---

23. A. A. Bonar, *A Commentary on Leviticus* (r.p. Banner of Truth, 1966, originally published 1861), pp. 214f.

hand on the animal's head and thereby transferring his sin and his desire for forgiveness to the animal.[24] Attractive though such an interpretation is, and it may contain an element of truth, it clearly fails as an explanation of the sin offering in particular, for all sacrifice involved the imposition of the worshipper's hands and the animal's death. Why does this action point to vicarious suffering in the sin offering but not in other sacrifices where it occurs, for example in the burnt offering, whose atoning significance Keil denies? Furthermore, Keil's interpretation of the sin offering, while attaching peculiar significance to those features it has in common with all sacrifices, completely fails to explain its distinctive features, namely smearing the blood on the altar, in the holy place or on the mercy seat.

The reason why these rituals are so difficult to understand is that they are so rarely explained in the Bible, or so briefly that several interpretations are possible. Descriptions of the rarer sacrifices, the sin offering (*ḥaṭṭā't*) and guilt offering (*'āšām*), give a number of clear hints as to their significance, but the very different interpretations placed on the sin offering by Milgrom and Keil merely highlight our problem. The more common sacrifices, the burnt offering, cereal offering and the peace offering, receive practically no explanation in the text. They are all said to be *'iššéh* (possibly 'fire or food offerings') making a 'pleasing odour to the LORD' (Lev. 1 – 3). Such a remark does not take us very far. To say that a sacrifice produces a 'pleasing odour' means that God likes them. But why? And what differentiates the burnt offering from the peace offering, apart from the outward ritual acts? Leviticus 1:4 says the burnt offering 'makes atonement' for the offerer, but again the interpretation of that word is uncertain, and raises the question whether the burnt offering differs at all in its function from the sin offering.

Faced with the apparent insolubility of arriving at an objective interpretation of the sacrifices, the majority of modern commentators on Numbers have more or less given up attempting to understand them and concentrate instead on discussing the

---

24. C. F. Keil, *Manual of Biblical Archaeology* I (Clark, 1887), p. 299; id., *The Pentateuch* II (Eerdmans, n.d. reprint), p. 305.

sources and redaction of the book. But that is to bid farewell to the commentator's central task, interpretation of the present form of the text.

Very little is said in the Old Testament itself about the significance of these sacrifices because it was so self-evident to writers that they did not need to explain them. But the modern reader of the Old Testament ritual texts feels he is watching charades; faced with some of the other religious symbols he is as perplexed as by a piece of abstract art. In charades the spectator can always ask the actors whether he has correctly guessed what they are doing. The human authors of the Pentateuch are dead and can no longer be questioned about their meaning, so the modern reader is left wondering whether his guess is right.

d. An anthropologically based approach to ritual symbolism

Into this apparently hopeless situation light has begun to shine from an unexpected quarter. Social anthropologists in seeking to understand primitive societies have developed an approach to the interpretation of ritual which can be applied with some modification to the biblical texts. Three seminal works[25] by anthropologists have pointed a way forward to determining with greater objectivity the significance of ritual and associated symbols. Of course, there are problems in applying anthropological methods to ancient texts. Their methods have been devised to interpret living societies where informants are available to test the investigator's hypotheses. Furthermore the data contained in the Old Testament are much less than a total description of Israelite society, which would be necessary to prove our interpretations beyond cavil. Yet just as the methods of modern linguistics have been successfully applied to the study of dead languages,[26] there is no reason in principle why

---

25. M. Douglas, *Purity and Danger* (Routledge and Kegan Paul, 1966); E. R. Leach, *Culture and Communication* (CUP, 1976); J. Soler, 'The Dietary Prohibitions of the Hebrews', *New York Review of Books*, 26.10, 14 June 1979, pp. 24–30.

26. E.g. F. I. Andersen, *The Hebrew Verbless Clause in the Pentateuch* (Abingdon, 1970); id., *The Sentence in Biblical Hebrew* (Mouton, 1974).

anthropological methods devised to study living cultures should not be applied with profit to extinct societies.

This is not the place to attempt to justify in detail the application of anthropological methods to the study of the Old Testament. The ultimate test must be the fruitfulness of the methods themselves. My main concern is to explain how I have sought very tentatively to apply these methods myself in the body of the commentary. Nevertheless it is worth setting out some of the reasons for supposing this general approach to be valid, even if some of the details remain open to question.

First, this approach seeks to understand the whole ritual system and not just parts of it, or more precisely to understand the parts in the light of the whole. This may be illustrated by Douglas' approach to the food laws. Earlier commentators picked on certain elements in the food laws as suggestive of a particular interpretation. For instance, sheep were clean because they reminded man of his divine shepherd, while serpents were unclean because they recalled the agent of the fall. But multitudes of animals in the list found no easy explanation of this type, for example, camels, eagles, grasshoppers, etc. Douglas drew attention to that feature of the lists in Leviticus 11 and Deuteronomy 14 that the biblical writers seem to concentrate on, namely the means of locomotion of the animals, how many feet and what type of feet they have. From surveying the lists as a whole she deduced that the animal world mirrors the human world. Just as there are three principal divisions among men, Gentiles, Jews and priests, so there are three classes of animals: unclean, that may not be eaten; clean, i.e. edible; and sacrificial beasts. Her theory of a correspondence between the human and the animal kingdoms is confirmed by other texts scattered throughout the Pentateuch.

Secondly, Soler has independently arrived at a similar analysis of the food laws to that of Douglas. Indeed his study represents an advance on her work, showing that the correspondences between animals and men run even deeper than earlier realized. The birds listed as unclean are unclean because they are birds of prey, i.e. eat flesh with blood in it, a mortal sin under Old Testament law (Lev. 17:10–14). It is the herbivorous land animals that are clean, and according to Genesis 9:3 (cf. 1:29f.) man too was vegetarian until after the flood.

It is also worth noting that Carmichael,[27] using more traditional methods of exegesis, has arrived at similar conclusions. He argues that in Genesis 49 and Deuteronomy 22:10 the ox, the best of the sacrificial and clean animals, symbolizes Israel, while the ass, an unclean beast, pictures Canaan. This convergence of interpretation, based on several different methods of study, suggests that the symbolic dimensions of biblical thought are at last being understood.

Thirdly, this interpretation is corroborated in the earliest commentaries on these laws. For example, the second-century BC Letter of Aristeas sees the behaviour of clean animals as models for human conduct.[28] Acts 10 links the preaching of Peter to the Gentiles with eating unclean animals. In other words, as soon as men of all nations could belong to the people of God, those food laws which had symbolized Israel's election and served to separate her from the nations became irrelevant too.

The anthropologists' interpretation of Old Testament sacrifice as substitutionary seems to be endorsed by the New Testament too. The New Testament writers employ the categories of Old Testament sacrifice to explain the death of Christ. He is the lamb of God who died in our place. Yet Old Testament scholars tend to deny or play down the substitutionary aspect of sacrifice.[29] By placing his hand on the animal's head, the worshipper is only saying he owns the animal. 'This animal belongs to me, therefore I should benefit by the sacrifice.' But the anthropologist Edmund Leach confidently asserts, 'The plain implication is that, in some metaphysical sense, the victim is a vicarious substitution for the donor himself.'[30] It may be added that in some Hittite rituals the animal is explicitly described as a substitute for the worshipper.[31]

27. C. M. Carmichael, 'Some Sayings in Genesis 49', *JBL*, 88, 1969, pp. 435–444; id., *The Laws of Deuteronomy* (Cornell UP, 1974), pp. 160–162.

28. 144ff.

29. E.g. R. de Vaux, *Studies in Old Testament Sacrifice* (University of Wales, 1964), p. 28; cf. R. Péter, *VT*, 27, 1977, p. 52.

30. E. R. Leach, *Culture and Communication,* p. 89.

31. E.g. *ANET*, pp. 350f., 355.

Now this recognition of the substitutionary concept of sacrifice fits in very well with Douglas's and Soler's observations on the tie-up between the animal world and the human situation. The Israelite, a member of the clean nation, chooses a clean animal to sacrifice on his behalf. The imposition of hands makes the equation even more explicit. But a sacrifice is not merely a suitable animal being offered for the group of people symbolically identified with it. The individual Israelite must choose it himself and then place his hands on its head in a dramatic declaration that he is this animal, that it is taking his place in the ritual.

Invaluable as these studies are, however, they can only provide a general pre-understanding of ritual symbolism. The next stage in the process of interpretation has been expounded by Edmund Leach in *Culture and Communication* (1976). Basically one must examine the whole ritual and symbolic system of ancient Israel and note the distinctions and gradations within it. It is the contrasts between similar elements within the system that are of primary importance, not the individual elements in it. Thus in the tabernacle different colours and materials are used in different parts: for example, the curtains round the outer courtyard were white, whereas those in the holy of holies were blue; the clasps for the courtyard curtains were silver, but those in the holy of holies were gold; the courtyard altar was covered in bronze, but that in the holy place was made of gold. This series of differentials points to the holy of holies being the most sacred spot, where God himself dwelt.

In interpreting rituals Leach insists similar procedures must be followed. (I find his own examples drawn from Leviticus rather too superficial to be convincing: Milgrom's work[32] illustrates Leach's principles much better, though he docs not in fact appeal to anthropological method to justify it.) To discover the meaning of a sacrifice, all the occasions on which it is offered must be examined: similar situations will demand a similar sacrificial response. Thus, if the reason for making an offering on a particular occasion can be discovered, one may assume that it was for similar reasons that the offering was required on other occasions. Rarely in fact are sacrifices

---

32. E.g. *Cult and Conscience* (Brill, 1976).

offered alone, and this complicates the situation. Then one must discover which combination of sacrifices is offered on what occasion.
For example, the Nazirite on completing his vow must offer burnt,
sin, peace, cereal and drink offerings all together (Num. 6:14f.).
These sacrifices were also required on the first and eighth day of the
priest's ordination (Lev. 8 – 9). This is one of several hints in the
Nazirite law that the sanctity of the Nazirite was on a par with that
of the priests.

The third stage of interpreting ritual has been pioneered by Victor Turner, though unlike the previous writers he has not applied his
methods directly to biblical texts. He insists that to find the full
meaning of a rite, one must not only examine its function within the
total system, but also take account of all the elements within the
rite.[33] On this basis it is not merely the sequence of colours and
metals within the tabernacle that is significant; the particular
materials themselves have symbolic significance. I would suggest,
therefore, that the holy of holies was decorated with gold, purple and
blue furnishings because these were the marks of royalty and divinity,
and because this part of the tabernacle was the throne-room of
Israel's divine king.

But how are we to arrive at such conclusions? Modern anthropologists can ask the natives; our would-be informants are long since
dead. This poses our greatest danger. Once admit that every element
possesses symbolic significance, and we may be tempted to invent
meanings indiscriminately, returning full circle to the unscientific exegesis of some older commentaries. We must have controls if symbolic interpretation is not to suffer from the whims of imaginative
commentators. The following principles, I suggest, may preserve us
from going too far astray in interpreting individual features within
a rite.

First of all, the meaning of an element should be suggested elsewhere in Scripture. Poetic metaphor may often provide a clue to the
meaning of symbols, as for example, when Israel is identified with
the ox, or blood with wine. Unfortunately this principle does not suffice to explain every feature in Old Testament rites and then we must

---

33. E.g. in *The Forest of Symbols* (Cornell UP, 1967).

look further afield for possible meanings. Some colours, e.g. black,
white and red, have almost universal significance.[34] Cultures from
very different places tend to view white positively, e.g. as symbolizing life and purity. Comparative studies particularly of ancient near
eastern sources may suggest interpretations of features of Israelite
ritual symbolism.[35] It must be borne in mind, however, that a particular animal or colour or gesture in one culture may have quite a
different symbolic value in another culture. A word in one language
may sound very similar to that in another language, and the meanings be quite different. The problem here is like that posed by those
comparative philologists who suggest new meanings for Hebrew
words on the basis of cognate languages. The same criteria should
apply to evaluating the meaning of symbolic elements in ritual: a
meaning suggested by a culture close in space and time to ancient
Israel is more likely to be valid than one derived from a more distant
culture.[36]

Secondly, though other passages of Scripture and neighbouring
cultures may suggest meanings for elements of rites, ultimately this
interpretation must be compatible with the overall purpose and
function of the rite as recovered by the systematic analysis of that
rite and similar ones. Just as in a sentence the context determines
which of several possible meanings fits a particular word, so the ultimate test of any proposed interpretation of a symbolic element is
the overall purpose and function of the ritual. For example, Numbers 19 prescribes a mixture of water and ash to purify people who
have had contact with the dead, and it therefore must be presumed
that all the ingredients burnt to make this ash had something to do
with purification. In other words the basic meaning of a rite as deduced by the methods of Leach and Milgrom outlined earlier must
control the interpretation of individual elements within it. In some
instances, a variety of symbolic interpretations seems to fit the

---

34. Ibid., pp. 59ff.
35. O. Keel, *The Symbolism of the Biblical World* (SPCK, 1978) contains useful
    comparative material relating to the psalms.
36. Cf. J. Barr, *Comparative Philology and the Text of the Old Testament*
    (Clarendon Press, 1968).

context, e.g. the dust added to the water in Numbers 5:17. In this instance we need not necessarily choose between the various meanings, for by their very nature symbols are multivocal,[37] bearing a variety of connotations simultaneously.

A few more detailed examples may clarify the method being advocated. Numbers 15 insists that the burnt offering and peace offerings should always be accompanied by a cereal offering and a libation of wine. However, it never explains why or what these accompanying rites signified. How should the cereal offering and the drink offering be interpreted?

The following approach is one possibility. Elsewhere in the sin offering (Lev. 5:11–13) a cereal offering may replace the offering of animals. Thus, if in the sin offering the animal represents the worshipper, it follows that grain when substituted for the animal also represents the worshipper. This hypothesis is confirmed I believe by the following observation: in animal sacrifice the animal chosen is always a clean animal, i.e. one that symbolizes Israel, or more exactly the Israelite priests. Wheat, the usual ingredient of the cereal offering, also represents Israel, for the twelve wheaten loaves of shewbread (Lev. 24) clearly symbolize the twelve tribes of Israel. Therefore in the cereal offering, the presentation of the grain to the priest and the burning of part of it on the altar represent the immolation of the worshipper himself. It echoes very clearly the meaning of the animal sacrifice it accompanies. Indeed burnt offerings, peace offerings and cereal offerings are all alike called *'iššēh*, 'food or fire offerings'.

Similarly the ritual of pouring out wine at the foot of the altar as a libation appears to equate wine, which is often red, with blood; and wine is a regular scriptural metaphor for blood (Gen. 49:11; Rev. 14:20). Furthermore one of the favourite descriptions of Israel is the vine (Ps. 80:8, 14; Isa. 5:1–7; Hos. 10:1); thus the material chosen for the libation, like the animals chosen for sacrifice, immediately suggests an identification between the offerer and his offering. The wine libation like the outpouring of animal blood portrays the worshipper dying for his sin and giving himself totally to the service of God.

---

37. V. W. Turner, *Forest of Symbols*, pp. 27ff.; *Ritual Process*, pp. 64ff.

It may then be objected that the burnt offering and its traditional accompaniments, the cereal offering and the drink offering, each symbolized much the same thing, thereby rendering the latter two redundant. However, this is characteristic of symbolism[38] and indeed of much great art. Saying the same thing in a variety of ways reinforces and enhances communication. Remarks made only once are generally unimportant and soon forgotten. Elegant repetition and variation characterize great music, drama, literature and liturgy. The message of the burnt-offering ritual, dramatically setting out the effect of sin and the need for total consecration to God's service, is powerful enough on its own. Intensified by the accompanying rites of cereal offering and libation, it becomes overwhelming.

It is on these lines that I have tried to understand the symbols and rituals of Numbers in the following commentary. Yet the reader is warned that the suggested interpretations are very tentative. Though totally persuaded of the importance of ritual and symbolism, I am far from certain that I have discovered the correct interpretation of the rites in Numbers. If these suggestions stimulate others to pursue the issues further, biblical interpretation could take a significant step forward in a field of great importance, hitherto sadly neglected.

7. The theology of Numbers

It is impossible to discuss the theology of Numbers in isolation from the other books of the Pentateuch, particularly Exodus and Leviticus. The outward structural devices that link the three middle books of the Pentateuch point to an inner unity of theological theme that underlies them all. All are concerned with the outworking of the promises to Abraham and the moulding of Israel into the holy people of God. But the focus of interest in each book is different. Exodus concentrates on the deliverance from Egypt, the covenant at Sinai and the erection of the tabernacle. Leviticus highlights the nature of true worship and holiness. Numbers focuses on the land of promise and Israel's journey towards it. God's character

---

38. E.g. *ANET*, pp. 349–356.

and his reactions to Israel's behaviour are constant throughout these books, but different aspects come to the fore in different books. If Leviticus emphasizes the importance of holiness and cleanness, Numbers reiterates the value of faith and obedience. Where Leviticus stresses the role of sacrifice in creating and maintaining right relations between God and man, Numbers accentuates the indispensability of the priesthood for preserving the nation's spiritual health. Yet these contrasts are not incompatible with one another. It is through obedience to the law that Israel is sanctified, and without priests there can be no sacrifice. The theological emphases of the different books do not contradict but complement one another. Therefore, in the exposition that follows, while I have picked out topics that are most prominent in Numbers, I have not refrained from utilizing passages from other parts of the Pentateuch bearing on these topics.

a. The character of God

Numbers, like other parts of Scripture, does not attempt to paint a detailed portrait of God's character. Nevertheless in its laws and narrative certain traits emerge very clearly.

Fundamental to Israel's experience was *the real and visible presence of God among them*. In one sense God was ever present with Israel; the recurrent refrain in the laws of Leviticus, 'I am the LORD your God', is a reminder that every deed is done unto the LORD. But Numbers speaks of God's frequent visible presence with his people during their wilderness wanderings. The fiery cloud covering the tabernacle showed that it was no empty royal palace, but that 'the LORD their God is with them, and the shout of a king is among them' (23:21). Wherever the cloud went the people followed; when the cloud stopped moving on, the people camped (9:15–23). So impressive was this phenomenon that not only did the Mesopotamian seer Balaam recognize it, but so did the Egyptians and Canaanites according to 14:14: 'They have heard that thou, O LORD, art in the midst of this people; for thou, O LORD, art seen face to face, and thy cloud stands over them and thou goest before them, in a pillar of cloud by day and in a pillar of fire by night.' Ultimately it would lead them to the land of promise which would be hallowed by the presence of God living among his people (35:34). The moving cloud and the ark were images of God going with his people to protect them and give them victory over their foes (10:33–36). In their absence defeat was inevitable (14:43–44). More ominous still, the cloud appeared in moments of crisis, when the people protested against the divinely appointed leadership or the planned journey into Canaan. The cloud's sudden appearance heralded some dire punishment on the wicked (11:25, cf. 33; 12:5, 10; 14:10; 16:19, 42; 20:6).

These judgments demonstrated *the holiness of God*, another aspect of his nature underlined throughout the Pentateuch. Just as Mount Sinai was fenced off and any trespasser stoned or shot (Exod. 19:12–13), so the tabernacle had to be separated off from the tribes encamped around it by a cordon of priests and Levites empowered to execute any unauthorized person drawing near (1:49 – 3:10). Even those Levites, the sons of Kohath, appointed to carry the sacred furniture of the tabernacle, such as the ark and golden candlestick, were not permitted to see these very holy objects uncovered. They had to be wrapped up first by the priests lest laymen saw them and died (4:1–20). In other words these most potent symbols of the presence and power of God partook of his holiness. Just as no man may see God's face and live (Exod. 33:20), so none but the priests could see these symbols of his presence without experiencing sudden death. Even the most privileged, those who had immediate and ready access to God such as the priests, could not with impunity flout the demands of divine holiness. Aaron's sons died for offering incense 'such as he had not commanded' (Lev. 10:1). Numbers 20:12 records that Moses and Aaron were sentenced never to enter the promised land for deviating slightly from God's instructions. The comment of Leviticus 10:3 on the former incident applies equally to the second: 'I will show myself holy among those who are near me, and before all the people I will be glorified.'

But God's holiness is tempered by *his graciousness*, a third attribute of his character on which Numbers lays great stress. The appointment of the priests and Levites to minister in the tabernacle is an act of mercy designed to prevent his wrath engulfing the nation (3–4, 16–18). Several times it is recorded that God's judgments are halted by Moses' intercession (11:2; 12:13; 14:13–20; 21:7) or by priestly acts of atonement (16:47; 25:7). Even Israel's experiences in the wilderness are proof of God's goodwill towards them; for the generation that came out of Egypt experienced the fulfilment of all the promises made to the patriarchs save that of entering the land of Canaan, for which they had only their unbelief to blame. It is to these promises that Moses appeals when God threatens to annihilate Israel for their unbelief (14:16; cf. Exod. 32:13). Balaam's oracles also allude to many features in these promises. Because God has blessed them, Balaam cannot curse them (23:8; 24:9; cf. Gen. 12:2–3). Israel is as numerous as the dust of the earth (23:10; cf. Gen. 13:16). They will settle and prosper in the land (24:6ff.; cf. Gen. 13:17). Kings shall arise from them (24:7, 17; cf. Gen. 17:16). Again, the census lists (chs. 1, 26), especially the second, emphasize the growth of Jacob's family, and serve as implicit reminders of the fulfilment of the promises, even though there is no explicit reference back to them. Similarly, the description of the cloud guiding the tribes through the wilderness (9:15–23) bears comparison with Genesis 28:15: 'Behold, I am with you and will keep you wherever you go, and will bring you back to this land.'

God's graciousness is revealed not only in his present actions and his past promises, but also in his laws for the future. This comes out most vividly in chapter 15. The whole project of entry to Canaan has suffered a catastrophic set-back as a result of the spies' report. The adults have been condemned to die in the wilderness. A sudden burst of penitence has prompted an attempt to enter the land, but it has ended in ignominious defeat. The next chapter, a set of laws about sacrifice, begins 'When you come into the land you are to inhabit, which I give you' (15:2). There follow detailed instructions about the amounts of wine, oil and flour, that must accompany animal sacrifices, materials available, at least in the quantities specified, only in a settled farming community. These laws, then, underline the promise of entry to the land. They assure the people that, notwithstanding their recent unbelief, their children will enjoy the fulfilment of the promises. Similarly, the laws at the end of the book about the land are a further assurance that it will soon be theirs. God will put the people in a position where they can obey these laws (33:50 – 36:13).

One final aspect of God's character stressed in Numbers is *his constancy*. Once again Balaam spells out what the whole story implies: 'God is not man ... that he should repent' (23:19). The two short travelogues in chapters 11 – 12, 20 – 21 record incidents similar to the earlier journey described in Exodus 13 – 18. Similarly, the revelations associated with Kadesh (13 – 19) and with the plains of Moab (22 – 36) recall, modify and expand the earlier legislation revealed at Sinai (Exod. 19 – Num. 10). This threefold repetition spanning forty years suggests that every generation must appropriate the law for themselves and experience both the grace and judgment of God. The briefer, less detailed itinerary of chapter 33, with its pattern of six cycles of seven stations, re-emphasizes that God is ever constant in working out his purposes, even when to the human observer nothing significant seems to be happening.

All these aspects of God's character are endorsed in the New Testament. In our Lord Jesus 'the Word became flesh and tabernacled among us' (John 1:14). Through the spirit the believer has become the temple of God (1 Cor. 3:16–17; 6:19). The heavenly Jerusalem is described as a place where the ideals of Numbers find their ultimate fulfilment: 'I heard a loud voice from the throne saying, "Behold, the dwelling of God is with men. He will dwell with them, and they shall be his people"' (Rev. 21:3).

Similarly the New Testament re-affirms the doctrines of the holiness, graciousness and constancy of God. 'He who called you is holy' (1 Pet. 1:15), and Paul sees the stories of judgment in Numbers as warnings for the Corinthians (1 Cor. 10:1–11; cf. Heb. 12:18–29). The grace of God is the principal theme of the New Testament: 'All the promises of God find their Yes in him' (2 Cor. 1:20). Finally, regarding his constancy: 'he remains faithful – for he cannot deny himself' (2 Tim. 2:13). 'Jesus Christ is the same yesterday and today and for ever' (Heb. 13:8).

b. The land

The whole book of Numbers looks forward to the occupation of the land of Canaan. Chapters 1 – 10 describe the preparations for the journey from Sinai to Canaan, 11 – 12 the journey itself, 13 – 14 the abortive attempt at conquest. The rest of the book describes the subsequent period of wanderings and their period of waiting in Transjordan prior to their entry. Canaan is the ever-present goal of the people, that is never quite reached in Numbers. The geographic limits of Canaan (34:2–12) from the Mediterranean in the west to the river Jordan, and from Mount Hor in the north to Kadesh-barnea in the south, correspond to the Egyptian administrative district with the same name known from 15th-century texts onwards.

Theologically three aspects of this land are emphasized in Numbers. First, *the LORD had given it to Israel* (32:7, 9). More precisely, he had sworn to give it to Abraham, Isaac, and to Jacob (32:11; cf. 14:16; Gen. 17:8; 26:3; 28:13). These promises guaranteed that Israel would be able to conquer the land at the right time; the spies' unbelief was all the more heinous because their mission had specially visited the Hebron area where Abraham had first been promised the land, and where he and his family were buried (13:22–24; cf. Gen. 13:14 – 18:1; 23; 35:27–29; 50:13).

Second, *the land of Canaan was to be a holy land*, sanctified by God dwelling among his people (35:34; cf. Lev. 26:11–12). For this reason the native inhabitants were to be driven out, and their sanctuaries and idols destroyed. The LORD alone was to be worshipped there (33:51–52). God's presence would ensure that it would indeed be a land 'flowing with milk and honey' (13:27; 14:8) where the people would continue to multiply and enjoy life (24:5–7; Lev. 26:3–10). But death, particularly violent death, would pollute the land. Only the execution of the murderer, or in the case of manslaughter the death of the high priest, could rid the land of blood guilt (35:31–34; cf. Deut. 21:1–9, 22–23).

Third, *the land was to be Israel's permanent possession*. This is stated more explicitly in Genesis than in Numbers (e.g. Gen. 13:15; 17:8), but this is the clear implication of the jubilee laws (Lev. 25) and the rules about the marriage of land-owning girls in Numbers 36: 'each of the tribes of the people of Israel shall cleave to its own inheritance' (36:9). Disobedience may mean exile from the land, but there is a pledge of ultimate restoration (Lev. 26:40–45; cf. Deut. 30:1–10).

Though the New Testament re-affirms the validity of the patriarchal promises, it sees their scope as universalized (Rom. 9:4). As membership of the people of God now includes all those who are sons of Abraham by faith, so Canaan has become an image of 'a better country, that is, a heavenly one', a new Jerusalem from which sin and death are excluded (Gal. 3:7; Heb. 11:16; Rev. 21).

c. The people of God

Nowhere is the general biblical principle that the people of God should imitate God so well illustrated as in the book of Numbers. Individually and corporately Israel is to express the character of their redeemer. Their unity, holiness and faithful fulfilment of their promises must reflect the unity, holiness and faithfulness of their Lord and Saviour. As the LORD is one, so Israel must be one nation (Num. 32). 'You shall therefore be holy, for I am holy' (Lev. 11:45). As the LORD keeps his promises, so those who make vows are expected to fulfil them (Num. 30). What is true of the nation as a whole is particularly true of its spiritual leaders. The priests represent Israel before God, and God before Israel, and therefore their behaviour must be altogether godlike. Moses and the high priest in yet fuller measure are expected to incarnate God's words and attitudes. These parallels between God, Israel, the high priest and Moses make it quite natural for the New Testament to see in them types of Christ, the living Word.

The importance of Israel's unity is brought out in various ways. The census lists (1, 26) tracing the descent of every member of the nation back to one of Jacob's sons is a reminder that they were in fact one people joined together by ties of blood. But this unity had to express itself in action: the censuses were held in order to list all those able to go forth to war (1:3; 26:2). Every tribe had to supply a spy indicating its willingness to join in the battle for Canaan (13:2). Each tribe had to supply a thousand men in the war against Midian (31:4). When later the two and a half tribes declared they would be content to settle in Transjordan, this was hailed as a most serious crisis. It suggested not only an indifference to settling in the land of promise, but also unconcern about preserving the unity of the nation. Only when the tribes of Reuben, Gad and Manasseh agreed to send their warriors across the Jordan to fight for Canaan were they permitted to settle in Gilead (32:1–33). When the tabernacle was dedicated, each tribe indicated its full support of the sanctuary and its ministry by presenting a silver plate and basin and a golden spoon and a selection of sacrificial animals. Each offered exactly the same, demonstrating that all equally backed the sacred institutions (ch. 7).

Holiness is intrinsic to God's character, but not to men. Israel was holy in virtue of God's presence with them and their holiness therefore rested ultimately on God's initiative rather than human effort. In the covenant ratification ceremonies described in Exodus

24:3–8 their holy calling was given symbolic expression by their sprinkling with blood and a promise to keep the commandments.[39] Though it was not possible for the nation to make itself holy through its own unaided efforts, it was perfectly possible for them to destroy their God-given sanctity. Numbers recognizes two main ways in which this may happen: through disobedience and through uncleanness. As a constant reminder of his duty to obey the commandments, every Israelite had to attach to his clothes a tassel with a blue thread in it, symbolizing his membership of the 'kingdom of priests and a holy nation' (Exod. 19:6). 'So you shall remember and do all my commandments, and be holy to your God' (Num. 15:40). It was because sabbath-breaking and idolatry were flagrant violations of fundamental covenant demands and incompatible with the holiness of the nation, that those who sinned in this way were punished with the utmost severity (15:32–36; 25:1–9). But unbelief was equally culpable. The spies who refused to believe God would give them the land died in a plague, while those who accepted their report were forced to wander in the wilderness until they had perished outside the land of promise (14:34–37).

Though sin and disobedience come more easily to men than holiness, Scripture refuses to countenance the idea that holiness is somehow unnatural. It is in fact the essence of normality. That is why uncleanness, which may be roughly equated with abnormality, is incompatible with holiness. Uncleanness is caused by skin diseases, 'leprosy', which make men look abnormal (5:2; 12:10–14; Lev. 13 – 14), bodily discharges (5:2; cf. Lev. 12; 15), especially illicit sexual intercourse (5:19) and death, the very antithesis of life, the goal of creation (5:2; 31:19; 35:33). All these things are regarded as deviations from the perfection that should characterize all creation, and are therefore incompatible with holiness.

The law prescribes two different remedies for uncleanness: isolation or purification. If a holy man such as a Nazirite or high priest came in contact with a dead body his holiness would be destroyed; elaborate sacrifices are therefore prescribed to restore the sanctity of a Nazirite (6:9–12). The high priest is simply banned from any

---

39. See fuller discussion in Wenham, pp. 18ff.

contact with the dead (Lev. 21:11). But even the lesser sanctity of the
nation is jeopardized by uncleanness. Again, those affected must be
isolated from the nation until their purity is restored. Numbers 5:2 lays
down 'that they put out of the camp every "leper", and every one having a discharge, and every one that is unclean through contact with
the dead'. When a skin disease cleared up, the sufferer became clean
again, but he had to undergo the seven-day procedure of cleansing
and re-sanctification described in Leviticus 14:2–32 (cf. Num. 12:9–
15). Different cleansing rituals are prescribed for those polluted by
discharges or dead bodies (Lev. 12; 15; Num. 19; 31:19–24), but essential in all these procedures was the offering of sacrifice: the ashes
of the red heifer were effectively an instant ever-ready sacrifice.[40]

Though every Israelite was holy because he belonged to the holy
people, there were different degrees of holiness within the nation.
The denial of these distinctions was at the root of Korah's rebellion.
He argued that because all Israel was holy, the priests had no right
to claim a special status. He said to Moses and Aaron: 'You have gone
too far! For all the congregation are holy, every one of them, and the
LORD is among them; why then do you exalt yourselves above the
assembly of the LORD?' (16:3). The subsequent story disproves Korah's assertion. The priests are more holy than laymen and therefore
enjoy certain privileges denied to laymen. Numbers distinguishes at
least four grades of permanent holiness: lay, Levitical, priestly and
high priestly; one grade of temporary holiness was acquired through
taking a Nazirite vow.

The Nazirite vow (6:1–21) could be undertaken by any lay man or
woman pledging to abstain from drinking wine or coming near dead
bodies for a time. As a symbol of his consecration the Nazirite did not
cut his hair during the period he was under the vow. Abstinence from
alcohol and separation from the dead were also required of priests (Lev.
10:9; 21:1), but the Nazirite enjoyed none of the privileges of the
priests such as offering sacrifice and receiving offerings. Nevertheless
he was still holy unto the LORD, his uncut locks reminding himself and
others that total dedication to God's service was the calling of all Israel.

The Levites were the descendants of Levi, one of Jacob's sons.

---

40. See chapter 19.

Originally they had been a secular tribe without sacred responsibilities; but they had demonstrated such devotion to God when the
golden calf was made (Exod. 32:26–29), that they were appointed
permanent wardens of the tabernacle. The Israelite tribes camped
in a square around the tabernacle with a cordon of Levites separating the tabernacle from the lay tribes (Num. 2 – 3). Their relative
closeness to the sanctuary symbolized the greater sanctity of the
Levites. Though thus separated from the other tribes, they were at
the same time their representatives before God. In the last plague before the Exodus the first-born of the Egyptians died, but the first-
born Israelites were spared. Thereafter all first-born boys had to be
given to God, and they were therefore expected to serve God in a
full-time capacity. However, in Numbers this rather impractical
arrangement is replaced by appointing the Levites to undertake the
duties of the first-born males (Num. 3). Thus every family in Israel
had a stake in the ministry: they could look at the Levites and remember that one of them was serving God instead of the eldest boy
in the family. In recognition that the Levites were performing a
vital but dangerous ministry on behalf of the whole people, Israel
was called to support them by giving them a tithe of all their
produce (18:21–24) and by assigning them 48 cities (35:1–8).

Running through all the legislation in Numbers are warnings
about the danger of unholy men approaching God. The Levites were
appointed to guard the tabernacle from incursions by laymen. Yet
even they were not allowed to look at the sacred furniture of the tabernacle or offer sacrifice. Only the priests could perform these holy
and dangerous tasks. The Levite Korah supported by men from
other tribes contested the special prerogatives of the priestly family. Chapters 16 – 17 relate three signal demonstrations of God's
choice of Aaron's family. First, Korah and his supporters offered incense, a priestly task; as a result, some were burned with fire, others
were swallowed up by an earth slip. Then a plague broke out, a second sign of God's anger, which was stopped by Aaron offering incense. Whereas incense offered by the official priesthood effects
atonement, freelance offerings provoke judgment. The same point
is made in the third episode. Sticks representing all the tribes were
placed overnight near the ark. In the morning Aaron's rod had
sprouted, all the others were dead. The implication was obvious: if

anyone but Aaron's family drew too close to God, he would die. Yet the offering of sacrifice was indispensable if Israel was to remain the holy covenant nation. To sustain their life-giving ministry the priests were therefore awarded a tenth of the tithes, firstlings, first fruits and parts of many of the sacrifices (18).

The priests who drew near to God had to be exemplary in their holiness. They therefore had to avoid pollution that would mar their holiness (Lev. 21:1); indeed, if they suffered from skin disease or discharges, they could not partake of sacrificial food (Lev. 22:2–8). They had to set forth the will of God in their teaching (Lev. 10:11), in their personal relationships (Lev. 21:7), and in their public actions (Num. 25:11). Slight infractions of the commandments by priests were dramatically punished (Lev. 10:1–3), for it was only through the priests' punctilious performance of their duties that atonement could be made for the nation (Num. 16:46; 25:13).

At the pinnacle of the system stood the high priest. He was hedged about with yet tighter restrictions than the ordinary priests (Lev. 21:10–14). His supreme holiness was symbolized by his high-priestly vestments, adorned with twelve jewels, one for each of the tribes. He wore these clothes when he entered the outer part of the tent of meeting 'to bring the names of the sons of Israel to continual remembrance before the LORD' (Exod. 28:29). But even he was permitted to enter the holy of holies, the very presence of God, only once a year (Lev. 16:3). It was a journey fraught with the danger of sudden death, yet indispensable, for 'thus he shall make atonement for the holy place, because of the uncleannesses of the people of Israel' (Lev. 16:16). These day of atonement ceremonies enabled God to continue dwelling among his people despite their sinfulness. The atoning work of the high priest culminated in his death. This purged the land of the blood guilt associated with violent death and allowed those convicted of manslaughter to leave the cities of refuge and return home (Num. 35:28, 32).

Finally, there is the figure of Moses. His office was unique. Whereas Aaron's son succeeded him and enjoyed a similar authority to his father, Joshua was invested with only a part of Moses' authority. Whereas Moses instructed Aaron what to do, Eleazar was to guide Joshua using the Urim and Thummin (Num. 20:24–28; 27:15–22). In his person Moses combined the roles of prophet, priest and king. He demonstrated his prophetic calling in declaring Israel's future, setting out God's will in the law and interceding for the people (cf. Deut. 18:18). Moses showed himself first of the priests at the ordination of Aaron, when he played the role of priest while Aaron acted the layman (Lev. 8). And as judge, military commander and shepherd of his people Moses fulfilled all the duties later generations expected of their kings (cf. Num. 15:32–36; 27; 31; 36).

The New Testament views Israel (Matt. 2:15), the high priest (Heb. 3 – 10) and Moses (Matt. 17:3; Luke 16:29, 31; John 5:46; Acts 3:22; Heb. 3:2ff.) as types of Christ, that is, their life and work anticipate his ministry in various ways. It also sees Israel as a type of the church. Like Israel the church is one body, and must express that unity in united action (Eph. 4:3–16; 1 Cor. 1:10–17). Like the ancient Israelites, all Christians are saints: 'You are a chosen race, a holy nation, God's own people' (1 Pet. 1:2 – 2:9; cf. Exod. 19:5–6). Yet they must work to make this holiness a practical reality (1 Pet. 1:15–16).

The death of Christ has made obsolete the sacrifices which the priests of the old covenant used to offer (Heb. 10), but their New Testament counterparts, the bishops and elders, still have to teach the word of God and set forth the character of God in the holiness of their lives (1 Tim. 3; Titus 1:5–9). Like the priests and Levites, the ministers of the gospel are entitled to ample material rewards in recognition of the great spiritual benefits they bring to the people of God (1 Cor. 9:13–14; 1 Tim. 5:17–18).

8. The Christian use of Numbers

The prime duty of every interpreter of Holy Scripture is the elucidation of the original meaning of the text. But from Paul onwards Christian expositors have recognized that there is more to interpretation than historico-grammatical exegesis: 'whatever was written in former days was written for our instruction' (Rom 15:4). The lessons of these ancient texts, must be re-applied to the problems of the church in later ages.[41] Our guide in relating the teaching of Numbers to the new covenant situation must be the New Testament;

---

41. Cf. de Vaulx, pp. 41ff.

to this end I have usually included at the end of each chapter a few remarks about the relationship between the passage and later biblical revelation. Here I offer a brief overview of the use of Numbers in the New Testament, to help the modern reader gain spiritual profit as well as historical knowledge from his study of the book.

For the writers of the New Testament the book of Numbers stands as a great warning. Despite the miraculous deliverance from Egypt, and the daily evidences of God's provision for their needs, Israel refused to believe and rebelled against their Saviour. Numbers records a trail of spectacular judgments that ought to provoke caution in every believer.

'I want you to know, brethren, that our fathers were all under the cloud (cf. Num. 9:15–23), and all passed through the sea, and all were baptized into Moses in the cloud and in the sea (cf. Exod. 14:19–31; Num. 33:8), and all ate the same supernatural food (cf. Exod. 16:4ff.; Num. 11:4ff.) and all drank the same supernatural drink. For they drank from the supernatural Rock which followed them, and the Rock was Christ (cf. Exod. 17:1–7; Num. 20:2–13). Nevertheless with most of them God was not pleased; for they were overthrown in the wilderness' (cf. Num. 14:28–35; 26:63–65).

'Now these are warnings for us, not to desire evil as they did. Do not be idolaters as some of them were; as it is written, "The people sat down to eat and drink and rose up to dance." (Exod. 32:4–6). We must not indulge in immorality as some of them did, and twenty-three thousand fell in a single day (cf. Num. 25). We must not put the LORD to the test, as some of them did and were destroyed by serpents (cf. Num. 21:4–9); nor grumble, as some of them did and were destroyed by the Destroyer (cf. Num. 11:1ff.; 14:1ff.; 16:42ff.)' (1 Cor. 10:1–10).

In this passage Paul describes the experiences of Israel in the wilderness in such a way as to make clear the parallels with the situation at Corinth.[42] Most of the sins of Corinth are thus prefigured

---

42. Baptism (1 Cor. 1ff.), Manna and Water (the Lord's supper) (1 Cor. 10:14ff.), Idolatry (1 Cor. 8; 10), Immorality (1 Cor. 5 – 7), Grumbling (1 Cor. 12ff.).

in Numbers, and if Israel was punished so severely, what can the church of the new covenant expect?

Similarly Hebrews reminds its readers of the spy incident. As disobedience and unbelief prevented the exodus generation from entering the promised land of rest, so the same sins can bar later generations from the enjoyment of a heavenly rest (Heb. 3:7 – 4:13). Jude too makes use of the stories in Numbers to warn the church of everpresent dangers from ungodly members. 'I desire to remind you ... that he who saved a people out of the land of Egypt, afterward destroyed those who did not believe' (Jude 5). He picks out immorality, the rejection of authority (Korah's rebellion) and covetousness (Balaam's error) as characteristic faults of these men (Jude 8, 11).

If the epistles focus on Israel's disobedience in the wilderness, the Gospels remind us of God's gracious provision then and the more wonderful era ushered in by the coming of Christ. In the Synoptic Gospels Jesus is in a sense the new Israel who succeeded where the old Israel fell. After his baptism by John (cf. Paul's association of baptism with the Red Sea crossing, 1 Cor. 10:2), he was driven into the wilderness and was hungry. His replies to the devil's temptations are all drawn from passages in Deuteronomy dealing with Israel's wilderness experiences (Matt. 4; Luke 4).

In John's Gospel Jesus is portrayed as the prophet who is greater than Moses (6:14; cf. 5:46), the good shepherd (10:1–18; cf. Num. 27:17), the life-giving serpent (3:14), the passover lamb (19:36), the water giver (4:10–15), the manna from heaven (6:26–58), and the glory of the Shekinah (1:14–18). In our Lord all the Old Testament symbols of the grace and presence of God find their ultimate fulfilment.

These examples of the way Numbers is used by the New Testament writers all demonstrate the principle of typology, a principle already enunciated in Numbers itself as it presents the history of Israel in a series of cycles. Typology is a natural, if not an inevitable, technique of historical writing once the constancy of God's character and human nature are understood. Though the light of revelation grows ever brighter with the passing of time, man's ability to respond to truth is little altered. Thus against the changing background of historical development there will be repeated cycles of sin, grace and judgment. God's ideals of holiness for Israel, the priests or Moses will prefigure the only one who ever embodied those ideals perfectly, while the actual performance of Israel or her leaders will anticipate the real experience of the church and the ministers of the gospel in every age.

The principle of typology may also be invoked to explain the relationship of the laws in Numbers to the Christian. But just as it is necessary to generalize to see the parallels between Moses and Christ or the church and Israel, so one must look behind the particular provisions of Numbers to the underlying principles if their validity and applicability in the Christian era are to be appreciated. Theologically and socially the modern church finds itself in a quite different situation from ancient Israel: this changed setting must be borne in mind when the ancient laws are interpreted.[43]

Thus the institution of cities of refuge (Num. 35) is no longer appropriate in our society. First, because we leave the arrest of criminals to the police, not to the relatives of the murdered man, there is no need for a sanctuary for homicides. Secondly, it would be difficult to devise a punishment for manslaughter in our secular society like that of detention in the city of refuge until the high priest's death, because there is no-one of comparable religious stature in our secular society. Even if the law is no longer applicable in detail, its underlying principle remains valid. The life of man, created in the image of God, is beyond price. Damages can never compensate for its loss. Traditional English and American law recognized this principle without creating cities of refuge,[44] and it is this principle that should inform the Christian conscience, whatever the mores of the society he lives in.

Similarly the sacrificial offerings of animals, flour, oil and wine prescribed in Numbers (7; 15; 28 – 29) are no longer valid expressions of Christian worship, because they point beyond themselves to the one atoning sacrifice of Christ which has made them obsolete (Heb. 10). Yet Christians are still reminded: 'let us continually

---

43. See B. N. Kaye and G. J. Wenham (eds.), *Law, Morality and the Bible* (IVP, 1978).

44. J. J. Finkelstein, 'The Goring Ox', *Temple Law Quarterly*, 46, 1973, pp. 169–290.

offer up a sacrifice of praise to God, that is, the fruit of lips that acknowledge his name. Do not neglect to do good and to share what
you have, for such sacrifices are pleasing to God' (Heb. 13:15–16).
The principle of whole-hearted dedication to the worship of God
links Old and New Testaments, even if our mode of devotion has
altered. Similarly if the tithe (Num. 18) remains a norm for Christian giving (Matt. 23:23), it may be noted that some believers evidently gave much more (Luke 19:8; Acts 2:45; 2 Cor. 8). If much of
the biblical legislation cannot be applied today, its thoroughness
and attention to detail should challenge the modern church to
ask whether our more casual attitudes may not be a cloak for
indifference.

ANALYSIS

1. **The people of God prepare to enter the promised land (1:1 – 10:10)**

    A. Censuses (chapters 1 – 4)
    B. Cleansing the camp (chapters 5 – 6)
    C. Offerings for the altar (chapter 7)
    D. Dedication of the Levites (chapter 8)
    E. The second passover (chapter 9)
    F. The silver trumpets (10:1–10)

2. **From Sinai to Kadesh (10:11 – 12:16)**

    A. Departure in battle order (10:11–36)
    B. Three complaints (11:1 – 12:16)

3. **Forty years near Kadesh (13:1 – 19:22)**

    A. The rebellion of the spies (chapters 13 – 14)
    B. Laws on offerings (chapter 15)

C. Prerogatives of the priests (chapters 16 – 18)
D. Laws on cleansing (chapter 19)

4. From Kadesh to the plains of Moab (20:1 – 22:1)

5. Israel in the plains of Moab (22:2 – 36:13)

A. Balaam and Balak (chapters 22 – 24)
B. National apostasy (chapter 25)
C. Census (chapter 26)
D. Laws about land, offerings and vows (chapters 27 – 30)
E. Defeat of Midian and settlement in Transjordan (chapters 31 – 32)
F. List of camp sites (33:1–49)
G. Laws about land (33:50 – 36:13)

COMMENTARY

I. THE PEOPLE OF GOD PREPARE TO ENTER THE PROMISED LAND (1:1 – 10:10)

A. Censuses (chapters 1 – 4)

The theme of the book of Numbers is the journey to the promised land of Canaan. Its opening ten chapters, covering a mere fifty days, describe how Moses organized Israel for the march from Sinai to the promised land. To appreciate their theological significance it is necessary to look backwards to the books of Exodus and Leviticus, as well as forwards to the conquest of Canaan. Exodus tells how God saved Israel from slavery in Egypt, and made a covenant with them at Sinai that he would be their God and that they would be his holy people (Exod. 19). This covenant relationship meant that God would actually live among them; Israel was therefore instructed to build a palace suitable for their divine king, the tabernacle. Just a month before Numbers opens, this tabernacle was consecrated and the glory of God descended on it (Exod. 40; cf. Num. 7:1; 9:15).

The book of Leviticus has as its theme the holiness of God. It therefore describes how the holy God must be worshipped through animal sacrifice (1 – 7). It notes the appointment of a high priesthood

to lead the nation's worship (8 – 10). It gives instructions for elimi-
nating the impurities of sin from people and from the tabernacle (11
– 16). It concludes by explaining the moral demands of holiness in
family life, good neighbourliness and care for the poor (17 – 25).

There is relatively little narrative in Leviticus: legal regulations
predominate. In Numbers the situation is reversed: the history is all-
important and the laws are fewer, generally discussing problems that
arose in the wilderness. These opening ten chapters show how the holiness principles of Leviticus were put into practice in the organization of the whole nation. Here symbolism is very important. At the
centre of the camp stood the tabernacle where God was enthroned
above the ark in the holy of holies. Round the tabernacle camped the
priests and Levites, guarding it to prevent ordinary Israelites entering without careful preparation. Beyond the Levites camped the
secular tribes, drawn up in battle order as befits the people of God.
Outside the camp lived the unclean, sufferers from skin diseases or
bodily discharges, who were unfit for the presence of God.

Both at rest and on the move the camp was organized to express
symbolically the presence and kingship of the LORD. It was God
who showed when and where they were to travel. 'Whenever the
cloud was taken up from over the tent, after that the people of Israel set out; and in the place where the cloud settled down, there the
people of Israel encamped' (9:17).

These opening chapters of Numbers are not arranged in strictly
chronological order. The regulations in chapters 1 – 6 are dated by 1:1
to the first day of the *second* month, whereas 7:1 – 9:15 fall between the
first and fourteenth day of the *first* month (cf. Exod. 40:2). Chapters
1 – 6 are probably placed before chapters 7 – 9 to explain the significance of the latter. For example chapter 4, specifying the tasks of the
Levitical clans, explains the gift of wagons to them in 7:1–9. Chapter
3 explains the purpose of dedicating the Levites, described in 8:5–26.
The book of Leviticus may also be arranged in a similar fashion. The
ordination of the priests described in chapters 8 – 9 is preceded by the
laws of sacrifice, so that the ordination offerings may be understood.[1]

---

1. The text itself hints at the non-chronological order. Leviticus 1:1 – 6:7
    were revealed from the tent of meeting, i.e. some time after the first day

i. Census of the people (1:1–19). Moses and Aaron are instructed to take a census of all the able-bodied men aged twenty or older (2–3). One man from each tribe is appointed to gather the numbers for his group (4–16). To underline the care with which this order was carried out, certain of the details are mentioned a second time in verses 17–19.

1. *The LORD spoke.* Because it is so common in the Pentateuch, the significance of this phrase can be overlooked. Saving history begins with God speaking (cf. Gen. 1:3; Lev. 1:1). *In the wilderness of Sinai.* A year after the law giving (Exod. 19:1) Israel is still to be found near the holy mountain of Sinai. Traditionally this has been located in the south of the modern Sinai peninsula at Jebel Musa. For a more detailed discussion of its location, the Additional note on the route of the Israelites should be consulted. The Hebrew word for *wilderness* (*midbār*) means a place for driving flocks. It is not a completely arid desert, but contains a little vegetation and a few trees. The rainfall in such areas is too light, a few inches per year, to support cultivation.

The tent of meeting (AV 'tabernacle', Heb. *'ōhel mô'ēd*) refers to the tent shrine that served as the portable divine palace. It housed the ark, the golden candlestick and the altar of incense, and is fully described in Exodus 25 – 40.[2] Though it housed these most sacred objects, and was decorated inside with brilliantly coloured hangings, its exterior was covered with goat's hair curtains, making it look like the black tents used by the bedouin today. But it was more than a shrine; it was a tent of meeting, because there God used to speak with Moses, and in front of it sacrifices were offered at the great altar of burnt offering. For this reason 'tent of meeting' is the preferred description in contexts of revelation and worship (cf. Exod. 29:42–43).

However, another term is also used to describe it, the *tabernacle* (Hebrew *miškān*) (e.g. Num. 1:50–53), literally 'dwelling'. In some passages this seems to describe the interior of the tent of meeting, but in many cases the terms are practically interchangeable. The word 'tabernacle' perhaps emphasizes the permanent dwelling of God

---

of the second year (Exod. 40:2), whereas 6:8 – 7:37 were revealed in Mount Sinai (7:38), suggesting some time in the first year.

2. See diagram below, p. 82.

among his people symbolized in the cloud and pillar of fire (Exod.
40:34–38; Num. 9:15–23).

*On the first day of the second month, in the second year after they had come
out of the land of Egypt* (cf. Exod. 12:2; 16:1; 19:1;   40:2; Num.
10:11). The exodus is usually dated to the first half of the thirteenth
century BC.[3]

2. *Take a census.* Literally 'calculate the total'. This seems to have
been the second census conducted during the wilderness wandering.
On the first occasion the purpose was simply to count all the
people over 20 years old and tax them half a shekel each, which was
put to the building of the tabernacle (Exod. 30:12–16; cf. 38:25f.). On
this occasion more details were required, the people were listed *by
families, by fathers' houses, according to the number of names.* *Family* (Hebrew
mišpāḥâ) would be more appropriately translated 'clan'. It is the
main social unit, intermediate in size between a tribe and the *father's
house* (Josh. 7:14). The *father's house* might be better rendered 'family',
though it was a somewhat larger unit than our nuclear families (cf.
Judg. 6:15). But in some cases the terms are used more flexibly
(Num. 4:18; 17:2).

3. This time the census had a military purpose: it was to count *all
in Israel who are able to go forth to war.* This phrase recurring repeatedly
throughout this chapter (1:3, 20, 22, 24 etc.) stresses that the nation
was being organized to invade the promised land. Everybody was
counted, because everyone had to support the war effort. To opt out
through doubt or fear was a great sin (14:1ff.; cf. Deut. 20:3f.).
Every man *from twenty years old and upward* was expected to join in.
Leviticus 27:3–4, by placing the highest valuation on people aged
between twenty and sixty, shows this was regarded as the prime of
life in ancient Israel. Generally men married before they were twenty,
but Deuteronomy 20:7 and 24:5 provide that those who were only
engaged or had just recently married were to be exempt from call-
up.

4–19. The representatives of each of the twelve secular tribes (the
Levites were not being counted) are named in verses 5–15. Most of

---

3. E.g. J. Bright, *A History of Israel*[2] (SCM, 1972), pp. 121f. For an earlier
date see J. J. Bimson, *Redating the Exodus and Conquest.*

the names are theophoric, that is they are compounds in which a name of God is used. Thus *Elizur* means 'my God is a rock', *Shedeur*, 'Shaddai is a light', *Shelumiel* means 'El (God) is my salvation'. It is interesting that Yahweh (the LORD) is not found in any of the names in this list, and this is one indication of its antiquity, for according to Exodus 6:3 the patriarchs knew God only as El Shaddai, not as Yahweh.[4] Another sign of the age of this list is the form of the names which suits a second millennium origin.[5]

These men reappear in chapter 7, and were probably the heads of their particular tribes (cf. 1:16). '*Clans*' (Hebrew *'elep*), literally 'thousands', seems to be an alternative name for the social unit rendered 'family' in verse 2 (Judg. 6:15; 1 Sam. 10:19) and, sometimes at least, designates the fighting members of a clan (cf. Num. 31:3–6).[6]

ii. The results of the census (1:20–46). The number of Israelites is given tribe by tribe. The formula is almost the same each time, emphasizing that these are the warriors that are being listed.

The grand total of all the warriors 603,550 (verse 46) is the same as that found in the first census (Exod. 38:26), and very similar to the total in the third census 601,730 (Num. 26:51) taken nearly forty years later. However, while the national totals stayed more or less constant over this period, the tribal totals show considerable variation. For example, the total of warriors in the tribe of Simeon declined over this period from 59,300 to 22,200 (1:23; 26:14), while the tribe of Manasseh increased from 32,200 to 52,700 (1:35; 26:34). These totals exclude women, children and Levites. When these are added, the total population of Israel must have come to about two million. Such

---

4. For discussion of Exodus 6:3 see G. J. Wenham, 'The Religion of the Patriarchs', in A. R. Millard and D. J. Wiseman (eds.), *Essays on the Patriarchal Narratives* (IVP, 1980), pp. 157–188.

5. See F. M. Cross. *Canaanite Myth and Hebrew Epic* (Harvard UP, 1973), p. 54.

6. For discussion of social terms, see J. Milgrom, 'Priestly Terminology and the Political and Social Structure of Premonarchic Israel', *JQR*, 69, 1978, pp. 65–81.

enormous numbers pose questions for the historian, and various interpretations of the figures have been advanced to alleviate the problem. They are discussed further in the additional note at the end of this chapter. Whichever solution to the historical problem is correct, the theological message of this section is clear. Every single man in Israel must prepare himself to fight in God's army. All the elect people of God are recorded in the book of life: but they have to identify themselves with this people by proving their pedigree and registering themselves on the national role (Exod. 32:32f.; Ps. 87:6; Isa. 4:3; Dan. 12:1; Mal. 3:16).

This census invites comparison with the opening chapters of the Gospels. Matthew begins by tracing the genealogy of Jesus, the new Israel, while Luke mentions that he was born in Bethlehem because his parents had gone there to be enrolled in a census (Luke 2:1–7). It is not clear if Luke saw this event as recapitulating the experience of the people of God in Numbers; but certainly many other parallels are drawn by the evangelists between our Lord's life and Israel's wilderness experiences. The great difference is that whereas Israel often failed the test, Jesus triumphed.

iii. The Levites' special role (1:47–54). The Levites were not included in this census, because it was concerned with establishing the number of fighting men. They had a different role, that of transporting, erecting and guarding the tabernacle. They had to camp round the tabernacle to prevent ordinary laymen approaching it unprepared. This would unleash God's wrath against the people (verse 53). Indeed, to prevent such a catastrophe they were commissioned to execute anyone who approached the tabernacle (verse 51). This drastic measure expressed the reality of God's presence in the tabernacle. Similar precautions were taken to prevent men straying on to Mount Sinai when God appeared on it (Exod. 19:11–13, 21–24). The New Testament also insists on men approaching God with reverent fear (Matt. 5:23–26; Acts 5:1–5; 1 Cor. 11:27–32; Heb. 12:18–29).

Additional note on the large numbers

The census results given in various chapters of Numbers are strikingly large. They are tabulated below.

	Numbers 1	Numbers 26
Reuben	46,500	43,730
Simeon	59,300	22,200
Gad	45,650	40,500
Judah	74,600	76,500
Issachar	54,400	64,300
Zebulun	57,400	60,500
Ephraim	40,500	32,500
Manasseh	32,200	52,700
Benjamin	35,400	45,600
Dan	62,700	64,400
Asher	41,500	53,400
Naphtali	53,400	45,400
Levi (Num. 3:46)	22,000	23,000
Total (excluding Levites)	603,550	601,730

According to Numbers 3:43 the number of first-born male Israelites was 22,273.

It should be noted that these figures interlock with each other. The grand totals are, of course, reached by adding up the tribal totals. The sum raised by the half-shekel tax was 100 talents 1,775 shekels, i.e. 301,775 shekels = ½ × 603,550 (Exod. 38:25–26). Also the number of first-born males is said to be exactly 273 more than the number of Levites (Num. 3:46–50).

There are four main problems with accepting the numbers as they stand. First, it is very difficult to imagine so many people surviving in the wilderness of Sinai for forty years. When women and children are included, the census figures suggest there were about two million people all told. Even allowing for heaven-sent quails and manna and occasional miraculous supplies of water, there would be great

difficulties in providing for all the physical requirements of such a
multitude, the more so when they are all supposed to have camped
neatly round the tabernacle (Num. 2) and marched together, and so
on. The bedouin population of modern Sinai amounts to only a few
thousand; and until relatively recent Jewish immigration into Israel,
the total population of Palestine, a much larger and more fertile area,
was only just over a million.

The second difficulty about accepting these figures is that they appear internally inconsistent. The most obvious point concerns the
ratio of adult males to first-born males, roughly 27 to 1. This means
that out of every 27 men in Israel only 1 was the first-born son in
his family. In other words an average family consisted of 27 sons, and
presumably an equal number of daughters. The average mother must
then have had more than 50 children![7] This figure would be reduced
if multiple polygamy were common in Israel and only the father's
first child counted as the first-born in the family. But other evidence
suggests bigamy was unusual in Old Testament times, and that multiple polygamy was restricted to the very rich.

The third difficulty arises from other texts which apparently acknowledge that initially there were too few Israelites to occupy the
promised land all at once (Exod. 23:29f.; Deut. 7:6f., 21f.). But two
million Israelites would have more than filled the land. Indeed, in the
judges period the fighting men of the tribe of Dan numbered only
600 (Judg. 18:16; cf. Num. 1:38–39).

The fourth point is a mathematical oddity, and does not prove
anything, though it may suggest these figures are not quite what they
appear. Not only are most of the figures rounded off to the nearest hundred, the hundreds tend to be bunched: 200, 300, 400, 500,
600, 700 occur but never 000, 100, 800 or 900. This concentration
of hundreds between 200 and 700 suggests the totals are not random
as might have been expected in a census.

There are four possible solutions:

1. The figures are accurate. Keil for instance argues that the number of first-born refers to those born *since the exodus*.[8] Given about

---

7. Keil, pp. 5ff.
8. Keil, pp. 5ff.

600,000 married couples in Israel it is not difficult to suppose that 22,273 boys were born in 13 months. As for the other objections one must remember that the land was more fertile in ancient times and that God provided for Israel in miraculous ways. Gispen[9] is the most recent writer to accept the authenticity of the figures. While not disputing these arguments, it still seems to me difficult to suppose there were so many people on the move in the wilderness. For example, most of the towns in the Bible excavated by archaeologists contained hundreds rather than thousands of people. In the Amarna letters (14th century BC) Canaanite kings have but a few hundred men in their armies, while in the great battle at Qadesh between the superpowers of Egypt and the Hittites (13th century), both armies mustered at most 20,000 men.

2. The figures are accurate but reflect the population of a later age, perhaps that of David. This was the view of Dillmann[10] and more recently W. F. Albright.[11] There are two problems with this view. First, that the figures are still large for the period of the united monarchy.[12] Second, by this time it seems that the tribe of Simeon was already being merged with the tribe of Judah, whereas this list presupposes the independence and strength of Simeon.

3. The figures have suffered textual corruption. The original figures were much smaller, but in the process of copying larger numbers have been substituted in error. These alterations may have been accidental because the manuscript being copied was hard to read, or deliberate: the scribe thought he understood what was meant and rewrote the text to clarify it.

This type of explanation has been adopted by a number of scholars. The first to propose this solution was Flinders Petrie.[13] He suggested that when the number of the tribe of Reuben is given as

---

9. Gispen, I, pp. 29–34.

10. Dillmann, p. 7.

11. W. F. Albright, *From the Stone Age to Christianity*[2] (Doubleday Anchor, Garden City, 1957), p. 253.

12. Cf. R. de Vaux, *Ancient Israel* (Darton, Longman and Todd, 1961), pp. 65–67.

13. W. M. Flinders Petrie, *Researches in Sinai* (John Murray, 1906), pp. 207ff.

forty-six thousand five hundred, the word translated thousand (*'elep*) has been misunderstood. It meant both thousand and family. In Numbers 1 it meant family. Thus the tribe of Reuben consisted of 46 families, containing 500 men. A later scribe misunderstood *'elep* to mean 1,000 and produced a grand total of Israelite men as 603,550. What he should really have done was to add up the families separately from the hundreds, which would have given 598 families, 5,550 men in the first census and 596 families, 5,730 men in the second census. This, Petrie suggested, would have been quite a plausible number of people to have inhabited the wilderness.

Flinders Petrie realized there was a weakness in his argument as far as the Levites were concerned. In the detailed breakdown of that tribe (Num. 3:21–34) the ratio of families to hundreds is very high compared with the secular tribes. He suggested that the list of Levites came from a later period soon after the conquest, when the population had greatly increased.

Petrie's suggestion has more recently been taken up by G. E. Mendenhall.[14] He points to census lists from Mari (18th century BC) and Alalakh (14th century) which also list those liable to war service. Both the overall totals of conscripts in the army and the size of units within the army (*'elep*) are of comparable size to those recorded here. However Mendenhall argues that these are lists of men of military age, not the whole population as Petrie suggested. This is what Numbers itself says (e.g. 1:3) and fits the practice of other ancient societies. Mendenhall thinks the lists date not from the wilderness period but from the judges era.

On the Petrie-Mendenhall hypothesis, the family group varied in size from 5 (300 ÷ 59) in the tribe of Simeon to 14 (650 ÷ 45) in the tribe of Gad. R. E. D. Clark[15] and my father, J. W. Wenham,[16] tried to improve the correlation between the number of families and tribal

---

14. G. E. Mendenhall, 'The Census of Numbers 1 and 26', *JBL*, 77, 1958, pp. 52–66.

15. R. E. D. Clark, 'The Large Numbers of the Old Testament', *Journal of the Transactions of the Victoria Institute*, 87, 1955, pp. 82–92.

16. J. W. Wenham, 'Large Numbers in the Old Testament', *TB*, 18, 1967, pp. 19–53.

size by postulating that *'elep* meant both 'family leader' or 'thousand'. Thus Reuben's total of 46,500 really meant 45 leaders, 1,500 men. By this means R. E. D. Clark reduced Israel's total population to 140,000, while J. W. Wenham reckons it was about 72,000, as against Petrie's estimate of 5,550 and Mendenhall's implied total of at least 20,000.

In evaluating these rival schemes, one is weighing the simplicity of Petrie's suggestion against the mathematical consistency of Clark and Wenham. With Mendenhall I do not see why there should not have been considerable variation in size between the different 'families'. Against Mendenhall I do not see why these figures should not have originated in the wilderness period. If one does adopt one of the text-critical solutions outlined here, one must suppose there was a thorough recension of the Hebrew text in which *'elep*, 'military group', 'family' was mistaken for '1,000', all the totals were inserted and then the other related figures made to tally with them. Since the Samaritan version and LXX by and large support the MT, this recension must have taken place no later than the fifth century BC.

4. The numbers are symbolic. The oldest attempt to interpret these figures uses gematria, that is each letter of the Hebrew alphabet is given a numerical value. On this basis 'children of Israel' comes to 603; whereas 'total of all the congregation of the people of Israel' (Num. 1:2) has been computed at 603,551. This is, of course, very close to the census total given in Numbers 1:46. However, this system explains only one of the numbers satisfactorily.

A completely different approach to the problem has been put forward by M. Barnouin.[17] In Mesopotamia mathematics and astronomy were well developed from early times. Quite complicated calculations were done using a sexagesimal system, and the length of the lunar and solar year and the synodic periods[18] of the planets were accurately known.

The census figures when divided by 100 can all be related to these

---

17. M. Barnouin, 'Les recensements du Livre des Nombres et l'astronomie babylonienne', *VT*, 27, 1977, pp. 280–303.

18. When a planet is in line with the sun and the earth it is invisible. The time from one passage behind the sun (or in front of the sun) to the next one is termed the synodic period.

astronomical periods. For example the number of Benjaminites is 100 × a short lunar year 354 days (Num. 1:37). This is the simplest case. The other figures in the list can be arrived at by combining pairs of census figures which then equal various astronomical periods. Thus in the first census (Num. 1) Issachar (544) + Ephraim (405) = Manasseh (322) + Dan (627) = Naphtali (534) + Asher (415) = 949 = solar year (365) + Period of Venus (584). In the second census (Num. 26) Simeon (222) + Asher (534) = 756 = 2 × period of Saturn (378). The grand totals can also be shown to have astronomical significance. In the first census the total is 603,550, in the second 601,730. These can be arrived at by adding up the respective tribal totals, but Barnouin suggests they have significance in their own right. 355 is a long lunar year. 1.73 = a long lunar year (355) − 2 × quarter solar year (91). 6,000 is a significant number in a sexagesimal system and is also equal to twice the sum of 365 (solar year) + 378 (Saturn's period) + 2,257 (sum of all planets' periods: Mercury, Venus, Mars, Jupiter, Saturn).

Barnouin gives reasons for believing that the relationship between the census lists and astronomical periods is more than coincidence. There are other texts in the Old Testament where numbers are used apparently with symbolic significance. The ages of the antediluvian patriarchs in Genesis may also be related to astronomical periods. Thus Enoch lived 365 years (Gen. 5:23) and Kenan's age 910 = 10 quarter years (Gen. 5:14). Furthermore, one of the promises to Abraham was that his descendants should be as numerous as the stars of heaven (Gen. 15:5). Indeed, Scripture frequently refers to the celestial bodies as God's heavenly host (e.g. Deut. 4:19), while the armies of Israel are his earthly hosts (e.g. Josh. 5:14 and throughout Num. 1). The earthly tabernacle was a replica of God's heavenly dwelling (Exod. 25:9, 40). Both were attended by the armies of the LORD. Finally, Genesis 37:9 compares Jacob and his sons (the ancestors of the twelve tribes) to the sun, moon and stars. These census numbers then affirm the sacred character of Israel. They remind us that God's promises to Abraham have been fulfilled, and that the holy people of God is called to struggle for him on earth as the stars fight for him in the heavenly places:

Barnouin's theory is very attractive, but it leaves some nagging questions. I tend to think that the theological symbolism he attaches to the numbers is correct, but I am not so sure that the procedures he uses for generating the numbers from astronomical periods is sufficiently simple to compel assent. In particular his scheme fails to offer a satisfactory treatment of the numbers of Levites. However, his is not the only system to break down at this point. Finally, it is tempting to ask how many in ancient Israel would have realized that the census numbers were related to astronomical periods. Barnouin side-steps the question of the historicity of these numbers by pointing to their symbolic value. However, it does not necessarily follow that because numbers are symbolic, they cannot also be historical. For example, in the Gospels Jesus chose twelve apostles and later sent out the seventy, and after the resurrection the disciples caught 153 fish. There is little doubt that these numbers are both symbolic and historical, whereas the numerous figures in the book of Revelation are pure symbolism. It depends on the type of literature whether symbolic numbers are also real.

Since these numbers claim to be census figures, the natural presumption is that they are to be taken literally, and that their symbolic significance is a matter of divine providence. However, given the difficulties of taking them literally (see opening paragraphs), we appear to be forced to take them as purely symbolic, unless it is postulated that the original census figures have been inflated by a factor of 100 in each case. But even this runs into problems with an odd 50 in Gad in the first census, and an extra 30 in Reuben in the second census. In short, there is no obvious solution to the problems posed by these census figures.

Barnouin also raises the question, where could Israel have acquired the astronomical knowledge that a symbolic interpretation implies they possessed? He suggests that they picked up the necessary data during the Babylonian exile. This is of course possible, but the evidence he cites does not demand it. Much of the astronomical information[19] was already known in the early second millennium BC, and the song of Deborah, universally recognized to be one of the

---

19. M. Rutten, *La Science des Chaldéens* (Presses Universitaires de France, Paris, 1960). H. W. F. Saggs, *The Greatness that was Babylon* (Sidgwick and Jackson, London, 1962), pp. 453ff.

earliest poems in the Bible, pictures the stars of heaven fighting alongside the armed tribes of Israel (Judg. 5:20). Thus the idea that the army of Israel corresponded to the heavenly host was an old one.[20]

iv. **Arrangement of tribes in camp and on the march (2:1–34).** This chapter describes how the tribes are to encamp around the tent of meeting in a square formation, and in which order they are to march. It is repeatedly said that they are to encamp *by their companies* (verses 9–10, 16, 18, 24–25, 32) and each company is described as the leader's *host* (verses 4, 6, 8, etc.). *Host* and *company* are alternative translations of the same Hebrew word *ṣābā'*, which could be rendered 'army'. Once again the picture is of the people of God organized as an army marching towards the promised land.

The Egyptian army under Rameses II (13th century BC) adopted this formation in camp. They camped in a square with the royal tent in the middle.[21] Likewise Israel's king dwelt in the centre of his armies in the tent of meeting. The *ensigns* (verse 2) by which the tribes camped were another piece of military equipment pictured in ancient inscriptions.[22] But unfortunately we have no idea what the Israelite tribal standards looked like. The *standard* (Hebrew *degel*, verses 2–3, 10, 18, 25, 31, 34) refers to the group encamped round each standard. Here it would be more appropriately translated 'company'.[23]

2. There was a space between the tribal encampments and the tent of meeting. The AV translation of *minneged* as *far off* (cf. NIV, 'some distance from it') seems preferable to NEB *facing it* (cf. 2 Sam. 18:13; 2 Kgs 4:25). Joshua 3:4 stipulates that a distance of 2,000 cubits (1,000 yards) should separate the ark from the secular tribes. This

---

20. I wish to thank my colleague, Dr Alan Hibbert, for his comments on the problems raised by these census lists.
21. See Y. Yadin, *The Art of Warfare in Biblical Lands* (Weidenfeld and Nicolson, 1963), pp. 236f. *Round* encampments of Assyrians are illustrated on pp. 292f. The gates of Shalmaneser III, however, illustrate both round and rectangular camps (Yadin, pp. 396f.).
22. See Yadin, pp. 123, 139.
23. Gray, p. 20.

The camp of Israel can be pictured diagrammatically:

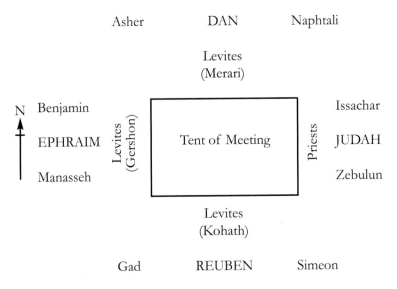

Asher   DAN   Naphtali

Levites
(Merari)

N   Benjamin   Issachar

EPHRAIM   Levites (Gershon)   Tent of Meeting   Priests   JUDAH

Manasseh   Zebulun

Levites
(Kohath)

Gad   REUBEN   Simeon

might be intended here as well. From 1:52f., 2:17 and chapter 3 we learn that the Levites were to encamp between the secular tribes and the tent of meeting.

3–31. The arrangement of tribes in camp and on the march suggests there was an order of precedence among them. Pre-eminent is the camp of Judah, which like the priests was stationed east of the tabernacle. Then came the camp of Reuben to the south, then Ephraim, then Dan. The same order was followed on the march (verses 9, 16, 24, 31). Verse 17 appears to say that the Levites carrying the tabernacle marched between the camp of Reuben and the camp of Ephraim. In fact, as 10:17–21 makes plain, some Levites marched before the camp of Reuben and some after it. 2:17 is making the point that, as the house of God had to be in the centre of Israel while they were encamped, so it had to be in the midst when they were on the march.

Verse 14 calls *Eliasaph*, the leader of Gad, *the son of Reuel.* Elsewhere (1:14; 7:42, 47; 10:20) MT always has 'son of Deuel'. R and D are very similar letters in Hebrew, and the confusion in the versions makes it difficult to decide which is the better reading. Since Deuel is more common it is more likely the earlier reading.

This picture of God dwelling among his people and guiding them on their journey towards the promised land aptly describes the present situation of the church. *The Word became flesh and dwelt* (tabernacled) *among us* (John 1:14). As God accompanied his people through the wilderness, he is present with the church today (1 Cor. 10:4). On the individual level 'your body is the temple of the Holy Spirit' (1 Cor. 6:19).

The book of Revelation takes the picture of the square camp with the tabernacle at its centre as the basis of its description of heaven, as a city which is a perfect cube with twelve gates named after the twelve tribes and 'its temple ... the Lord God the Almighty' (Rev. 21:10ff.). Adapting the imagery of Numbers in a different way, Revelation 19:14ff. speaks of the great battle in the last days when the armies of heaven will do battle with the kings of the earth. These ideas have been further developed in hymns like 'Onward, Christian soldiers'.

v. Census of all the Levites (3:1–51). Chapters 3 and 4 contain two censuses of the Levites. Chapter 3 counts all male Levites more than a month old, whereas chapter 4 numbers all male Levites between thirty and fifty years of age. So both these censuses are working on different bases from the censuses of the secular tribes recorded in chapters 1 and 26, which list the number of men over twenty years of age. The reason for these different age groupings is quite clear. The secular tribes were being organized into fighting units, but the Levites had a different function. Their primary task was the service of God: all the men in the tribe of Levi took the place of all the first-born men in Israel. The purpose of the census in Numbers 3 was to check that the number of Levites tallied with the number of first-born children among the other tribes. It was found that in fact the number of male Levites fell short of the number of first-born Israelites. So these extra Israelites had to be redeemed in a different way: by paying money.

The census in chapter 4 served a quite different purpose: to distribute the work of dismantling, transporting and erecting the tabernacle among the different Levitical clans. This work was dangerous, because it involved handling sacred equipment, and heavy. For these reasons it was restricted to men who were most likely to be of sober outlook and physically strong, i.e. those aged between thirty and fifty years.

2–4. The family of Aaron did belong to the tribe of Levi (1 Chr. 6:1–15), but as priests possessed superior status to the rest of the tribe. They alone had the right to handle the sacrificial blood, to touch the altar and to enter the tent of meeting. They were the authoritative teachers of the nation (e.g. Lev. 10:11; Deut. 24:8), the official mediators between God and Israel. With great privilege went immense responsibility. Those who represent God before men must be punctilious in obeying God's word. And Aaron's two elder sons were not: they *offered unholy fire before the LORD*, such as he had not commanded them (Lev. 10:1). This brief reference to the earlier incident explains why only Eleazar and Ithamar are mentioned as in charge of the Levites in 3:32; 4:16, 28, 33. It also serves to set the tone for chapters 3 – 4, which repeatedly allude to the mortal danger men face in dealing with God (3:10, 13, 38; 4:15, 18–20; cf. Acts 5:1–11; 12:22–23; 1 Cor. 10:6–11; 11:29–30).

5–10. This paragraph defines the Levites' duties. They are *to serve Aaron the priest and to minister to him* (NEB). More specifically *they shall perform duties for him … as they minister at the tabernacle*. The Hebrew phrases *šāmar mišmeret* (here translated by the RSV *perform duties*) and *'ābad 'ăbōdâ* (*minister*) are translated so vaguely in the various English versions, that the reader may well be left wondering what exactly the duties and ministry of the Levites consisted of. In fact the Hebrew phrases have a quite precise meaning in these chapters; they specify the two main functions of the Levites, to 'keep guard'(*šāmar mišmeret*), and 'to do the heavy work' of dismantling, transporting and erecting the tabernacle (*'ābad 'ăbōdâ*).[24] This second task is described more fully in chapter 4. They only had to do this heavy work whenever the camp was on the move. But they had to be permanently on guard, ready to kill any unauthorized person approaching the tent of meeting, its furniture or the altar. The phrase *he shall be put to death* implies a judicial execution, though in this context it is more like a policeman

---

24. See J. Milgrom, *Studies in Levitical Terminology* I (University of California, Berkeley, 1970).

shooting a bank robber (1:51; 3:10, 38; 18:7). The purpose of this summary execution was to prevent God punishing the whole people for one individual's transgression (cf. 1:53; chapters 16 – 17; cf. 25:8). Indeed, even the priests had to be ready to execute anyone who attempted to assume priestly prerogatives (verse 10). Examples of priests and Levites exercising this judicial role are to be found in Exodus 32:25–29 and Numbers 25:7–12.

11–13 explain the purpose behind the first Levitical census. All first-born creatures belong to God. Firstling animals such as cattle and oxen must therefore be offered in sacrifice (verse 13; cf. Exod. 22:29f.; 34:19f.), while every first-born boy in Israel was consecrated to the service of God in the sanctuary. But since the golden calf episode, the Levites had taken the place of the first-born in Israel (Exod. 32:25–29). The principle that all the first-born belong to God went back to the exodus. In the tenth plague all the first-born Egyptians and the firstling of cattle had died, but the Israelites were spared. In remembrance of their salvation the first-born Israelites had to be consecrated to the LORD (Exod. 11:4 – 13:15).

14–39. This section lists the number of Levites in each clan and assigns them their position in camp (see diagram on p. 77) and mentions briefly which parts of the tabernacle each clan is responsible for. Again a clear order of precedence among the clans is symbolized in their position and the items assigned to their care. The priests encamp in the most prestigious site east of the tent (verse 38). The Kohathites, the next most favoured group whose job is to carry the sacred vessels, encamp *on the south side of the tabernacle* (verse 29). The Gershonites charged with the care of the curtains camp to the west (verse 23), while the Merarites who are responsible for the poles and tent pegs camp *on the north side* (verse 35). On the march the Gershonites and Merarites go before the Kohathites, but that is for a practical reason: they have to erect the tent before the Kohathites arrive carrying the ark and the other vessels which are housed inside the tabernacle (10:17–21).

The total of 22,000 Levites given in verse 39 does not tally with the totals of the individual clans given in verses 22, 28, 34 which come to 22,300. The discrepancy is most easily explained as textual corruption in verse 28. The number of Kohathites may originally

have been 8,300. 3 (Hebrew *šlš*) could quite easily have been cor-
rupted into 6 (*šš*).[25]

40–51. The number of first-born Israelites exceeds the number
of Levites by 273. Therefore these excess Israelites must be redeemed by the payment of five shekels per person; this is the tariff
laid down in Leviticus 27:6 for boys between a month and five
years of age. This chapter lays down how much must be paid to the
sanctuary when someone is dedicated to God. Through dedication
a person becomes God's slave, as it were, but since only Levites may
actually serve as divine slaves other Israelites must be redeemed.
They do this by paying a sum equivalent to what they would fetch
if sold as slaves on the open market.[26] In the second millennium an
ordinary labourer could expect to earn less than a shekel per month.
The passage does not make it clear who paid the five shekels. Was
the whole sum (1,365 shekels) collected from all the (22,273) first-
born, or was it just the 273 who had to pay 5 shekels each for their
redemption? It is more natural to take verse 49 in the latter sense,
but certainty is impossible.

In the principle that the servant Levites redeem the first-born Israelites, Christians may see an anticipation of Jesus the great suffering servant who redeemed his people. This chapter's insistence that
the Levites must prevent other Israelites from sinning by warning and,
if necessary, killing encroachers anticipates New Testament challenges, particularly to elders, to correct erring brethren (Matt. 18:15ff.;
Acts 18:26; Gal. 2:11ff.; 6:1; 1 Thess. 5:12–14; 1 Tim. 5:19f.; Jas 5:19f.).

vi. Census of mature Levites (4:1–49). The second census of
Levites was designed to establish the number of male Levites aged
between thirty and fifty. These men were judged fit to carry the tabernacle on the march and assemble it wherever the nation camped.
A diagram of the tabernacle and court will clarify the instructions
in this chapter.[27]

---

25. This reading is supported by a few LXX manuscripts and the Armenian
    version.
26. See G. J. Wenham, 'Leviticus 27:2–8 and the Price of Slaves', *ZAW*, 90,
    1978, pp. 264f.
27. Detailed instructions about the design of the tabernacle are found in

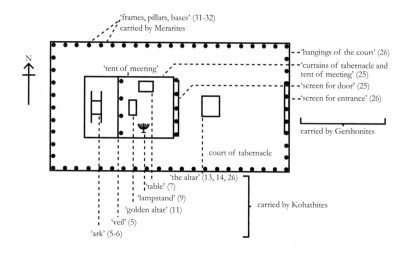

The Kohathites carried the furniture of the tabernacle, such as the ark, lampstand and golden incense altar. But they were not allowed to pack and unpack these items. Aaron and his sons, i.e. the priests, had to do this, because if the Kohathites had looked at these holy things uncovered, or touched them, they would have died (verses 5–20; cf. 1 Sam. 6:19f.; 2 Sam. 6:6f.).

4–15. The different vessels of the tabernacle were wrapped in different coloured cloths marking their different degrees of holiness. The most holy ark, the very throne of God, was wrapped first in the veil, then in *a covering of goatskin*[28] (AV 'badgers' skins', NEB 'porpoise-hide'), and finally in a blue cloth. The vessels from the next most holy

---

Exodus 25ff. For a full discussion on the interpretation of these chapters see *IBD*, 'Tabernacle', pp. 1506–1511.

28. As the different translations make plain, it is uncertain what the outer cover was made of. Hebrew *taḥaš* (RSV *goatskin*) was taken by the early versions to be a colour. But early Jewish scholars suggested that *taḥaš* was the name of an animal, *tuḥas* in Arabic means 'dolphin' and this underlies the NEB's suggested translation 'porpoise-hide', and NIV's 'hides of sea cows'.

part of the tabernacle were wrapped in a blue cloth, then in an outer goatskin covering (verses 7–12). The altar for burnt offering that stood in the court of the tabernacle was wrapped first in *a purple cloth*, and then in a goatskin cover. Thus, when the camp was on the move, the ark was distinguished from all the other pieces of furniture by its blue outer cover.

The same set of colours was used in the tabernacle. Deep blue curtains were used in the holy of holies, purple in the holy place, and the outer cover was again of goatskin. Undoubtedly these colours had significance, but discovering what they signified is difficult.[29] Evidently blue marked out the holiest objects, those most closely associated with the presence of God, perhaps because blue is the colour of heaven, God's real dwelling-place (cf. Exod. 24:10; 1 Kgs 8:27), and the tabernacle was built on the pattern of God's heavenly house (Exod. 25:9, 40; Heb. 8:5). Elsewhere blue and purple hangings adorned royal tents (Esth. 1:6). Similarly, kings and nobles wore blue and purple garments (e.g. Ezek. 23:6; Judg. 8:26). The use of the same colours here reminded Israel that the tabernacle was the palace of their divine king and that the ark was his throne.

The Kohathites carried their items on poles or a carrying frame (verses 6, 8, 11, 12, 14), but did not actually pack them up. The Gershonites and Merarites on the other hand packed and unpacked their parts of the tabernacle themselves, under priestly supervision (verses 28, 33), but did not carry these parts. They were transported on oxcarts. The curtains which were the Gershonites' responsibility required two carts, while the poles and tent pegs, for which the Merarites were responsible, needed four carts. Because their items were small and numerous, each Merarite was responsible for one particular item, so that none of them would be lost (verse 32).

Running through these censuses are two important biblical principles. First, that every member of the people of God has his part to play. The priests offered sacrifice, the Merarites carried the tent

---

29. On colour symbolism see V. W. Turner, *The Forest of Symbols* (Cornell University Press, 1967), pp. 59ff. For a discussion of the symbolism of the tabernacle see I. Hart, *Typology as a Hermeneutical Principle* (Belfast MTh Thesis, 1977).

pegs, the other tribes fought in the army. Each was indispensable to the smooth functioning of the whole body. Without full mutual cooperation the people would not reach the promised land. Similarly, in Christ's body every member has been endowed with spiritual gifts which contribute to the welfare of the whole church. But as in ancient Israel 'there are varieties of gifts, but the same Spirit; and there are varieties of service, but the same Lord; and there are varieties of working, but it is the same God who inspires them all in every one' (1 Cor. 12:4–6). Paul devotes the rest of the chapter to working out these principles in more detail.

The second great principle that is clearly enunciated in these chapters is that Israel was a hierarchy or, more precisely, a theocracy. God spoke to Moses and Aaron, and they passed on God's words to the people. The priests, Aaron's sons, obeyed their father. The Levites were subordinate to the priests, while in their turn the Levites served as religious policemen preventing the ordinary Israelite falling into deadly sin. Similarly, the New Testament pictures the church as well organized with a hierarchical order among its office-bearers. This organization goes back to our Lord himself who appointed twelve apostles in evident imitation of the twelve-tribe organization of Israel. Under Christ the apostles are the supreme authority in the church. Beneath them are the other office-holders such as prophets, teachers and elders (cf. 1 Cor. 12:28ff.; Eph. 4:11f.). The ordinary Christian is urged: 'Obey your leaders and submit to them' (Heb. 13:17; cf. 1 Cor. 16:16; 1 Thess. 5:12ff.; 1 Pet. 5:5); and the leaders are encouraged to 'command' and 'reprove with all authority', for by holding to scriptural teaching 'you will save both yourself and your hearers' (1 Tim. 4:11–16; Titus 2:15).

Additional note on the history of the priests and Levites

The book of Numbers sets out the relationship between the priests and Levites more clearly than any other part of the Old Testament. Both priests and Levites were descended from Levi, one of Jacob's twelve sons. The tribe of Levi was divided into three clans, Kohath, Gershon and Merari. The priests were one Levitical family, whose father was Aaron. According to 1 Chronicles 6:2–3, Aaron belonged to the Kohathite clan; this seems to be corroborated by Numbers

3 – 4 which gives the Kohathites more prestige than the other clans. According to Numbers, only the priests could offer sacrifice; the Levites' duties were to guard, transport and erect the tabernacle. Numbers assumes, and Exodus 32:25–29 confirms, that this relationship between the priests and Levites goes back to the wilderness period.

However, since Wellhausen popularized the idea in his *Prolegomena to the History of Israel* (1878), it has been commonly held that this relationship between priests and Levites originated only in much later, even post-exilic, times. It is argued that the real history of the priests and Levites ran somewhat as follows. In the earliest period every man could become a priest. At a later stage this right was restricted to the tribe of Levi, who ministered at various shrines throughout the land. In Jerusalem the priests descended from Zadok were in control. When Josiah abolished the high places in his great reformation between 630 and 622, the Levitical priests of the high places were brought into Jerusalem and allowed to serve in an auxiliary capacity assisting the Zadokite priests. To console the Levites for the loss of priestly rights at the high places, the Zadokites of Jerusalem claimed that they too were descended from Levi. Thus, although the Levites could no longer actually minister at the high places, it could be said that members of the tribe of Levi were the priests of the capital city. This was a legal fiction, for according to Wellhausen the Zadokite priests were not really members of the tribe of Levi. Variations on this theory can be found in most modern histories of Israelite religion and in more detailed studies of the Old Testament priesthood.[30]

A thorough refutation of this theory cannot be attempted here, but some of its weaknesses may be pointed out.[31] First, the role of the Levites as described in P (the priestly material in the Pentateuch)

---

30. E.g. A. H. J. Gunneweg, *Leviten und Priester* (Vandenhoeck and Ruprecht, Göttingen, 1965). A. Cody, *A History of Old Testament Priesthood* (Pontifical Biblical Institute, Rome, 1969).

31. These arguments are more fully set out in J. Milgrom, *Studies in Levitical Terminology* I (University of California, Berkeley, 1970). See also M. Haran, *Temples and Temple Service in Ancient Israel* (Clarendon Press, 1978),

does not correspond to that found in the later books of the Old Testament, such as Ezekiel and Chronicles. In Numbers the Levites' tasks are guarding and moving the tabernacle. The technical term *'ăbōdâ* for the physical labour of moving the tabernacle does not have the meaning of helping in the temple worship that it does in Chronicles. In Chronicles and Ezekiel the Levites never move the temple, because it was a fixture. Instead they sing, clean the sanctuary, and kill the sacrificial animals. Leviticus in fact instructs the layman to kill his own animal, but in later times this right was restricted to the Levites, and later still to the priests alone. Apart from transporting the tabernacle, the main job of the Levites according to P was guarding it (see Num. 1:51, etc.). This fits in with remarks in other early texts about the tribe of Levi, which is portrayed as warlike and keen to defend the LORD's rights with the sword (Gen. 34:25–30; 49:5–7; Exod. 32:25–29; Deut. 33:8f.). As for the distinctions between the priests and Levites, so clearly enunciated in Numbers and said to be a late innovation, a similar distinction is already found in a second-millennium Hittite text dealing with temple guards. It is also apparently presupposed in Deuteronomy, a book which is dated before P by most critics.[32]

B. Cleansing the camp (chapters 5 – 6)

i. **Purifying the camp (5:1–4).** The preparations for departure from Sinai continue with the expulsion of the unclean from the camp. They are not permitted to dwell in the tribal encampments described in chapter 2, but must separate themselves from the people and live in caves or in tents in the wilderness (cf. Lev. 13:46; 2 Kgs 7:3).

Uncleanness is a most important concept in the Old Testament. Leviticus 11 – 15 are devoted to expounding its meaning, but it is

---

pp. 58–111, and the articles of R. Abba, *IDB*, 3, pp. 886–889; *VT*, 27, 1977, pp. 257–267; *VT*, 28, 1978, pp. 1–9; and D. A. Hubbard, *IBD*, pp. 1266–1273.

32. See J. G. McConville, *Cultic Laws in Deuteronomy* (Belfast PhD thesis, 1980), pp. 205–248.

hard for secularized Western man to grasp.[33] It is of course related to being dirty, for one of the standard ways of removing minor uncleanness is washing (Lev. 11:40; 15:18; 17:15). But it means much more than dirt. It is caused by death, sins, especially of sex, and certain bodily conditions we might class as abnormal. If a person was affected in any of these ways he became unclean and unfit for the presence of God. Indeed, to approach God in such a condition was positively dangerous and could lead to the death of the individual concerned (Lev. 7:20). But unclean people were a danger to the whole community. In some cases their uncleanness could be directly transmitted to other people, thus making them liable to divine judgment if they partook of a sacrifice. But more important still, uncleanness could defile the tabernacle, which would make it impossible for God to dwell there (Lev. 15:31). Thus the very purpose of Israel's existence would be nullified. Once a year on the day of atonement the priest conducted a purification of the tabernacle to ensure God's continuing presence with his people (Lev. 16). The measure described here is preventive. By the exclusion of the seriously unclean from the camp the chance of polluting the tabernacle would be reduced.

Three categories of unclean person are mentioned here: lepers, those with discharges, and those who have come in contact with the dead. Despite the translation *leper* (RSV) or *malignant skin disease* (NEB), neither leprosy nor skin cancer is meant by the Hebrew term *ṣāraʿat*. Careful study of such passages as Leviticus 13 and Numbers 12:10–16 suggests that patchy, scaly skin diseases are meant, such as psoriasis or favus.[34]

The discharges which make people unclean are those from the sexual organs (see Lev. 15). It seems likely that only the longer-term discharges, that required a sacrifice to be offered when they cleared up, are meant here.

Being the antithesis of perfect life, which points to God the

---

33. See Wenham, pp. 18ff.
34. See E. V. Hulse, 'The Nature of Biblical "Leprosy"', *PEQ*, 107, 1975, pp. 87–105 and Wenham, pp. 194ff.; cf. S. G. Browne, *Leprosy in the Bible* (Christian Medical Fellowship, London, 1970).

creator, death is patently most unclean. Contact with dead animals makes a man unclean for a day, but contact with human corpses, for a whole week. Thus the holy men of ancient Israel, such as the priests and Nazirites, were forbidden to join in mourning for their relatives (Lev. 21:2f., 11; Num. 6:6f.). Here these requirements are extended to all Israel, to impress on them the need for total dedication to the LORD. Similar rules about purity in war were still observed in David's time (1 Sam. 21:5; 2 Sam. 11:11; cf. Judg. 20:8).

The unclean were expelled from the camp because God was dwelling in the midst of it. The book of Revelation uses the same ideas to describe the new Jerusalem: 'God himself will be with them; he will wipe away every tear from their eyes, and death shall be no more ... But nothing unclean shall enter it' (Rev. 21:3f., 27). In anticipation of the heavenly consummation, the early church exercised a discipline over its members who blatantly erred in practice or belief (1 Cor. 5; 2 Cor. 6:14 – 7:13; 2 Thess. 3:14; Titus 3:10f.; 2 John 10f.). Patristic commentators also saw this passage as justifying the excommunication of heretical or immoral church members.[35]

But if the New Testament upholds the moral side of these uncleanness regulations, it abolished the symbolic physical distinctions. Our Lord healed lepers and the woman with a flow of blood, and raised the dead through his touch (Luke 17:12ff.; 8:40ff.). In these ways he declared that those conditions which for centuries had separated even the elect people of God from God no longer mattered. God has himself drawn nigh. The kingdom of heaven is now open to all who repent and believe the gospel.

ii. Repayment of debts (5:5-10). The narrative pauses for a moment for the revelation of three pairs of laws[36] illustrating how the unclean should be treated. Whereas the expulsion of 'lepers' and others from the camp was an immediate response to the presence of unclean persons among the holy people of God, these laws could be

---

35. de Vaulx, p. 91.
36. For this pattern of three pairs of law on similar subjects cf. chapter 15; 33:50 – 36:13; Deut. 21; 22:13–29; G. J. Wenham and J. G. McConville, 'Drafting Techniques in Some Deuteronomic Laws', *VT*, 30, 1980, pp. 248–252.

applied beyond the wilderness situation and hence function as implicit promises that ere long Israel would reach the promised land.[37]

Each pair of laws begins, *The LORD said to Moses, 'Say to the people of Israel'* (5:5–6, 11–12; 6:1–2) and falls into two parts (5:6–7/8–10; 5:11–31;[38] 6:2–12/13–20). In two of the three cases the sin is described as breaking faith (*mā'al ma'al*, 5:6, 12, 27), and where atonement was possible the appropriate sacrifice was a guilt offering (*'āšām*, 5:8; 6:12). As elsewhere in Numbers the right of the priests to a share in the sacrifices is emphasized (5:8–10, 25; 6:10–12, 14–20).

The first pair of laws is an invitation to all those who have stolen things, or otherwise defrauded their neighbours, to put things right. The sort of offence envisaged is described in Leviticus 6:1–5. Someone has acquired goods that he has no right to and has then denied his offence under oath. By so doing he is *breaking faith with the LORD* (verse 6) as well as sinning against his neighbour.

The following verses describe what must be done 'when that person feels guilty'[39] (verse 6b), *he shall make full restitution for his wrong, adding a fifth to it, and giving it to him to whom he did the wrong* (verse 7). This provision corresponds exactly to the rules enunciated in Leviticus 6. Numbers then proceeds to a case not covered by Leviticus. What is to be done if the defrauded man is dead? Restitution must instead be made to his near relatives; if they are all dead, it must be made to the priest. In all cases involving fraud with false oaths a ram had to be offered as a reparation (guilt) offering (cf. Lev. 5:14–19). Where the defrauded man was dead, the priest received the returned goods as well (verse 8). This prompts a reminder about always giving the priests their rightful dues (verses 9f.). Fuller regulations

---

37. The prohibitions against consuming any grape products in 6:3–4 is the clearest pointer that a settled agricultural life is envisaged (cf. 13:23ff.).

38. The law on the suspected adulteress also covers two cases, the guilty and the falsely accused, but since the prescribed ritual is the same in both cases it is only in the introduction and concluding summary that they are formally distinguished (5:12–14a/14b; cf. 29/30).

39. The translation 'feels guilty' is an apter rendering of *wĕ'āšēmâ* than *is guilty* (RSV) or *incurred guilt* (NEB). See J. Milgrom, *Cult and Conscience* (Brill, Leiden, 1976), pp. 9ff.

about priestly perquisites are to be found in Leviticus 6:14 – 7:36; 27; Numbers 18 and Deuteronomy 18:1–8.

The practical importance of this law is obvious. Israel had been drawn up in battle array to march towards the promised land. But their unity would be shattered if they were squabbling among themselves and taking God's name in vain. Through restitution and sacrifice, peace with God and harmony within the nation could be restored. The New Testament underlines these points: 'If you are offering your gift at the altar, and there remember that your brother has something against you, leave your gift ... first be reconciled to your brother' (Matt. 5:23f.; cf. Luke 19:8f.; 1 Cor. 6:7f.; Gal 5:15, etc.).

iii. The ordeal of jealousy (5:11–31). It is most unusual in the Bible for descriptions of biblical rituals to include the words that accompanied them. In the many sacrifices described in Leviticus, the prayers of the participants are hardly ever recorded, we have just the rubrics. Here both the prayers and the ritual are recorded, and this makes the interpretation of the ceremony relatively straightforward. It is a ritual both to determine the guilt or innocence of a woman suspected of adultery, and to punish the guilty while leaving the innocent unscathed. Drinking ordeals like this are best attested in African societies, but parallels are also found in Mari (18th century BC) and Hittite texts[40] (cf. Exod. 32:20).

As often in Numbers, it is not immediately apparent what this law has to do with its context. It seems out of place in a section concerned with purifying the camp and the people. Closer inspection shows that this ritual is indeed related to the preceding laws. Adulterous wives are picked out for special attention, because adultery pollutes those involved, making them unclean (verses 13f., 19f., 28f.; cf. Lev. 18:20, 25, 27). They should therefore be eliminated from the camp (cf. verses 3f.). Second, both adultery and the offences described in verses 5–11 are described as *breaking faith* (verse 6) or *acting unfaithfully* (verses 12, 27). The same Hebrew word (*mā'al*) is used in both cases: false oaths break faith with God, adulterers break faith with their spouses. Thirdly, it may be noted that Leviticus 19:20–22

---

40. See M. Weinfeld, 'Ordeal of Jealousy', *Encyclopaedia Judaica*, XII, pp. 1448–1449; T. S. Frymer, 'Ordeal, Judicial', *IDBS*, pp. 638–640.

prescribes a guilt offering for adultery with a slave girl. This association with guilt offerings serves to link these three consecutive sections (5:5–10; 11–31 and 6:1–21; NB verse 12). A fourth point of contact with verses 5–10 is that this ordeal is essentially an elaborate oath to establish a wife's fidelity or otherwise. Such oaths were also used to determine rights in property claims (e.g. Exod. 22:7–13) and are alluded to in verse 6 'breaking faith'. Whereas in the case of debt repayment we have a guilty man owning up to misusing an oath, in this ordeal we have a suspicious husband imposing a solemn oath on his wife. Finally, throughout Scripture the covenant relationship between God and his people is compared with marriage. As he is concerned with the purity of Israel shown in the expulsion of the unclean from the camp, so husbands are right to be worried if they suspect their wives have polluted themselves through infidelity. Indeed, early Jewish exegesis likened the drink made from the ashes of the golden calf to the draught administered to suspect women. This law and the golden calf episode may lie behind prophetic references to the cup which the LORD will make faithless Israel drink (Isa. 51:17, 22; Ezek. 23:30–34).

A certain repetitiveness in this law (cf. 16b and 18a, 19a and 21a, 21b and 22a, 24a, 26b and 27a) has led some commentators to surmise that two different laws have been combined in this chapter, though they admit it is difficult to reconstruct both sources in their entirety. I noted that both the preceding law (5:5–10) and the immediately succeeding law (6:2–21) fell into two parts. Something similar is discernible here. The law is concerned with two possibilities: the woman is guilty of adultery but her husband has no proof (5:12–14a, 27, 29), or she is innocent and her husband's suspicions are groundless (14b, 28, 30). The double heading and subscript to the law show that it is concerned with these two distinct cases.[41] But since the procedure is the same in both, it is described only once (15–26). This section makes good sense as it stands. It is unnecessary to postulate the presence of two sources here. The repetition

---

41. Cf. M. Fishbane, 'Accusations of Adultery: A Study of Law and Scribal Practice in Numbers 5:11–31', *HUCA*, 45, 1974, pp. 25–45. Fishbane, p. 35, thinks the twin heading is 12–13/14 not 12–14a/14b.

sometimes results from the law dealing with the two possibilities, guilt or innocence (19–22). Elsewhere it is typical Hebrew style, which may anticipate or resume a point out of strict chronological sequence[42] (e.g. 16a/18a; 24/26/27). A summary of the ceremony will make this clear.

1. the suspicious husband brings his wife and an appropriate cereal offering to the priest (15).
2. the priest takes the woman into the court of the tabernacle *before the LORD* (16).
3. the priest takes an earthenware vessel, puts water in it, and mixes it with dust from the tabernacle floor (17).
4. the priest goes back to the woman, *unbinds her hair* and puts the cereal offering in her hand (18).
5. holding the water in his hands the priest recites the curse to the woman, and she assents to it (19–22).
6. the priest writes down the curses and then washes them off into the holy water (23).
7. the priest takes the cereal offering from the woman, and burns part of it on the altar (25–26).
8. the woman drinks the water (26b).
9. the water affects the woman if she is guilty (27–28).

TEV makes the sequence of events quite clear.

The oath administered to the woman makes the purpose of this ritual perfectly clear (19–22). The modern reader may wonder why an oath was not sufficient on its own. Would not God have answered the priest's prayer without resorting to the mumbo-jumbo of magic? Does not this ceremony imply an unbiblical notion of a God subject to human manipulation, or at least an unscientific belief in the efficacy of holy water? Similar objections could of course be raised against the practice of animal sacrifice. Why does the Old Testament

---

42. Cf. H. C. Brichto, 'The Case of the *Sōṭā* and a Reconsideration of Biblical "Law"', *HUCA*, 46, 1975, pp. 55–70. TEV and Brichto, p. 61, are probably right to regard verse 24 as anticipating the climax of the rite in verse 26b.

insist on the slaughter of lambs and bulls to propitiate God's wrath? Would not prayer alone have been adequate to secure divine forgiveness?

Since ritual plays such a major role in the Bible and its function is rarely appreciated by modern readers, it is worth while examining very briefly the role ritual plays in social life, before we attempt to interpret this particular ceremony. 'Rituals reveal values at their deepest level ... men express in ritual what moves them most, and since the form of expression is conventionalized and obligatory, it is the values of the group that are revealed.'[43] Monica Wilson was talking about African tribal societies, but her observations are equally applicable to the conventional rites of our society. Monarchs are crowned with elaborate ceremonial: prime ministers and presidents are installed with next to none. University degrees are conferred in person at grand graduation ceremonies: A or O-level (high-school examinations) certificates are sent out by post. It is not simply because coronations and graduation are archaic customs that more ritual is associated with them. Monarchs are supposed to enjoy the allegiance of their whole people and to personify the values of the nation, whereas prime ministers are elected by majority vote. Similarly, the holding of a degree ceremony indicates that a degree is more highly valued than an O-level pass. The rituals accompanying graduation, baptism or marriage indicate the importance society attaches to these institutions. Similarly, here the offering of sacrifice and the drinking of the bitter waters underlines and dramatizes the curses imposed on the woman. Whether the potion was effective in making a guilty woman sterile no more depends on magic than does intercessory prayer. Prayer and symbolic rituals both depend ultimately on the will of God for their efficacy.

The ceremony begins with the husband bringing an offering of barley meal. Though it is called a cereal offering, he is forbidden to offer oil and frankincense which usually accompanied cereal offerings (Lev. 2). This makes it much more like the poor man's sin offering (Lev. 5:11–13) offered when someone had contracted

---

43. M. Wilson, *American Anthropologist*, 56, 1954, p. 241, quoted by V. W. Turner, *The Ritual Process* (Routledge, 1969), p. 6.

uncleanness (Lev. 5:1–4). This then is the first hint in the ritual that the woman is regarded as unclean. For the sin offering fine flour (possibly wheat flour) was prescribed; here cheap barley meal is required, making this the lowliest sacrifice in the Bible. Oil and frankincense symbolize joy and the Spirit of God (cf. Ps. 45:7; 1 Sam. 10:1). Their omission here is clearly deliberate. The barley is given to the woman by her husband, and she then gives it to the priest (15, 25–26). Hosea 2:8–9 states that God will cut back the rations of faithless Israel, and it may be that the offering of barley without oil in this instance mirrors what has been happening at home: the husband has been depriving his wife of oil and frankincense (cf. Ezek. 23:41).

The draught is prepared from holy water, probably taken from the laver between the altar and the tent of meeting (Exod. 30:18), dust from the tabernacle floor, and the curses (17, 23). Every component in a ritual has symbolic significance, but without living informants it is difficult to recover the full meaning of a ceremony. It may be that the mixing of the water and dust in the vessel is supposed to picture what is happening inside the woman's body. *Vessel* can refer to a body (1 Sam. 21:5; Jer. 18:4; 22:28; cf. Acts 9:15; 1 Thess. 4:4). *Water* symbolizes life and fertility[44] (Ps. 1:3; Jer. 17:13), and occasionally is a metaphor for male semen (Prov. 5:16; cf. 9:17). Several of the symbolic meanings associated with *dust* might be appropriate here. Abraham's seed were to be as numerous as the dust of the earth (Gen. 13:16; cf. Num. 23:10). The unclean beast, the serpent, ate dust (Gen. 3:14; cf. Exod. 32:20). God created man from the dust of the earth (Gen. 2:7). The last meaning may be primary here, but the other ideas may be in the background as well, for symbols evoke a multiplicity of associations.

If the interpretation of individual items in the rite is uncertain, the overall thrust is very clear. Holy water and dust from the tabernacle are to be administered to a woman suspected of uncleanness. Even without the addition of an oath, such a procedure should have proved fatal, if the woman was guilty. Someone who ate of a sacrifice while he was unclean was liable to sudden death (Lev. 7:21; 22:3; cf. Num. 9:6). This dust taken from the very presence of God

---

44. Cf. V. W. Turner, op. cit., p. 66.

himself was likely to have been more lethal still. It is not likely that
the dust would have made the water taste bitter (*mārîm*), and the
phrase *and cause bitter pain* (24, 27), literally 'for bitterness', suggests
that another translation may be more appropriate, NEB 'contention'
supposes *mārîm* is a noun derived from *mārâ*, 'to rebel', while
Brichto[45] suggests it comes from *yārâ*, 'to show, teach' and translates
it 'portent'. If the traditional translation 'bitter waters' is retained, the
reference must be to their effect rather than their taste.

The unbinding of the woman's hair is another hint that she was
viewed as unclean. 'Lepers' had to let their hair hang loose as a mark
of their uncleanness (Lev. 13:45) whereas priests, forbidden to contract pollution through touching the dead, had to refrain from un-
tidying their hair even in mourning (Lev. 10:6; 21:10–11).

The effect of the curse on a guilty woman is to make 'her thigh
fall away and her belly to swell' (verses 21, 27). The Mishnaic comment on this passage (*Sotah* 1:7) 'In the member she sinned with she
will be punished' has hit the nail on the head. This is a case of a punishment mirroring the crime, a favourite principle of oriental law. In
adultery the woman sinned with her 'thigh' and conceived in her
'belly'. Therefore it is fitting that these organs should be the scene
of her punishment. What this means in medical terms is uncertain.
Josephus[46] suggested dropsy. More recent suggestions include a
miscarriage (NEB), thrombophlebitis,[47] or a false pregnancy.[48] Exact
diagnosis is unimportant; as the contrast with the innocent wife
makes clear (verse 28), the adulteress will be childless and therefore
an *execration among her people* (verses 21, 27). Genesis 20:17 mentions
that Abimelech's wives became sterile as a result of his intention to
commit adultery with Sarah. Leviticus 20:20f. predict that the same
penalty will befall couples guilty of incestuous relationships.

Though childlessness may seem to be quite a mild penalty to modern urbanized man, it was regarded as a catastrophe in biblical times
(e.g. Gen. 15ff.; 30; 1 Sam. 1:8, etc.) and still is in primitive societies.

---

45. *HUCA*, 46, p. 59.
46. *Antiquities* iii.11.6.
47. J. M. Sasson, *Biblische Zeitschrift*, 16, 1972, p. 251, n. 15.
48. Brichto, *HUCA*, 46, p. 66.

For this reason the ordeal should not be thought of as a mild alternative to the death penalty prescribed for adulterers caught red-handed (cf. Lev. 20:10; Deut. 22:22). It was designed to reassure suspicious husbands that, even if they had no proof themselves of their wives' infidelity, God would assuredly punish the guilty and demonstrate the innocence of the faithful (cf. verses 27–28, 31).[49] It was also a graphic and dramatic representation of the importance of purity in marriage; and as every human marriage is an image of the relationship between God and his people, it also reminds us of the faithfulness God requires in his servants.

Our Lord forgave penitent adulterers (e.g. John 8:2–11; cf. Luke 7:37–50). But his 'Go and sin no more' is echoed in the clear warnings in the epistles that persistence in sexual immorality excludes men from the kingdom of God (1 Cor. 5:9f.). Such people must be driven out of the church (1 Cor. 5:11–13). Fornicators are among those shut out from the holy city (Rev. 21:8; 22:15). Thus Numbers 5, Paul and Revelation make the same point: unfaithfulness in marriage is incompatible with membership of the people of God.

iv. **The Nazirite (6:1–21).** The Nazirites were the monks and nuns of ancient Israel, lay men or women who consecrated themselves to the total service of God, usually for a specific period of time, though more rarely for life. The laws on Nazirites were included here because they fit the general theme of this part of Numbers. The nation is being organized as the holy people of God. Israel was called to be 'a kingdom of priests' (Exod. 19:6), and the rules voluntarily assumed by the Nazirites resembled those governing the behaviour of priests, while their distinctive hairstyle reminded the laity that even they were called to be kings and priests to God (cf. Rev. 5:10). Thus as marriage symbolized the relationship between God and Israel (Num. 5), so the Nazirites epitomized the holy calling of the nation (Jer. 7:29). If pollution through dead bodies demanded the expulsion of ordinary laymen from the camp (5:2–3), it had an even more drastic effect on the Nazirites, the quintessence of sanctity (6:9–12).

---

49. *The man shall be free from iniquity* (31) indicates that no blame will be attached to him for making his wife submit to the ordeal.

Formally these laws also cohere well with their context. There is
the same opening formula (6:1–2; cf. 5:5f., 11f.), and, as in the preceding laws, the subject is dealt with under two main heads: the pollution of Nazirites (6:2–12) and their deconsecration (6:13–21). The
reminder to give the priests their full dues links these laws with what
precedes and what follows (6:19–20; cf. 5:8–10; 6:22–26).

Vows to God were a regular feature of life in Israel. They traditionally took the form of a promise to give or do something for God,
if he helped the votary (Gen. 28:20–22; Lev. 27; Judg. 11:30ff.; 1 Sam.
1:11ff.; Ps. 66:13f.; Jon. 1:16; Acts 23:12ff.). However, the Nazirite vow
is here described as a *special vow* (verse 2; cf. Lev. 27:2); the Hebrew
word (*hipli'*) indicates something outstanding and unusual (e.g. Judg.
13:19; Isa. 28:29), in that the person gave himself to God for a period
of time. At least, this was the usual arrangement envisaged in this law.
The phrase *all the days of his vow* (verse 5; cf. 4, 6 , 8 , 12) and the regulations about the sacrifices to be offered when the vow was complete
(13–20) show that the Nazirite vow normally had a time-limit on it
and was undertaken voluntarily by the person concerned. However,
Samson and probably Samuel[50] were dedicated by their parents to be
life-long Nazirites even before they were born (Judg. 13:4–5; 1 Sam.
1:11).

The English word *Nazirite* (2, 13, 18–21) transliterates Hebrew
nāzîr,[51] meaning 'set apart'. Negatively the Nazirites were separated
(hiphil of *nāzar*, verse 3) from wine, grape products and dead

---

50. One of the Qumran MSS calls Samuel a Nazirite: this is implied but not
explicit in the MT. See *BASOR*, 132, 1953, p. 18, n. 5.

51. *nāzîr* sometimes means 'prince' (e.g. Gen. 49:26; Deut. 33:16; Lam. 4:7)
and twice 'unpruned vine' (Lev. 25:5, 11). These homonyms may also
help to elucidate the symbolic significance of the Nazirites. They were
lay 'princes' whose uncut hair was their crown (*nēzer*). The vine
symbolizes Israel (e.g. Isa. 5:7; Mark 12:1) and the fruit of the unpruned
vines was not gathered in the seventh year as a sign of that year's
dedication to the LORD. It may be that the unpicked, unpruned vines
symbolized Israel's consecration to God's service; this would fit our
interpretation of the Nazirite vow. On the multivocality of symbols see
V. W. Turner, *The Forest of Symbols*, pp. 19ff.

bodies. Positively they were separated *to the* L ORD (2, 5, 6, 12). He was *holy to the* L ORD (8). The same root *nēzer*, translated *separation* (7) or *consecrated* (*head*) (9), denotes the characteristic mark of the Nazirite, his uncut hair. The same term is used of the high priest's diadem and anointing oil and the royal crowns (Lev. 8:9; 21:12; 2 Kgs 11:12). The Nazirite's long hair was regarded as God's special gift to him (Judg. 16:17, 22), which had to be returned to God in the sacrificial fire when the vow was completed (18).

It is not a coincidence that the Nazirite's long hair and the high priest's diadem and anointing oil are all called *nēzer*, for in both cases these were outward symbols of the holiness expected of high priest and Nazirite. The restrictions placed on Nazirites suggest that their sanctity exceeded that of ordinary priests and resembled that of the high priests. Priests were prohibited from drinking alcohol only before going on duty in the tabernacle (Lev. 10:9); Nazirites were forbidden to consume any products of the vine at any time[52] (3–4). Whereas ordinary priests could mourn their closest relatives, high priests and Nazirites could not (7; cf. Lev. 21:2f., 11). On completion of his vow the Nazirite had to offer the same range of sacrifices as Aaron did at his ordination, another pointer to the comparable holiness of Nazirite and high priest (13–20; cf. Lev. 8).

The exceptional holiness of the Nazirite is again underlined by the rules governing his reconsecration should he contract pollution through contact with a corpse. Minor uncleanness could be cleansed through washing with water and waiting till evening (e.g. Lev. 11:39f.; 15:17f.). More serious pollution demanded a seven-day wait and the offering of cheap sin offerings (Lev. 12; 15:1–15). As Numbers repeatedly stresses, the pollution caused by human death is particu-larly serious. Nevertheless the ordinary layman may be cleansed from it through washing in the special mixture prescribed in Numbers 19.

This was inadequate in the case of the Nazirite. He had to bring birds as a burnt offering, a sin offering and, most expensive of all,

---

52. The words translated juice, seeds, skins (3–4) occur only here and are of uncertain meaning.

a lamb for a guilt offering.[53] This sacrifice was reserved for severe infringements of God's rights.[54] In addition, contact with the dead polluted his holy hair, which therefore had to be shaved off. Because it was defiled it could not be burnt in the altar fire (cf. 18). In addition the period of Naziriteship started all over again (9–12). The Mishnah relates how Queen Helena had almost completed seven years of a Nazirite vow when she was defiled and therefore had to keep it for another seven years.[55]

If in holiness the Nazirite was regarded as equal to the high priest, in other respects he was quite different. The priesthood was restricted to men, but women could become Nazirites (2). The priests could enter the tent of meeting, offer sacrifice, bless the people and give authoritative teaching. The Nazirites could not. The priests wore distinctive vestments and trimmed their hair (Ezek. 44:20), but the Nazirites did neither. The priests lived off the offerings of the laity; the Nazirites, as laymen, gave sacrifices to the priests.

When the Nazirite had fulfilled his vow, he brought the four main types of sacrifice: burnt, cereal, peace and sin offerings (13–20; cf. Lev. 1 – 4) together with the drink offerings of wine that traditionally accompanied burnt and peace offerings (Num. 15). Laymen were normally allowed to bring pigeons as a cheap alternative to lamb for burnt and sin offerings (Lev. 1:14–17; 5:7–10); here three lambs are mandatory, another reminder of the cost and sanctity of the Nazirite vow (14).

Another variation in the peace-offering ritual makes a similar point. The peace offering was the only animal sacrifice in which the worshipper enjoyed a share of the meat. The priest usually received the breast and the thigh (20). The breast was *waved*, traditionally supposed to mean a ritual side-to-side motion, and the thigh was *offered*

---

53. For full description see Lev. 1 – 7 and Additional note on Old Testament sacrifice, pp. 226ff.
54. Cf. J. Milgrom, *Cult and Conscience* (Brill, 1976), pp. 66–70; Wenham, pp. 104ff.
55. *Nazir* 3:6.

(AV *heaved*), an up-and-down action.[56] But on this occasion *the shoulder of the ram* and two cakes (19) were waved as well and donated to the priest, who thus received an extra part of the lamb for his own consumption (cf. Deut. 18:3). This departure from normal practice is no doubt significant: the Nazirite gives more of the peace offering than usual, thereby asserting once again in a different way that the vow involves an extra degree of consecration to God's service. These sacrifices and the shaving off of his holy hair reintegrated the Nazirite into the ranks of the ordinary people of God. So afterwards he *may drink wine* again (20; cf. 3–4).

The summary of the law in verse 21 implies by the phrase *apart from what else he can afford* that some Nazirite vows included extra commitments not mentioned here. These too had to be fulfilled before a man could be released from his vow. The regulations in 2–20 set out the minimum requirements for a Nazirite vow.

Throughout the biblical period the discipline of Nazirite vows was highly respected. Samson, Samuel and contemporaries of Amos (Amos 2:11f.) took the vow. Josephus[57] mentions that these vows were popular in the first century AD. The vows mentioned in Acts (18:18; 21:23) may have been Nazirite. It has often been suggested that John the Baptist and James the brother of Jesus were Nazirites.[58] These examples suggest that vows and other self-imposed obligations may still have a place in church life, pointing to the total dedication to God's service that is the goal of all Christian disciples (e.g. Matt. 6:16; Mark 2:20; Luke 14:26; Matt. 8:21–22). Like the other holy men of the old covenant, the Nazirite also prefigured the ministry of our Lord (Matt. 2:23).

v. The Aaronic blessing (6:22–27). This short and beautiful prayer is so familiar that its meaning may be easily taken for granted and not appreciated. Its strange context, immediately after the Nazirite law and before the offerings of the princes (ch. 7), forces the reader to consider why it is placed here. Its introduction (verse 22) links it with the regulations designed to purify the camp (5:1ff., 5ff., 11ff.; 6:1ff.), and

---

56. J. Milgrom, *IEJ*, 22, 1972, pp. 33–38, suggests waving was a ritual giving to God, whereas offering did not involve any special gestures.

57. *Antiquities* xix.6.1.

58. E.g. Eusebius, *Ecclesiastical History* ii.23.4.

thereby to prepare the people for the great act of worship, the march towards the promised land. The blessing which invokes God's protection on the people comes at a very apposite moment. It also serves to show that God's permanent purpose is to bless all his people, not merely those who undertake the Nazirite vow. Whereas Nazirites generally undertook their vows for a short period, the priests were always there pronouncing this blessing at the close of the daily morning service in the temple and later in the synagogues. The proclamation of this prayer by the priests was a guarantee that God would indeed *bless the people of Israel* (verse 27).

The prayer is cast in poetic form and is probably one of the oldest poems in Scripture.[59] The first line consists of three words in Hebrew with a total of twelve syllables, the second five words and fourteen syllables, and the third seven words with sixteen syllables.[60] Even the number of Hebrew consonants builds up steadily, fifteen, twenty, twenty-five. If one subtracts the thrice-repeated name of the LORD, there are twelve words left, no doubt symbolizing the twelve tribes of Israel.[61] Grammatically there is no need to repeat God's name, but the repetition emphasizes that the LORD is the source of all Israel's benefits, as does the last clause *I will bless them* (27): 'I' is emphatic in the Hebrew.

As the lines of the blessing lengthen, their content becomes richer, producing a crescendo that culminates in the word *peace* (26). Each line has the LORD as its subject and is followed by two verbs, the second of which expands on the first: *bless, keep; shine, be gracious; lift up, give peace.* 'The first clause of each line (invokes) God's movement towards his people, the second clause, his activity on their behalf.'[62]

Though blessing is a broad term, it has a quite specific content in the Old Testament. God blesses people by giving them children, property, land, good health, and his presence (Gen. 17:16; 22:17f.;

59. See D. N. Freedman, 'The Aaronic Benediction', in *No Famine in the Land*, Studies in honor of J. L. McKenzie, eds. James L. Flanagan and Anita Weisbrod Robinson (Scholars Press, 1975), pp. 35–48.

60. Ibid., p. 36.

61. Gispen I, p. 117. Vowels were not indicated in early Hebrew.

62. P. D. Miller, 'The Blessing of God: An Interpretation of Numbers 6:22–27', *Interpretation*, 29, 1975, pp. 240–251. The quotation is from p. 243.

Lev. 26:3–13; Deut. 28:2–14). Psalm 121, which apparently alludes to Numbers 6:24 in verses 7 and 8, explains what is involved in being kept by God. Those in God's keeping will be protected against 'all the changes and chances of this mortal life' (cf. 1 Pet. 1:5).

Make his face to shine upon you (25). This vivid metaphor,[63] likening God to light, is characteristic of the biblical picture of God (cf. Pss. 31:16; 67:1; 80:3, 7, 19). When God smiles on his people, they can be sure that he will *be gracious* to them, that is, he will deliver them from all their troubles. He will answer their prayers and save them from their enemies, sickness and sin (Pss. 4:1; 6:2; 41:4; 51:1).

Lift up his countenance (26). Whereas 'shining' refers to the benevolent look on God's face, to lift up one's eyes or face means to pay attention (Gen. 43:29; Pss. 4:6; 34:15). Peace (*šālôm* in Hebrew) means more then the absence of war. It means well-being, health, prosperity and salvation: in short, the sum total of all God's good gifts to his people.

This Aaronic benediction is echoed in many of the Psalms,[64] most clearly in Pss. 67 and 121. This is perfectly natural since both psalms and blessing were used in the temple. Many branches of the church have adopted this blessing for use at the close of Christian worship. And this is entirely appropriate, for not only are its petitions of abiding relevance, but in the threefold repetition of the divine name theologians have traditionally seen an adumbration of the Trinity. The New Testament affirms that Jesus is Lord, and that the Holy Spirit is Lord (Rom. 10:9; 2 Cor. 3:17). In Jesus the full meaning of peace is revealed: he gave peace, made peace and is our peace (John 14:27; Eph. 2:14f.). This new covenant dimension gives an added depth to a prayer that in its Old Testament setting is already extraordinarily meaningful.

C. Offerings for the altar (chapter 7)

Exodus 40 to Numbers 6 describe what happened from the erection of the tabernacle on the first day of the second year until the

---

63. D. J. Wiseman compares it with the ancient Semitic idiom, 'to make light shine upon', i.e. 'to set free'.

64. K. Seybold, *Der aaronitische Segen* (Neukirchen, 1977), pp. 56ff.

census one month later. Numbers 7 – 9 record other less important events that fell within that same period, and constitute a digression whose beginning and end are marked by the inclusion, *on the day when Moses had finished setting up the tabernacle* (7:1; cf. 9:15).[65] The dated events in Exodus 40 to Numbers 10 are as follows.

Day				
1.1.2	Tabernacle erected	Exod. 40:2	Tabernacle erected	Num. 7:1
	Laws from tabernacle begin	Lev. 1:1	Offerings for altar begin	Num. 7:3
	Ordination of priests commences	Lev. 8:1		
8.1.2	Ordination completed	Lev. 9:1		
	Death of Nadab and Abihu	Lev. 10:1–3		
	Blasphemer dies	Lev. 24:10–23		
12.1.2			Offerings for altar end	Num. 7:78
			Appointment of Levites	Num. 8:5
14.1.2			Second passover	Num. 9:2
1.2.2	Census begins	Num. 1:1		
14.2.2			Delayed passover	Num. 9:11
20.2.2	Cloud moves	Num. 10:11		

65. On the use of inclusion to mark a digression see S. Talmon, 'The Presentation of Synchroneity and Simultaneity in Biblical Narratives', *Scripta Hierosolymitana*, 27, 1978, pp. 9–26.

It would no doubt have been possible to have included the material in Numbers 7 – 9 at appropriate points in the main narrative of Exodus 40 to Numbers 1. But the present arrangement makes for a clearer exposition of the main themes of Leviticus and at the same time permits the reader to see the full significance of the tribal gifts to the altar. Had the narrative in Leviticus been interrupted by twelve notices of tribal gifts on twelve consecutive days, it would have obscured the focus of that book on the sacrifices and the ordination of Aaron. Describing the organization of the camp and the tasks of the Levites in Numbers 1 – 6 before recording the gifts of the princes and the appointment of the Levites (Num. 7 – 8) enables the reader to appreciate the significance of these events. For example, Numbers 4 gives directions about dismantling and transporting the tabernacle. The Kohathites were to carry the most sacred items of tabernacle furniture, such as the ark and golden candlestick, but that chapter does not make clear how the other Levites were to carry the heavier items. This chapter clarifies it: the Gershonites, responsible for the tabernacle curtains (4:24–28), were given two ox-carts; the Merarites, responsible for the poles and curtains (4:31–33), received four (7:7–8).

This technique of anticipatory explanation is also to be seen in Leviticus: there the laws explaining the sacrifices (1 – 5) precede the description of the ordination of Aaron (8 – 9), because his ordination involved offering these sacrifices. It seems probable, however, that Leviticus understands these laws to have been revealed after the erection of the tabernacle, the day on which the ordination began.

Finally, placing this record of the princes' gifts for the altar at this point in the narrative serves a theological purpose. It follows the Aaronic blessing (6:22–27). The priesthood and the altar belong together. The princes are thus portrayed as responding to the prevenient grace of God shown in the establishment of the tabernacle and priesthood. Their generosity leads in its turn to greater divine blessing, God's continued presence among them (verse 89; cf. Lev. 26:11f.). This pattern – divine blessing/believing human response/greater blessing – is basic to Old Testament theology.

Verses 12–88 describe with much redundant repetition the offerings made by the tribal leaders on the occasion of the altar's dedication. Each leader gave a silver plate weighing about 3 lb (1.4 kg), a silver basin weighing nearly 2 lb (840 g) and a gold spoon[66] weighing about 4 oz (120 g). The plates and basins were full of oil mixed with flour, and the spoon contained incense. These were the principal ingredients for the cereal offering (Lev. 2). They also presented suitable animals for the usual animal sacrifices, burnt, peace and sin offerings[67] (Lev. 1, 3 – 4). Only guilt offerings (Lev. 5:14 – 6:7), which were reserved for specific serious sins, were not brought. The tribal leaders are listed in the same order as in chapter 2.

What was the point in bringing these particular gifts when the altar was dedicated, and why are they described in such detail? Hebrew narrative, even in ritual texts, tends to be sparing in its use of words.

The altar was the focal point of daily worship, and it was therefore appropriate that when it was dedicated a representative from every tribe should offer all the regular sacrifices. It set a precedent and demonstrated that the worship was for every tribe and supported by every tribe. It may be significant that the cereal offering is mentioned first of all on this occasion. Usually it was simply an accompaniment to the burnt offering. The cereal offering was the main source of income for the priests, and so, by mentioning it first, the leaders' commitment to the support of the priestly ministry is underlined. This would be fitting, since the seven-day ordination of the priesthood began on the day the altar was dedicated (Lev. 8:11) and the gifts are described immediately after the priestly blessing.

It has been suggested that the repetitiveness of the list of sacrifices shows it is based on a temple archive.[68] This could be so, but it fails to explain why the writer retained this form here when it is not his custom elsewhere to be so long-winded. It seems likely that a theological purpose underlies his wordiness: to emphasize as strongly as possible that every tribe had an equal stake in the

---

66. AV *spoon* seems a more likely rendering of Hebrew *kap*, literally 'palm of the hand', than either RSV *dish* or NEB *saucer* in view of its light weight. A shekel weighed about 12 grammes (0.42 oz) according to R. de Vaux, *Ancient Israel* (DLT, 1963), p. 205; cf. 'Weights', *IBD*, pp. 1634ff.

67. On these see Additional note on Old Testament sacrifice, pp. 226ff.

68. B. A. Levine, 'The Descriptive Tabernacle Texts of the Pentateuch', *JAOS*, 85, 1965, pp. 314–318.

worship of God, and that each was fully committed to the support of the tabernacle and its priesthood.

Their sacrifices were not in vain. The chapter closes with a reminder of how God used to speak to Moses from the cloud resting on the mercy seat in the holy of holies. The tabernacle was no empty shrine, but the palace of the living God (89).

This chapter's insistence that sacrifice and ministry are essential to the life of the people of God is taken up in the New Testament. The sacrifice of Christ on the cross is the heart of the gospel (1 Cor. 1:17ff.), and the New Testament writers use the various Old Testament sacrifices to interpret the meaning of his death. Calvary has now replaced the bronze altar as the place of sacrifice (Heb. 9 – 10), but believers are still expected to respond to God's grace by giving themselves to him and their money to maintaining the gospel ministry (Rom. 12:1; 1 Cor. 9:3ff.).

D. Dedication of the Levites (chapter 8)

i. **Aaron and the lampstand (8:1–4).** As elsewhere in Numbers, the connection between this section and those that precede and follow it is not immediately obvious. A few rather hesitant suggestions are to be found in the commentaries. 7:89 relates how God used to speak to Moses when he went into the holy place; 8:1–3 describes what Aaron had to do when he entered the holy place every morning and evening[69] (Exod. 30:7–8). Chapter 7 describes how the heads of each secular tribe made offerings for the service of God; 8:1–3 prescribes how Aaron the head of the priestly tribe of Levi had to attend to the lampstand each day in the holy place.[70] This command to Aaron forms a fitting introduction to the account of the dedication of the Levites to their tabernacle service.[71] It may also be noted that the altar in the court of the tabernacle and the lampstand in the tent of meeting were the two parts of the sanctuary which required the priest's attention twice a day, for the offering of the

---

69. Cf. Heinisch, p. 39.

70. Cf. Rashi, p. 41; Keil, p. 46.

71. Cf. Keil, p. 46.

morning and evening sacrifices and tending the lights (Exod. 29:38–42; 30:7f.). In both places fire had to be kept burning continually (Lev. 6:8–13; 24:2–4).

The lampstand or menorah is more fully described in Exodus 25:31–40. It was made out of solid gold sheet, *hammered work* (4), unlike some other items in the tabernacle such as the ark and the table of shewbread which were gold-plated wood (Exod. 25:10–30). Its form, a seven-branched flowering tree, symbolized the life-giving power of God. Like the rest of the tabernacle and its furniture, it was modelled on the heavenly sanctuary which Moses had seen when he was up on Mount Sinai (4; cf. Exod. 25:40; Heb. 8:5; Rev. 1:12–2:1). By comparing the biblical descriptions of the menorah with other ancient oriental lampstands it has been possible to clarify its design and demonstrate its antiquity. In shape it closely corresponds to Late Bronze Age designs[72] (15th–13th centuries BC).

This paragraph particularly insists on one point: Aaron is so to position the seven oil lamps placed at the end of each branch of the lampstand that they *give light* (Hebrew *hē'ir*, shine, 6:25) *in front of the lampstand* (2–3). It is not explained why the direction of light should have been so important.

The meaning of this action becomes apparent when the design of the holy place is taken into account. If the light beamed forwards it would have fallen on the table of shewbread, where twelve loaves of bread, symbolizing the twelve tribes of Israel, were heaped up (Lev. 24:5–9). Light and fire represent the life-giving presence and blessing of God (e.g. Exod. 13:21–22). Thus Aaron had to arrange the lamps so that their light always illuminated the shewbread. This arrangement portrayed visually God's intention that his people should live continually in his presence and enjoy the blessing mediated by his priests. This section therefore expresses symbolically what 6:23–27 affirms verbally: 'So shall they put my name upon the people of Israel, and I will bless them.' Hebrews 8 – 9 reminds us that Christ is now ever present in the heavenly sanctuary making intercession for his people.

---

72. C. L. Meyers, *The Tabernacle Menorah* (Scholars Press, 1976), esp. pp. 31ff., 182ff.

ii. The dedication of the Levites (8:5–22). With the official
dedication of the Levites to their various tasks the people are almost
ready to depart. Chapter 3 reports the census of the Levites, chapter 4 their various tasks in dismantling and transporting the tabernacle, chapter 7 the gift of oxen and carts for its transport, and at
last the ceremony in which they were dedicated to their role as
guardians and movers of the tabernacle is described.

5–19. The command to set apart the Levites is quite elaborate in
its detail and structure. In characteristic fashion the second half of
the command goes over the same topics in reverse order, cf. A *to
make atonement for the Levites/for the people of Israel* (12, 19), B *to do service at the tent of meeting* (15, 19), C *given to me/to Aaron* (16, 19), D *instead of all the first-born* (16, 18). This chiastic pattern (ABCDEDCBA)
helps to underline the points made explicitly in the text, that the
Levites are to take the place of the first-born Israelites and make
atonement through their service in the tent of meeting. It also
draws attention to item E at the centre (i.e. verse 17), which recalls
the great redemption from Egypt when the first-born Egyptians died
in the last great plague while God passed over the first-born Israelites
(Exod. 11 – 13). Thus the dedication of the Levites to take the place
of the first-born is very appropriate here, for the next chapter describes the second passover.

Whereas the ordination of the priests involved their elevation to
a special level of sanctity, through the offering of sacrifice, anointing with oil and blood, and dressing in priestly vestments (Lev. 8),
the Levites had simply to be cleansed. Every layman who contracted any impurity and wished to join in worship and eat of the sacrifices had to be cleansed (cf. Exod. 19:10ff.; Lev. 7:19–21). Verses
6–8 explain the cleansing procedures required in this case (cf. Lev.
11; 14–15). It is uncertain whether *the water* of purification (7) was
simply pure water out of the laver or the specially prepared 'water
for impurity' (19:9, 13, etc.).

The peculiar feature of the dedication of the Levites is described
in verses 10–13. The Israelites, i.e. their representative leaders, *the
whole congregation* (9), lay their hands on the Levites' heads, and then
Aaron offers them *as a wave offering.* This was the way animals used
for peace offerings were treated. The worshipper laid his hand on the
animal's head, and after it had been chopped up, the priest waved its

breast and retained that portion for himself (Lev. 3; 7:28–34). Traditionally waving has been supposed to involve moving the object from side to side horizontally, but if that is the case the form is used metaphorically here. Alternatively, waving may mean ritual dedication within the sanctuary.[73] Whatever the precise meaning of the term, the significance of the action is clear: the Levites are being substituted for the first-born Israelites, who as a result of the passover were given to the Lord and therefore, in theory, to be sacrificed (Exod. 13:2). Numbers 3:45ff. has already mentioned that the Levites are to take the place of the first-born. Through the laying on of hands this substitution is symbolized, and by being waved they are given to Aaron and the priests (13, 19). The Levites thereby *make atonement*[74] (Hebrew *kipper*) *for the people of Israel* (19), that is pay the ransom price (*kōper*). However, the Old Testament never countenances human sacrifice; so the Levites in their turn lay their hands on two bulls to make atonement for them (12), and their lives are given *to do service at the tent of meeting* (15, 19), i.e. the work of carrying and erecting the tabernacle (cf. ch. 4). Because the Levites have undertaken the work of handling the sacred tent, the Israelites are protected from 'plague' (19), i.e. mass death for provoking God's anger (cf. Exod. 12:13; 30:12; Num. 16:46, 48; Josh. 22:17; cf. Num. 25:9); for wherever men defiled by sin dare to approach the holy God, such judgment is a possibility (cf. Exod. 19:10–24).

20–22 records the faithful fulfilment of the divine commands given in the previous section (cf. 1:17–19, 54; 2:34; 3:42, 49–51; 4:37, 41, 45–49; 5:4).

New Testament parallels to the Levites are hard to find. In their role as sacrificial victims who ransom the people from their sins one may view them as a type of Christ. In their role as lay assistants to the priesthood they foreshadow the deacons, who were appointed to relieve the apostles of church administration (Acts 6:1–6; 1 Tim. 3:8–13).

---

73. J. Milgrom, 'The Alleged Wave Offering in Israel and in the Ancient Near East', *IEJ*, 22 (1972), pp. 33–38.

74. For fuller discussion of this phrase see Wenham, pp. 28, 59ff. and J. Milgrom, *Studies in Levitical Terminology*, pp. 28–30.

iii. **The retirement of the Levites (8:23–26).** The section dealing with the appointment of the Levites is followed by a regulation
about their retirement, and this brings the discussion of their ministry to an appropriate conclusion.
   At the age of fifty they must withdraw from the 'workforce' (25).
(Hebrew *ṣĕbā' hā'ăbōdâ* literally *'army of service'*, RSV *work of the service*.)
Here as in chapter 3, *'ăbōdâ* means the heavy work of erecting, dismantling and transporting the tabernacle, a job suited to men in the
prime of life, defined as 25[75] to 50 years old in verse 24. However,
even after retirement older Levites may still help the younger men
by 'doing guard duty', RSV *keep the charge* (26; cf. chapter 3).

---

75. *From 25 years old and upward* (24). This regulation conflicts with the
    provision in chapter 4, that the Levites between the ages of 30 and 50
    (see verses 3, 23, 30, 35, 39, 43, 47) are to be in the labour force. The
    LXX already tried to harmonize these figures by reducing the age limit to
    25 in chapter 4. Jewish commentators suggest that Levites served an
    apprenticeship for the first five years. Critical commentators argue that
    8:23–26 is from a different, probably later, source than chapter 4, a step
    towards the 20 years of 1 Chronicles 23:24; 2 Chronicles 31:17; Ezra 3:8.
        1 Chronicles 23:24ff. mentions that David reduced the age of
    Levitical service from 30 to 20 years, because they no longer had to
    carry the tabernacle but help the priests clean the temple, assist with
    various cereal offerings and form a temple choir. It looks therefore as
    though the age limit on Levite service was reduced because more
    Levites were needed for temple worship than in the tabernacle. But
    whether Numbers 8:24 should be regarded as a step in this direction is
    doubtful. Apart from the different age, there is nothing stylistically to
    indicate that 8:23–26 is from a different source from chapter 4. The
    context of this regulation between 7:1 (cf. Exodus 40:2) and 9:1
    suggests it is dated about the 13th day of the first month, which is
    before the regulations in Numbers 1:1ff. It therefore seems preferable
    to suppose that the minimum age for Levitical service was increased
    from 25 to 30 years. No reason is given. Did the censuses show that
    there were more Levites than necessary for the work of transporting the
    tabernacle? Raising the age limit from 25 to 30 would have cut the
    number required by at least 20%.

E. The second passover (chapter 9)

i. The passover at Sinai (9:1–14). 1–5. The passover, combined with the feast of unleavened bread which immediately followed it, was the great festival celebrating the exodus from Egypt. It began on the 14th day of the 1st month, that is about April, and lasted eight days (Lev. 23:5–6). The offerings of the tribal leaders began on the 1st day of the month and lasted twelve days (7:1; cf. Exod. 40:2). This episode therefore concludes the digression from 7:1 to 9:15, relating events that took place before the census recorded in 1:1. It is not clear whether the dedication of the Levites took place within this fortnight, but its present place is appropriate since the Levites took the place of the first-born who had been consecrated to the LORD on the first passover night (8:17f.).

The passover had to be celebrated according to *all its statutes and all its ordinances* (3). Exactly how the regulations in Exodus 12 were carried out is not stated: possibly the blood was smeared on the tents instead of on the lintels and doorposts. *In the evening* (NEB 'between dusk and dark', NIV 'twilight') renders a problematic Hebrew phrase that may be more literally rendered 'between the evenings'. Jewish tradition holds that it means between mid-day and sunset. In New Testament times they began to slaughter the passover lambs at about 3.00 p.m. Modern commentators generally suppose that Deuteronomy 16:6 'at the going down of the sun' is the oldest interpretation of the phrase, and this is the basis of the NEB translation.

6–8. Sacrifices could be eaten only by those who were clean, i.e. free from the pollution caused by discharges, skin disease and dead bodies. If someone ate sacrificial meat when he was unclean, he might be cut off (Lev. 7:19–21). There is no mention of the danger of uncleanness in Exodus 12, but, given all the regulations set out in Leviticus 11 – 15, such a concern was now appropriate. *Certain men who were unclean through touching the dead body of a man* therefore asked Moses what they were to do. This problem and the divine answer to their predicament is the central concern of this section. The opening verses (1–5) about the passover merely set the scene.

9–14. The reply is straightforward. Any Israelite who for any reason cannot celebrate the passover at the normal time must celebrate it one month later in the traditional way. Verses 11–12 mention some of the standard regulations (cf. Exod. 12:8, 10, 46). However, a rider is added: anyone who abstains from celebrating the passover *shall be cut off from his people* (13). This punishment is repeatedly referred to in the Pentateuch for various religious and sexual sins (e.g. Lev. 17:4, 9; 20:6, 18; 23:29; Num. 15:30f.; 19:13). It is a threat of sudden death at the hands of God, and may also hint at punishment in the life to come.[76] Thus, both participation in the passover when unclean and abstention for no good reason are equally dangerous.

The New Testament sees Jesus as the true paschal lamb 'who takes away the sin of the world' (John 1:29; 1 Cor. 5:7). At his crucifixion none of his bones was broken 'that the scripture might be fulfilled' (John 19:36; cf. Num. 9:12). Furthermore, 'unless you eat the flesh of the Son of man and drink his blood, you have no life in you', but those who eat and drink unworthily are 'guilty of profaning the body and blood of the Lord … that is why many of you are weak and ill, and some have died' (John 6:53; 1 Cor. 11:27, 30). In this way the New Testament re-asserts the threat of cutting off, both on those who fail to participate in the Christian passover when they can, and on those who do eat it when unclean (Num. 9:7, 13; cf. Lev. 7:20).

ii. Following the cloud (9:15–23). *On the day the tabernacle was set up* (15; cf. 7:1) brings us back to the first day of the second year (Exod. 40:2). This passage elaborates and develops the shorter statement in Exodus 40:34–38, in an almost poetic fashion using parallelism and repetition. The poetic quality is most obvious in verses 17–23:

> 17 Whenever the cloud lifted from over the tent
>   afterwards the Israelites set out;
> Wherever the cloud settled
>   there the Israelites encamped.
> 18 At the command of the LORD the Israelites set out,
>   and at the command of the LORD they encamped.
> As long as the cloud settled over the tabernacle,
>   they encamped.

---

76. See Wenham, pp. 241f. for further discussion.

19 When the cloud remained many days over the tabernacle,
    the Israelites kept the LORD's watch,[77]
    they did not set out.

20 Sometimes the cloud was a few days over the tabernacle –
    at the command of the LORD they encamped,
    and at the command of the LORD they set out, –

21 And sometimes the cloud was (over the tabernacle) from evening
    till morning.
    When the cloud lifted up in the morning
    they set out.
    Or a day and a night, when the cloud lifted up
    they set out.

22 Or two days, a month, or a year,
    when the cloud remained settled over the tabernacle
    the Israelites encamped,
    they did not set out.
    And when it lifted up,
    they set out.

23 At the command of the LORD they encamped
    and at the command of the LORD they set out.
They kept the Lord's watch[77] at the command of the LORD given
    by Moses.

The irregularity of the lines shows this is not true poetry: rather
it is elevated prose, expressing the excitement of the occasion. The
newly organized nation with its God-given system of worship is
about to set out from Sinai for the promised land. This section describes how this journey is to be undertaken. The thrice-repeated refrain sums it up, 'At the command of the LORD they encamped, and
at the command of the LORD they set out' (20, 23; cf. 18). The cloud
hovering over the tabernacle provided the perfect means of divine
guidance: the people had to respond with perfect obedience.

The real and visible presence of God among his people was his
response to their obedience in building the tabernacle (15). But this
section is placed immediately after the account of the celebration of

---

77. On this phrase see on 3:7.

the second passover. The cloud of God's presence first appeared after the first passover (Exod. 13:21–22). The tabernacle could be built only once, but the festivals of redemption were to be celebrated regularly. This narrative, therefore, looks beyond the wilderness situation, in which Israel could follow God's leading in an immediate way, to a time when its faithfulness to the LORD would be demonstrated by their keeping of the festivals.

The New Testament also uses cloud imagery to describe the presence of God. Our Lord was overshadowed by the cloud at his transfiguration, and disappeared into a cloud at his ascension (Luke 9:34; Acts 1:9). He indeed was the perfect tabernacle in which 'the Word ... dwelt among us' (John 1:14). Paul and Peter both compare the body to a tent, a temporary dwelling to be replaced after death (2 Cor. 5:1–4; 2 Pet. 1:13–14). Like the tabernacle, the Christian's body is no empty tent, but a temple for the Spirit (1 Cor. 6:19). Filled by the Spirit he may follow in his Lord's footsteps and resist the temptations of Satan even in the wilderness (Luke 4:1ff.). 'Let the fiery, cloudy pillar lead me all my journey through.'

F. The silver trumpets (10:1–10)

The last directions given at Sinai deal with the manufacture and use of two silver trumpets to co-ordinate the movements of the tribes on their march through the wilderness. Though they were to be guided by the cloud, more precise means of control were necessary if the people were to march in the tight-knit formations envisaged in chapters 2 – 3. Though the passage gives no indication when these instructions were received by Moses, their present position is very appropriate. They complete and complement the means of divine guidance described in 9:15–23, so that the whole nation is poised to begin its sacred march from Sinai to the promised land.

The trumpets are described by Josephus[78] and pictured on the arch of Titus in Rome. They were straight pipes, a little less than 18 in. (45cm) long with a flared opening at the end. They could be blown in various ways to give different signals. What distinguished

---

78. *Antiquities* iii.12.6.

blowing and sounding an alarm is uncertain. But if we follow
Jewish tradition, long blasts (Hebrew *tāqa‘*, RSV *blow*) were used to
assemble people to Moses, to the tent of meeting and for worship
(3–4, 10).[79] Short staccato blasts (Hebrew *tāqa‘ lěrû‘â*, RSV *blow an
alarm*) were used in battle and to order the camps to move off. Each
time an alarm was sounded a group of tribes moved off. At the first
alarm the tribes to the east of the tabernacle moved off, at the second alarm those on the south, at subsequent blasts those on the west
and north (5–6; cf. 2:1–31). It is significant that, as in ancient
Egypt,[80] the trumpets were used in war and to summon people to
worship. Like the arrangement of the camp with the tabernacle at
the middle, and the ordering of the tribes in battle formation, the silver trumpets declare that Israel is the army of the King of kings
preparing for a holy war of conquest.

Other biblical passages mention trumpets being used in the worship of the temple (2 Kgs 11:14; Ps. 98:6; Ezra 3:10). In Europe the
faithful have traditionally been called to worship by church bells, but
in the last day the elect will be once again summoned 'with a loud
trumpet call', 'and the dead shall be raised incorruptible' (Matt.
24:31; 1 Cor. 15:52 AV; cf. Rev. 8 – 9).

---

79. *Congregation* (3) refers to the adult males, representing all Israel; *assembly*
    (7) to the community gathered for worship.
80. H. Hickmann, 'Die kultische Verwendung der altägyptischen Trompete',
    Welt des Orients, 1:5, 1950, pp. 351–355. The evidence cited by Hickmann
    comes from the New Kingdom period, 16th to 11th centuries BC,
    another pointer to the antiquity of the biblical tradition.

2. FROM SINAI TO KADESH (10:11 – 12:16)

According to most commentators the second great section in Numbers runs from 10:11 to 22:1. It covers the thirty-eight years that elapsed between Israel's departure from Sinai and their arrival in the plains of Moab. For reasons set out in the introduction[1] it seems preferable to divide this central section of the book into two travelogues, 10:11 – 12:16, 20:1 – 22:1, and a period of revelation centred on Kadesh (chapters 13 – 19). There are sufficient parallels between the three stages on the journey from Egypt to Canaan, i.e. from the Red Sea to Sinai (Exod. 13 – 19), from Sinai to Kadesh (Num. 10 – 12), from Kadesh to Moab (Num. 20 – 21), to make the analysis of these central chapters a probability. It is enhanced by the parallels between the content of revelation at the three great centres of Sinai, Kadesh, and the plains of Moab.

Nevertheless it is not completely clear where the travelogues end and begin and where the Kadesh material opens and closes. Do

---

1. See above, Introduction, 2. Structure, pp. 16ff.

chapters 13 – 14 belong with the preceding travelogue, or with the Kadesh material? Does chapter 20 belong to the Kadesh material, or with the subsequent travelogue? It could be argued that the rebellion at Kadesh following the spies' report marks the climax of a series of rebellions described in chapters 11 and 12. I prefer to see chapter 13, with its descriptions of the bounty of Canaan, as a triumphant re-affirmation of the divine promise of the land (cf. the great promises opening the Sinai narrative Exod. 19, and Balaam's prophecies, Num. 22 – 24). Then chapter 14, the great apostasy, can be compared to the golden calf episode which took place while Moses was receiving the ten commandments (Exod. 32). Furthermore, if the travelogue ends with 12:16, we have three stories of complaint in chapters 11 – 12, and such triads are a favourite device of Hebrew writers (cf. Num. 16 – 17; 22 – 24). Though most of the events in chapter 20 are located in or near Kadesh, the parallels with other travelogues and the mention of movement make it more plausible to associate chapter 20 with 21 rather than with chapters 13 – 19.

A. Departure in battle order (10:11–36)

11–12. After spending eleven months in *the wilderness of Sinai* (12; cf. Exod. 19:1) preparing themselves as described in Exodus 19 to Numbers 9, the people set out for *the wilderness of Paran*. Verse 12 summarizes several days journeyings. Stops were made at Kibroth-hattaavah and Hazeroth before they finally reached the wilderness of Paran (11:35; 12:16). This is the largest and most barren of the wildernesses traversed by the Israelites, covering much of the Northern Sinai peninsula and some of the Southern Negeb and Arabah[2] (Gen. 21:21; Num. 13:26; 1 Kgs 11:18).

13–20. The march begins exactly as prescribed in the previous

---

2. This is the view of M. Harel, *Masei Sinai*, pp. 208f. Y. Aharoni, *Encyclopedia Miqrait*, 6, pp. 433f., thinks Paran covers all the wilderness area, of which other wildernesses Shur, Sinai, Sin are parts. See map and further discussion of itinerary in the Additional note on the route of the Israelites, pp. 246ff.

chapters. The cloud lifted, and the people followed *at the command of the LORD by Moses* (13; cf. 9:23). *By Moses* may be an allusion to the blowing of the trumpets (10:5–6). The tribes moved off in groups of three in the order specified in chapter 2. At the front of the procession went the standard of the tribe of Judah, with the tribes of Judah accompanying it (14–16; cf. 2:1–9). Then came the Gershonites and Merarites carrying the curtains and poles of the tabernacle on the oxcarts (17; cf. 4:21–45; 7:2–8). This detail is not mentioned in chapter 2, which does not differentiate between the Kohathites marching in the middle of the procession, and the Merarites and Gershonites going ahead of them. The latter arrangement was adopted so that the tabernacle could be set up before the most sacred objects carried by the Kohathites arrived (21). These could then be immediately placed inside the tent.

21–28. After the Gershonites and Merarites marched the tribes of Reuben, Simeon and Gad. Then came the Kohathites *carrying the holy things* (21), i.e. the table for the shewbread, the lampstand, the incense altar and the altar of burnt offering and maybe the ark as well (4:5–15), though verse 33 implies that this went first of all, some way ahead of the main procession.[3] After the Kohathites came the tribes of Ephraim, Manasseh and Benjamin. The final group consisted of Dan, Asher and Naphtali (22–27; cf. 2:18–31).

---

3. It is often supposed that the apparent difference between verses 21 and 33 can be explained source critically: that 21 is P, whereas 33 is E or J. The earlier source pictured the ark going ahead of the people, whereas the later one made it travel in their midst. However, such a source division creates its own problems. Verse 34 with its mention of the cloud is typically P. And we must ask why the final editor of Numbers, either identified with P or strongly influenced by him, should have left a remark that flatly contradicts his own view that the ark travelled in the middle of the people. Even if the existence of two sources is admitted, it seems likely that the final editor supposed the ark went at the front of the procession (cf. Josh. 3:3f.). It was standard oriental practice for divine symbols or statues to precede armies on the march; cf. T. W. Mann, *Divine Presence and Guidance in Israelite Traditions* (Johns Hopkins UP, Baltimore, 1977), pp. 169ff.

29–32 relates how Moses invited his brother-in-law[4] Hobab to accompany Israel on their journey to Canaan. His father-in-law, Reuel or Jethro, had earlier given Moses valuable advice about organizing the people (Exod. 18; cf. Exod. 2:18). Now Moses requests Hobab to *serve as eyes* for them (31), that is show the Israelites where to find water and give them other practical advice in the places God will lead them through. The Midianites were a group of tribes living in the desert areas surrounding Canaan, and Hobab would therefore be well acquainted with the area they were travelling through. Elsewhere Hobab's descendants are called Kenites, evidently a sub-group of the Midianites (cf. Judg. 1:16; 4:11). Hobab's response is not recorded here, but Judges 1:16 indicates he did accede to Moses' request.

33–36. The first stage was a three-day journey. The text does not say it took the Israelites only three days to cover the distance: with their children and herds they may well have progressed more slowly. But they set out triumphantly, with the ark and the cloud hovering ahead of them. Moses' faith and elation is particularly emphasized. He tells Hobab *'the LORD has promised good to Israel'* (29). As the ark set out each morning he called out, *'Arise, O LORD and let thy enemies be scattered'* (35; cf. Ps. 68:1), and at evening he prayed with poetic hyperbole, *'Return, O LORD to the ten thousand thousands of Israel'* (36).[5] The faith which Moses affirms so confidently stands in ironic contrast to what happens in the succeeding chapters: whereas Moses is sure God will do good to Israel, the people begin to complain of the evil (11:1) that he is doing them. Moses prays that all God's enemies will be scattered: the spies declare Israel will be defeated (chapter 13). This chapter's triumphant conclusion deepens the poignant tragedy of the succeeding scenes.

---

4. On *ḥtn*, 'father-in-law', 'brother-in-law', 'relation by marriage', see T. C. Mitchell, *VT*, 19, 1969, pp. 93–112.
5. In the Hebrew text verses 35 and 36 are bracketed by inverted *nuns* (n). These are also found in Ps. 107. The significance of these signs is uncertain. It may indicate that early scribes considered the verses misplaced. LXX puts verse 34 after verse 36.

B. Three complaints (11:1 – 12:16)

i. Taberah (11:1–3). Leaving the relative fertility of the area around Mount Sinai, the Israelites soon found themselves in the most inhospitable desert of Et-Tih, and they began to complain. A modern traveller would sympathize. But the biblical writers did not (cf. Deut. 9:22; Ps. 78:17ff.). For them the complaints of Israel were proof of national rebelliousness and unbelief. Numbers makes the same point by describing God as angry and his fire consuming 'at one end of the camp' (1, NEB). Fire is a sign of divine activity, either in blessing or in judgment (cf. Lev. 9:24; 10:1). The text does not make clear what was burnt on this occasion, whether it was just shrubs near the tents, or some of the tents themselves. However, the people realized the danger they were in and appealed to Moses to pray for them. As on previous occasions God heeded his intercession (Exod. 15:25; 32:11–14). To commemorate the event the place was called Taberah, 'burning'. Since Taberah is not included in the list of camp sites in chapter 33, it was probably a name given to an area near Kibroth-hattaavah (cf. verses 4–35).

This episode heads a series of stories in which every group among the Israelites rebels at God's provision and plans. On each occasion the sin is described, and then the subsequent divine judgment. As a result of unbelief and disobedience all the adult males except Joshua and Caleb die in the wilderness, not in the land of promise. Even Aaron and Moses die before arriving in Canaan. The complete reversal of national attitudes is emphasized in traditions about Kibroth-hattaavah. The triumphant optimism of Moses, urging Hobab to accompany Israel to the *good* land promised by the LORD, is replaced by grumbles about the *evil* (RSV *misfortunes* verse 1, *wretchedness* verse 15) they are actually experiencing. Instead of looking forward to Canaan, they nostalgically yearn for Egypt (10:29; 11:5, 18, 20). Whereas Moses assured Hobab that the LORD would treat Israel well, he was soon to ask, 'Why hast thou dealt ill with thy servant?' (10:32; 11:11). Other great saints experienced similar crises of faith in times of adversity, e.g. Elijah, John the Baptist, and Peter (1 Kgs 19:4ff.; Matt. 11:2ff.; 26:69ff.). Both Moses and the people are treated gently at first; the fire is only at the edge of the camp (verse 1), and Moses is not rebuked for his doubts. It was their repeated acts of unbelief that led to their exclusion from Canaan.

ii. Kibroth-hattaavah (11:4–35). A prominent theme in the travel sections of Exodus and Numbers is the supply of food and water and the people's discontent with God's provision (Exod. 15:22ff.; Num. 20). It is again noticeable how the Red Sea to Sinai and the Sinai to Kadesh travelogues run in parallel here. A short murmuring tradition (Exod. 15:23–26 // Num. 11:1–3) is in both cases followed by a detailed account of the manna and quails[6] (Exod. 16//Num. 11:4–35). Both Exodus and Numbers date the arrival of the quails in the second month of the Hebrew year (Exod. 16:1; Num. 10:11), which would coincide with the northward migration of the quails across the Sinai peninsula.

4–6. In the wilderness of Sin it was lack of food that prompted complaint (Exod. 16:3): at Kibroth-hattaavah it was the lack of variety. Instigated by the *rabble* (4), a term found only here, probably denoting the non-Israelites who joined in the exodus from Egypt (cf. Exod. 12:38; Lev. 24:10), the people *wept again*. The year-long diet of manna, which had first appeared just before they reached Mount Sinai, and is described in Psalm 78:24–25 (cf. Exod. 16:4) as 'the grain of heaven' and 'the bread of the angels', had become monotonous. They longed for the fresh vegetables, fish and meat they had eaten in Egypt (5–6). With these nostalgic remarks the people express their opposition to God's purpose that they should settle in Canaan (cf. 11:18, 20; 14:2ff.; 20:5; Exod. 14:11f.; 16:3; 17:3).

7–9. The manna is described as looking *like coriander seed* or *bdellium*.[7] Exodus 16:14, 31 says it was flaky, like hoarfrost, and white and tasted like honey. Modern travellers in the Sinai have tried to identify the biblical manna with substances which may still be found there today. Tamarisk trees and some insects exude sweet globules. Some kinds of lichen also have a sweet taste.[8] None of these

---

6. Cf. D. Jobling, *The Sense of Biblical Narrative* (University of Sheffield, 1978), p. 59.

7. Bdellium is a pale yellow translucent resin.

8. Cf. F. S. Bodenheimer, 'The Manna of Sinai', *Biblical Archaeologist*, 10, 1947, pp. 2–6.

modern mannas exactly fits the description of the biblical material. But if one does suppose a naturally occurring product is meant, it must still be acknowledged that the large and regular quantities provided for Israel were miraculous. The narrative hints at its divine origin, for like the cloud of God's presence it came down (Hebrew *yārad*) on the camp (11:9, 25; cf. Exod. 16:4; John 6:1–58).

10–15. Again, the modern reader may be tempted to sympathize with the complaints of the Israelites. But neither God nor Moses did. *The anger of the LORD blazed hotly, and Moses was displeased* (lit. 'it was evil in his sight', 10). In a long and angry prayer[9] he vents his frustrations before God. Israel is like a little child. It is really hard work being nursemaid to him all day. It would be better to die than have to look after them alone (11–15; cf. Exod. 33:15; Rom. 9:3).

16–23. Moses complained about the general burdensomeness of the people and the particular problem of their demand for meat. God's reply (16–20) deals with both points. Some seventy elders are to be given some of Moses' spirit and thereby enabled to share his burdens with him. Since his administrative duties were already shared with others (Exod. 18:13ff.), these elders must have been intended to give him spiritual support (cf. Exod. 24:9). An apparent 600,000 people[10] are to be inundated with an overabundance of meat, a blessing that will prove to be a judgment. Moses' incredulity is answered by a divine 'wait and see'. *Is the LORD's hand shortened?* (23; cf. Isa. 50:2; 59:1.)

24–33. In fulfilment of the double-sided divine promise, the

---

9. The prayer is constructed to give a balanced palistrophic pattern, clearer in the Hebrew than in the English. A. deal ill. B. found favour. C. burden of all this people (11). D. all this people. E. carry them to the land. Where am I to get meat? (12–13). D'. all this people. C'. carry all this people (14). B'. find favour. A'. wretchedness (15). The structural unity of this prayer, linking as it does the people's demand for food with Moses' plea for aid, casts doubt on the suggestion that in 11:4–35 two stories, one dealing with the quails and another with the provision of seventy elders to assist Moses, have been combined.

10. On the number of men see Additional note on the large numbers, pp. 68ff.

spirit of the LORD is distributed to the seventy elders (25, 29) and *a wind from the LORD* (31) (*rûaḥ* in Hebrew means both *spirit* and *wind*) brings swarms of quails for the people to eat. Thus the story emphasizes from beginning to end the interrelatedness of the popular demand for meat and Moses' prayer for spiritual support. Yet the outcome of the requests was very different. The spirit was bestowed within the court of the tabernacle, in the clean and holy area; the quails fell outside the camp, in the zone associated with uncleanness and death. The gift of the spirit drew men towards God; the quails led them away from God. Consequently *the anger of the LORD was kindled ... and the LORD smote the people* (33).

26–30. Other passages also show that prophecy is a mark of God's spirit (1 Sam. 10:6–13; 19:20–24; Joel 2:28; Acts 2:4; 1 Cor. 12:10). As with Saul, the prophecy described here was probably an unintelligible ecstatic utterance, what the New Testament terms speaking in tongues, not the inspired, intelligible speech of the great Old Testament prophets and the unnamed prophets of the early church (1 Kgs 18:29; Acts 21:10–11; 1 Cor. 14). It is not explained why Eldad and Medad did not gather with the rest of the seventy in the tabernacle court, but through their prophesying in the camp the phenomenon became more widely known and allowed Moses to give it his public approval (cf. 1 Cor. 14:5).

31–35. Quails are small birds of the partridge family. They migrate northwards from Arabia and Africa in the spring (from the middle of March) and return again in the autumn (August to October). Their route takes them over Egypt, Sinai and Palestine. Earlier this century Arabs living around El-Arish in northern Sinai used to catch between one and two million quails during the autumn migration in nets spread out to catch the low-flying birds.[11] The NEB, following the Vulgate and some Jewish commentators, understands *about two cubits* (3ft, 90 cm) *above the face of the earth* to refer to the height at which the birds flew. But the verb in verse 31 (Hebrew *nāṭaš, let fall*, 'leave'; cf. 1 Sam. 17:20, 22) suggests that there were piles of birds up to three feet high. It is also difficult to imagine a man

11. Gispen, I, pp. 186–187.

catching 10 homers of birds[12] (possibly 500 gallons, 2,200 litres), but
it would have been feasible to gather that number if they were lying
on the ground. After capture the quails were *spread out* to dry and
preserve them. Neither Kibroth-hattaavah (Graves of Craving) nor
Hazeroth (courtyards) can be precisely located (34, 35).

The manna and quails are mentioned in several other passages in
the Old Testament (Deut. 8:3; Ps. 78:23–31; Neh. 9:20). Jesus seems
to have seen himself as reliving the experiences of Israel in the
wilderness. When invited to turn stones into bread he quoted
Deuteronomy 8:3, 'Man shall not live by bread alone, but by every
word that proceeds from the mouth of God' (Matt. 4:4). His feeding
of the five and four thousand (Matt. 14:13ff.; 15:32ff. and parallels)
recalls God's provision for Israel. This parallel is explicitly alluded
to in John 6:25ff., where Jesus identifies himself with the true bread
from heaven: the disciples must eat his flesh if they would enjoy
eternal life. Paul warns the Spirit-filled church of Corinth to
remember the judgments that befell Israel in the wilderness, lest a
similar fate overtake them (1 Cor. 10:1 – 11:32).

iii. Miriam and Aaron rebel against Moses (12:1–16). In
form and content this story of Miriam and Aaron's challenge to
Moses' supreme authority has many points in common with the
previous two episodes.[13] Though this protest appears to be much less
serious than the widespread popular discontent described in the
previous chapter, it was in fact a peculiarly piquant and fundamental
one. It was not just a case of petty family jealousy, for Aaron,
Moses' brother, was also the high priest and therefore supreme
religious leader and most holy man in Israel; while Miriam, his
sister, was a prophetess and thus head of the spirit-filled women
(Exod. 15:20f.). Here, then, is an alliance of priest and prophet, the
two archetypes of Israelite religion, challenging Moses' position as
sole mediator between God and Israel. His vindication is at once

---

12. de Vaux, *Ancient Israel*, p. 202.
13. Cf. 'spoke against' (cf. 11:1, 4–6); *the LORD heard* (2; cf. 11:1, 10); *anger
    of the LORD* (9; cf. 11:1, 10, 33); judgment (10; cf. 11:1, 33); appeal for
    mercy (11; cf. 11:2); Moses' intercession (13; cf. 11:2); journeying (16; cf.
    11:35).

decisive and dramatic: indeed the description of his position and office clearly prefigures that of our Lord in the New Testament.

1–2. Once again a personal grumble is coupled with a questioning of Moses' spiritual authority (cf. 11:4–34). This time Miriam and Aaron first complain about Moses' Cushite wife, before broaching the real issue: '*Has the LORD indeed spoken only through Moses?*' Of this Cushite woman we know nothing except what verse 1 tells us. She may be identical with Zipporah, more usually described as a Midianite (Exod. 2:16ff.); Habakkuk 3:7 and some Assyrian[14] texts suggest the identity of Midian and Cushan. Cush, however, normally refers to Ethiopia (e.g. Gen. 10:6). So most commentators think that she may have been Moses' second wife and that she had come from Ethiopia (e.g. Gen. 10:6). The text does not explain why Miriam and Aaron objected to this woman, because in reality their objections to her were only a smokescreen for their challenge to Moses' spiritual authority. Nevertheless, the linking of Moses' marriage with his relationship to Israel may not be as arbitrary as first appears. Regularly marriage is seen as symbolizing God's covenant with Israel. Moses, as God's representative *par excellence*, must therefore demonstrate in his relationship with his wife how God acts towards Israel. But it would be pure speculation to attempt to figure out the objections of Miriam and Aaron on the basis of this analogy.

Miriam and Aaron claim that the LORD speaks with them in the same intimate way that he speaks with Moses. 'Speak with' is a better rendering of the Hebrew *dibber bĕ* than RSV *speak through* (2), for the same phrase is used in verses 6 and 8 of the close and intimate discussions between God and his servants. Their questioning of Moses' unique authority follows the account of the sharing of Moses' spirit with the seventy elders, which could be interpreted as showing that Moses was just first among equals. However, the very terms in which Aaron and Miriam phrased their challenge shows they recognized there was a difference in fact between their authority and Moses'. This is confirmed by God's words in verses 6–8, the judgment on Miriam in verse 10, Aaron's

---

14. Gray, p. 121.

inability to help her (11–12) and her cure through Moses' intercession
(13–15).

3–8. On earlier occasions when the people complained about God
failing to provide them with food or water, Moses passed on their
complaint (11:4ff.; Exod. 17:2–4). This time, when his own status was
questioned, he remained silent, for *the man Moses was very meek, more
than all men that were on the face of the earth* (3). NEB and TEV 'humble'
conveys the sense of the Hebrew *'ānāw* better than *meek*. It is a word
that elsewhere is used only in poetry. It sometimes refers to those in
real poverty, or those who are weak and liable to be exploited (Amos
2:7; Isa. 11:4). Such people must look to God for aid, because they
are unable to help themselves. But more frequently the word seems
to denote an attitude of mind, more characteristic of the poor than
of the rich, one of humility and dependence on God. The Psalms
repeatedly assure the humble that God will deliver them, 'The LORD
lifts up the humble'; 'he adorns the humble with victory' (Pss. 147:6;
149:4; cf. 22:26; 25:9; 37:11; 76:9; cf. Matt. 5:5; 1 Pet. 5:6).

Rarely has a humble man been so signally and spectacularly
vindicated as Moses. Moses, Aaron and Miriam are summoned to the
tent of meeting. There God appears in the pillar of cloud. Then in
a poem eleven lines long[15] the Lord proclaims that Moses is without
peer among holy men.

There is little doubt about the meaning of the second and third
lines: *If there is a prophet among you, I the LORD make myself known to him
in a vision* (6); but the grammar of the Hebrew has puzzled
commentators, most of whom resort to emendation. However this
is probably unnecessary.[16] The lines can be literally rendered: 'If there
is among you a prophet of the LORD, in a vision to him I make

---

15. The NEB gives only ten lines, but the last line is really two:
    'And why were you not afraid
    to speak against my servant Moses?'
16. The problem arises with the phrase *nĕ'bî'akem yhwh*, literally 'your
    prophet of the LORD'. Nouns with pronominal suffixes are rarely
    construed as constructs and followed by another genitive, though there
    are some clear examples, e.g. Lev. 26:42. Hence the text is commonly
    emended to *nĕ'bî'akem*, 'a prophet among you'. *yhwh* 'the LORD' may be

myself known.' Whereas ordinary prophets had to be content with receiving God's word through dreams and visions and in riddles, Moses is in a different class. He is God's servant entrusted with looking after all his estate,[17] i.e. Israel, and like other men in his position he has immediate access to the owner of the estate (Gen. 24:2; 40:20). He speaks to God directly *mouth to mouth* and therefore can interpret God's will for Israel with total authority. Other men in the Old Testament, e.g. Abraham, Joshua, David and Elijah (Gen. 26:24; Josh. 24:29; 2 Sam. 7:5; 2 Kgs 10:10), are called God's servants, but only Moses is described as *entrusted with all my house*. Finally he sees the very *form* (*tĕmûnâ*) *of God* (8). That is not to say he saw God directly and unveiled. This, apparently, was the privilege that Moses requested when he asked to see God's 'face'. On that occasion he had to be content with seeing God's 'back' (Exod. 33:18–23). The word 'form' (Hebrew *tĕmûnâ*) is used of visual representations, pictures or images, of earthly and heavenly beings (Exod. 20:4). Job saw someone's form, but could not identify the person from it (Job 4:16). Thus, although Moses enjoyed a much closer relationship with God than any ordinary prophet, he saw only God's form, not the very being of God.

9–10. Their guilt pronounced, sentence immediately followed. For

---

taken as subject of the next clause, 'I make myself known'; but this creates another anomaly, in that the 1s. verb has a 3s. subject, NEB and TEV therefore omit 'the LORD'. Alternatively, one may retain *yhwh* in the previous clause but prefix it by *l* /'for' and read: 'If there is a prophet among you for the LORD'. But this makes the line too long metrically. I therefore prefer D. N. Freedman's suggestion ('The Aaronic Benediction', *J. L. McKenzie FS*, pp. 42–43) that this is an example of a broken construct chain. This allows the MT to be retained and translated as above.

17. J. S. Kselman, 'A Note on Numbers 12:6–8', *VT*, 26, 1976, pp. 500–505, attractively reinterprets *lō' kēn*, 'not so', as 'surely' (*lō'* asseverative) 'loyal', pointing out that this improves the parallel with the next line of the poem (cf. 2 Sam. 7:16; Pss. 78:8, 37; 89:37). He translates verse 7

'But my servant Moses is surely loyal:
in all my house he (alone) is faithful.'

her sacrilegious talk Miriam came out with 'leprosy' (cf. 2 Kgs 5:27; 2 Chr. 26:19). Aaron was spared, perhaps because as high priest his role was vital to the divine economy. Though 'leprosy' is the traditional translation of the Hebrew root *ṣāraʿ*, it is inaccurate. True leprosy (Hansen's disease) did not reach the Middle East until New Testament times at the earliest. Nor does true leprosy spontaneously disappear, as the various complaints listed in Leviticus 13 – 14 may do. Rather, biblical leprosy is a patchy, scaly skin complaint, such as psoriasis or severe eczema. It may be that the flaking, peeling scales associated with such complaints prompts the comparison with snow[18] and a still-born infant.[19]

11–16. Leviticus 13 – 14 prescribes no cure for 'lepers', it only lays down what rituals a man who recovers must follow if he is to be received back into the people and resume life in the camp. The ceremonies last a total of seven days. In final clinching proof of Moses' special relationship to God, his prayer for his sister's healing is immediately answered. But the LORD still insists that she must live outside the camp for seven days like other cured lepers, and undergo the normal rites of purification. Her affront to Moses' spiritual authority is as gross as if her father had spat in her face (cf. Deut. 25:9). By way of a footnote hinting at her great standing in the nation, it is mentioned that the whole nation waited for her before moving on (15; cf. Exod. 2:4ff.; 15:20–21; Mic. 6:4).

The New Testament draws many comparisons between Moses the mediator of the old covenant and Jesus the mediator of the new. Jesus is the prophet like Moses (Acts 7:37). Like Moses, Jesus is meek and lowly in heart (Matt. 11:29), and kept silent before his accusers (1 Pet. 2:23ff.). But whereas Moses was but a servant in God's house, our Lord was the son of the house (Heb. 3:1–6); Moses saw God's form and heard his word, but Jesus was the Word and in the form of God (John 1:14–18; Phil. 2:6).

---

18. In verse 10 the Hebrew reads 'like snow' not 'white as snow'.
19. For further discussions see E. V. Hulse, 'The Nature of Biblical Leprosy', *PEQ*, 107, 1975, pp. 87–105; Wenham, pp. 194ff.

3. FORTY YEARS NEAR KADESH
(13:1 – 19:22)

According to Numbers 34:4 and Joshua 15:3, Kadesh-barnea lay on the southern frontier of Canaan. These chapters then tell how Israel arrived at its goal and then turned away. The far-reaching significance of the events at Kadesh is underlined both by the narratives and the laws, which serve to point up the analogy with the periods of revelation at Sinai and in the plains of Moab.[1]

A. The rebellion of the spies (chapters 13 – 14)

Tragedy. These chapters should relate how the drama of the exodus and wilderness wanderings reached a triumphant conclusion. The

---

1. See Introduction, 2. Structure, pp. 16ff. In fact only chapters 13 – 14 are explicitly associated with Kadesh (13:26), and 14:25 and 20:1 may imply that the intervening episodes occurred elsewhere. Nevertheless the arrangement of this material does suggest that a deliberate parallel is

people of Israel, having survived the very difficult trek from Mount
Sinai to Kadesh, one of the most fertile oases in the Sinai peninsula,
find themselves on the borders of the promised land. Obeying
God's instructions, Moses sends out spies to see what the land is
really like. They bring back magnificent bunches of fruit, a vivid
proof that it is, as God said, a land flowing with milk and honey.

But instead of encouraging Israel to claim their inheritance, the
spies advise them that the land is too difficult for Israel to conquer.
They will die in the attempt. In despair the people propose returning to Egypt. God suggests annihilating them for their unbelief. In
response to Moses' intercession he mitigates his judgment. Only the
faithless spies die immediately; the people are condemned to wander in the wilderness for forty years until the older generation has
passed away. They will not enter Canaan, but their children will. As
the people refused to believe God's promise of victory over the
Canaanites, so they would not accept his judgment. The episode concludes with their attempting to conquer the land without divine aid,
and being chased all the way to Hormah.

Marking as it does the collapse of the national plan, and the postponement of God's promises to the patriarchs, the incident of the
spies is more than just another example of Israel's rebellion in the
wilderness. It is a historical watershed. Here the final break with
Egypt is made. Those who yearned for the luxuries of Egyptian slavery die in the desert; their children chastened by their wilderness experiences enter the promised land.

The narrative style of these chapters reflects the significance of
the events they describe. The terse restraint which characterizes
much of Numbers is here cast off. The actors speak passionately and
at length about the issues at stake. Repetition, vivid imagery and deliberate irony accent the main thrust of the story. Once again Moses'
intimacy and influence with God is brought into focus (cf. ch. 12),
thereby showing that this is no mere dispute about the politics of
conquest, but that the very core of the covenant, the promise

being drawn between the events and laws described in Num. 13 – 19
and those associated with Sinai (Exod. 19 – Num. 10) and with Moab
(Num. 22 – 36).

of Canaan itself, is being brought into question. At heart the issue is spiritual. Will God's people believe his word? It stands as a warning to subsequent generations not to put the LORD to the test. **13:1–16.** Twelve tribal leaders are selected to go from *Paran* (3; cf. 10:11–36) and *spy out* (2) the land of Canaan. Their job is described more fully in verses 17–20: they were to bring back a report on the quality of the land and the morale of its inhabitants (cf. Josh. 2; Judg. 18). From Deuteronomy 1:22 it seems that the purpose of the mission was to strengthen the Israelites' faith, not to bring back tactical information. The list of tribal leaders (4–15) given here is quite different from those found elsewhere in Numbers (chs. 1 – 2; 7). Maybe on occasions such as the census and the dedication of the altar the most senior leader from each tribe represented his tribe, while for the more energetic task of spying younger leaders were chosen. The order in which the tribes are listed here also differs from other passages for no apparent reason. In this list Joshua is called Hoshea (8; cf. Deut. 32:44), which probably means (God) 'is salvation', or (God) 'saves'. Verse 16 explains that Moses later renamed him Joshua, which means 'the LORD is salvation', or 'the LORD saves'. It is not explicitly stated that it was on this occasion that his name was changed to Joshua.² Indeed, that the list of spies calls him Hoshea suggests it was done later and indirectly confirms the antiquity of this list.³ Though some earlier passages use the name Joshua, they must be anticipating his subsequent change of name (e.g. Exod. 24:13). Other important name changes include Abraham's (Gen. 17:5), Sarah's (Gen. 17:15) and Jacob's (Gen. 35:10). The Greek version of the Old Testament translates Joshua by Jesus.

17–20 specify the spies' mission precisely. They are *to spy out the land of Canaan*, starting from the *Negeb* in the south and working northwards through the *hill country* (17). The boundaries of the land

2. Cf. Keil, p. 86.

3. According to Exod. 6:3 the divine name Yahweh, i.e. the LORD, was first revealed to Moses at the burning bush. It may be surmised that Hoshea was the name given to Joshua at birth, and that it was later changed to Joshua in the light of the new revelation, and as a mark of his identification with the work of Moses.

of Canaan are more closely defined in 34:1–12 (see map, p. 260), approximately the present territory of modern Israel, Lebanon and much of Southern Syria. In the el-Amarna letters (14th century BC) a similar understanding of the boundaries of Canaan is presupposed, and it was this area that was under Egyptian control in the New Kingdom (16 – 13th centuries BC) period.[4]

The Negeb is the dry area, unsuitable for cultivation, that runs southwards from Beersheba (cf. Gen. 20:1; 24:62; Num. 21:1). *The hill country* means the chain of hills that run north through the tribal territories of Judah, Ephraim and into Galilee (cf. Josh. 20:7).

In their travels the spies were told to observe what the land was like, in particular the strength of its inhabitants, whether its cities were fortified, and to bring back some of its fruit (18–20). *The season of the first ripe grapes* (20) is late July, approximately two months after the departure from Sinai (10:11). Deuteronomy 1:2 says that it is only eleven days' journey from Horeb to Kadesh-barnea; that would represent steady uninterrupted progress by a small group. Israel was a much larger group and there had been various delays on their way (cf. 11:20; 12:15).

21–26 briefly describe how the spies carried out exactly Moses' directions in 17–20. They traverse the land of Canaan from south to north: the wilderness of Zin[5] lies on the southern border to the north-east of Kadesh (cf. 20:1; Josh. 15:1), while Rehob, by Lebo-hamath (NEB), lies on the northern frontier[6] (Num. 34:8). This was a distance of about 250 miles each way, so forty days (25) would be a realistic estimate of the time for them to cover the distances involved.

Moses had instructed them to go up into the Negeb and into the hill country (17), and so they did: Hebron is the largest town in the hills of Judah (22). Some of the inhabitants of the town are named (22; cf. verse 19; Josh. 15:14; Judg. 1:10), and described as *descendants of Anak*. Though Anak[7] was probably a genuine clan name, *'ānāq* in

---

4. See Y. Aharoni, *The Land of the Bible* (Burns and Oates, 1966), pp. 61–70; R. de Vaux, 'Le Pays de Canaan', *JAOS*, 88, 1968, pp. 23–30.

5. See map (p. 260) and chapter 33.

6. See discussion on 34:8 and associated map, p. 260.

7. See 'Anak', *IBD*, p. 48.

Hebrew also means neck, and this group were famed for their
height (cf. 33). They also discovered that Zoan, to be identified with
Tanis in the Nile delta, near the land of Goshen (cf. Ps. 78:12, 43),
was built seven years after Hebron. If Tanis was founded by the Hyk-
sos kings of Egypt (c. 1700 BC), it may be surmised that Hebron was
too.[8]
At any rate, it implies that Hebron was a large, well-fortified
town (cf. 19). Finally, they brought back a selection of the fruits of
the land, grapes, pomegranates and figs, which they carried back on
a *pole*: though *pole* is the traditional rendering of Hebrew *môṭ*, it may
mean something more elaborate like the frames for carrying the tabernacle in 4:10, 12. These grapes came from a valley called Eshcol,
which means 'cluster'. Its location is uncertain, but it is assumed it
must be near Hebron, which is still a centre for growing grapes.
There is no contradiction between verse 23, which suggests the valley already had this name before the spies arrived, and the following verse which attributes its name to them. If the name of the valley was coined by the spies, then verse 23 is proleptic. If the name
is pre-Israelite (one of Abraham's allies in Gen. 14:13, 24 was called
Eshcol and lived near Hebron), then the spies in verse 24 are giving
a new interpretation to an old word.

It may well be significant that the narrative devotes so much attention to Hebron. It was near Hebron that God first promised
Abraham that he would inherit the land (Gen. 13:14–18). It was from
that area that he set out to defeat the coalition of kings (Gen.
14:13ff.). It was in Hebron that he acquired his only piece of real estate for the burial of his wife, and where he and the other patriarchs
were buried (Gen. 23; 25:9; 35:27–29; 50:13). The narrator knew these
traditions, and he assumes the spies did and that the reader does. It
is essential that they be borne in mind as the rest of the story un-
folds.

27–29. After the cool objective description of what the spies

---

8. However J. J. Bimson, *Redating the Exodus and Conquest*, p. 202, suggests
   that this verse may be referring to the rebuilding of Hebron and Tanis
   in the 11th century BC. Hebron was destroyed at the end of the Middle
   Bronze Age and apparently not rebuilt till the Iron Age.

discovered in Canaan in the preceding paragraph, these verses describe in more colourful terms the impression Canaan made on the majority and the report they gave to Moses in the presence of the *congregation*, i.e. the leading men in the nation (26; cf. 30). A hint of the spies' attitude is given in their very first words. They call Canaan *the land to which you sent us*; usually when the land is qualified by a relative clause, it is described as the land 'which the Lord swore to give them', or something similar (cf. 13:2; 14:16, 23, 30, 40; 15:2, etc.). Whenever the spies describe the land, they pointedly avoid this phraseology (cf. 13:32). They continue in apparently more positive vein, saying the land *flows with milk and honey* (27) and show the fruit they have picked.

But then, with a strong adversative *yet* (Hebrew *'epes kî*; cf. Judg. 4:9; 2 Sam. 12:14; Amos 9:8), they draw attention to the obstacles in the way of conquest: *the people are strong* (28; cf. 18) and *the cities are fortified and very large* (28; cf. 19). Then they list some of the inhabitants of the land, *the descendants of Anak* (28; cf. 22). The Amalekites, a bedouin-like people, lived on the southern borders of Canaan and in the Sinai peninsula (cf. Exod. 17:8ff.; Num. 14:45; 1 Sam. 15); the Hittites lived in the Hebron region (Gen. 23); the Jebusites in Jerusalem (Josh. 15:63; 2 Sam. 5:6ff.); the Amorites also lived in the hills, while the Canaanites proper lived along the sea coast and in the valleys. The Canaanites gave their name to the whole area, and in some passages any of the pre-Israelite inhabitants are called Canaanites[9] (cf. 14:45; Gen. 13:7).

These first-hand details about the residents of the land gave the spies' report a touch of authority, and no doubt helped to convince the people of the impossibility of its conquest. But at the same time they obliquely, but totally, challenged the divine promises. Up to this point the phrase *a land flowing with milk and honey* has always been coupled with the promise that God would give the land and its inhabitants, often listed as here, to Israel (Exod. 3:8, 17; 13:5; 33:3; Lev. 20:24). The spies question this conclusion. They look on the presence of these other nations as an insurmountable obstacle to entry, not as a confirmation of God's purpose.

---

9. For further discussions on these peoples see the relevant articles in *IBD* and D. J. Wiseman, *Peoples of the Old Testament Times* (Clarendon, 1973).

30–33. Caleb's attempt to calm the people and rekindle their faith in the promises (*go up, occupy*, Hebrew *'ālâ, yāraš* are key words in Exod. 3:8, 17; 33:3 and Lev. 20:24) is immediately rebuffed by the other spies with more outrageous misrepresentation (31–33). This time their words are dubbed an *evil report*, that means not simply that they describe the land as evil, but that their accusations about it are untrue (cf. TEV 'false report'). They claim it 'eats' *its inhabitants* (32), that is they tend to die due to the hostile environment (Lev. 26:38; Ezek. 36:13). For a similar personification of the land, cf. Leviticus 18:25, 28. Finally, they revert to the tall men, the sons of Anak, whom they describe with fantastic hyperbole as Nephilim, that is the demigods who lived on earth before the flood (Gen. 6:4). 'We felt as small as grasshoppers, and that is how we must have looked to them' (33, TEV; cf. Isa. 40:22).

Under ancient oriental law those who made false accusations were punished by receiving the sentence those they accused would have received if convicted (Deut. 19:16–19). The spies had wrongfully accused the land of homicide; therefore they could expect to receive the death penalty themselves. This principle is worked out in the rest of the story. The spies meet sudden death (14:37). The people who accept the false testimony of the majority and not the counter evidence of Caleb and Joshua suffer similarly. The fate they feared they would meet in Canaan actually overtakes them in the desert (14:3, 29–34).

14:1–4. Now the rebellion reaches its climax. Appalled by the spies' description of the promised land, the people break down completely. In the Hebrew (1–2; cf. AV) the verbs pile up in an attempt to express the passions unleashed. They reflect that anything they have experienced up to now will be better than Canaan. The thought moves from Egypt to the wilderness to Canaan and then back to Egypt. Time had already dulled their more bitter memories of Egypt, and in an earlier rebellion they had looked back on it with a certain wistfulness (cf. 11:5, 18, 20). But this time they actually propose returning to Egypt, thereby completely rejecting the whole plan of redemption. From Exodus 1 to the mission of the spies there is but one plot: how Israel was brought out of Egypt to the borders of Canaan. Now within sight of their goal they suggest giving it all up. Not only that, they propose electing an alternative leader to

Moses, their divinely appointed mediator of salvation. 'Let's choose a leader and go back to Egypt!' (4, TEV).

5. No wonder *Moses and Aaron fell on their faces*, not to plead for their lives, but to express their awe at the sacrilegious blasphemy of the people. To fall on one's face is the Old Testament's ultimate mark of religious worship and awe (Gen. 17:3; Lev. 9:24). But in Numbers it usually anticipates some great act of judgment (cf. 16:4, 22, 45; 20:6). Moses and Aaron, sensing the presence of God, fall to the ground in fear at what he is about to do. But God's glory is not immediately manifest (10): the narrative leaves us in suspense. The people are to be given one last chance to repent, as Caleb and Joshua forthrightly plead with them to trust in the Lord. Yet the prostration of Moses and Aaron intimates that this appeal will not be heeded and that the people will fall in the wilderness (cf. 29ff.).

6. Joshua and Caleb *rent their clothes*, a more conventional gesture of deep distress (cf. Gen. 37:29, 34; Lev. 13:45). Its traditional association with mourning for the dead may be another hint of subsequent events (cf. Judg. 11:35). This is the first time that Joshua has publicly associated himself with Caleb's minority report. His silence hitherto makes good psychological and literary sense. Had he spoken out earlier in defence of the plan of conquest, his testimony could have been too easily dismissed as biased; he was Moses' personal assistant and therefore entirely associated with the Mosaic programme of exodus and conquest. But in the context of this programme his intervention is most appropriate here. The people have just stated that their children will be taken captive if they enter Canaan and that they should, therefore, select a new leader to bring them back to Egypt. Though Joshua's appointment as Moses' successor is not discussed for many chapters, the stepping forward of Joshua at this moment adumbrates the future. He will be their new leader, who will bring their little ones into possession of the land.

7–9. Joshua and Caleb's speech closely echoes[10] the speeches by

---

10. Cf. *the land to which you sent us, through which we have gone*// *which we passed through* (13:27, 32; 14:7) *flows with milk and honey* (13:27; 14:8). *Yet ('epes ki)*// *Only ('ak)* (13:28; 14:9) *devours its inhabitants*//*they are bread for us* (13:32; 14:9).

the other spies (13:27–29, 32–33). They do not dispute their colleagues' account of its inhabitants, but they do insist that they are not to be feared. They may look like demi-gods, but *their protection* (literally 'shadow', an apt picture of divine protection in the hot lands of the Middle East, Pss. 91; 121:5) *is removed from them, and the* LORD *is with us.* The whole balance of power is altered.

10. *But all the congregation said to stone them.* This is not simply a mob-lynching (cf. Exod. 17:4; 1 Kgs 12:18). The congregation had judicial authority, and stoning was reserved for the punishment of major religious crimes (e.g. Lev. 20:2, 27; 24:23; Num. 15:36; Deut. 13:10) and sins within the family which symbolize breaches of the covenant (Deut. 21:21; 22:21, 24). Joshua and Caleb have accused them of rebelling against the LORD (9); the congregation rejects this charge as false and proposes to exact the appropriate penalty for false witness. At the critical moment the LORD appears in glory over the tabernacle (cf. Exod. 16:7, 10; 24:16–17; Lev. 9:6, 23; Num. 16:19, 42; 20:6; 1 Kgs 8:11).

11–12. The divine accusation is similar to Joshua's. 'This people treat me with contempt' (NEB; cf. 14:23; 16:30; Deut. 31:20). They will *not believe in me, in spite of all the signs which I have wrought among them.* By signs are meant the plagues, the crossing of the Red Sea, the miracles of feeding, and so on (Exod. 7:3; 10:1). Though words for faith and belief in God are fairly rare in the Old Testament, that man must exercise faith in God and his word is a fundamental presupposition of all the writers. To believe in God means to accept all he says and to act accordingly: to trust his promises and obey his commands. Faith makes a man to be counted righteous before God (Gen. 15:6): its absence damns him (cf. Num. 20:12). In this instance God proposes destroying Israel and starting afresh with Moses and his descendants (12).

13–25. The worship of the golden calf prompted a similar suggestion. Then Moses persuaded God to relent, on the grounds that the Egyptians would conclude he was powerless and that it would break the promises made to the patriarchs (Exod. 32:10–14). Moses invokes the same arguments here and reminds the Lord of the promises he had made before, that he would forgive Israel when they sinned (cf. Exod. 34:6–9).

As usual Moses' plea is heard: *the* LORD *said, 'I have pardoned,*

according to your word' (20). The divine pardon does not mean Israel will
escape all punishment for their sin, only that they will not suffer the
total annihilation they deserve. A similar understanding of forgiveness is found in many sacrificial texts. After the worshipper has performed the full ritual involving very often the heavy expense of
killing an animal, it is stated 'he shall be forgiven' (e.g. Lev. 4:20, 26,
31; 5:6, etc.). In other words, the man is restored to fellowship with
God, but he has still paid for his offence by offering a sacrifice. Similarly here, though forgiven the people may still not enter the promised land. The very next day they must turn and head toward the Red
Sea (25).

Geographically this probably means they were to head south-east
from Kadesh toward the Gulf of Aqabah, one of the recognized
north-south routes across the Sinai Peninsula.[11] But theologically *the
way to the Red Sea* suggests they are returning to Egypt. Typical of the
irony in this story, their punishment is made to fit their crime. They
wanted to die in the wilderness and return to Egypt: in a way rather
different from the one they intended, God grants their request.
The long-term programme of entering Canaan will be postponed to
let the generation of rebels die where they wanted.

26–38. This theme, that the rebellious generation will receive their
deserts, literally what they asked for, is developed in Moses' address
to the nation. They said, *Would that we had died in this wilderness!* (2).
Four times they are warned, *Your dead bodies shall fall in this wilderness*
(29, 32, 33, 35). Their children, who they said would perish in
Canaan, would eventually arrive there and take possession of it (3,
31, 33). In immediate confirmation of these warnings all the faithless spies die in a heaven-sent plague. Only Joshua and Caleb, whose
entrance to Canaan was guaranteed, survived (30, 36–38).

39–45. Mourning (39) was indeed appropriate, given Moses' message about their certain death in the wilderness. But evidently the
people did not really believe it, thinking that simple acknowledgment
of their mistake would be adequate. They set out on their own, un-
accompanied by Moses, the ark or the LORD, and they were defeated
near Hormah, a village on the southern borders of Canaan (cf. Josh.

11. See G. I. Davies, *The Way of the Wilderness* (CUP, 1979), p. 77.

15:30).[12] This short episode underlines the message of the whole spy story. Israel still does not take God seriously, or listen to Moses his appointed representative. They will not enter Canaan until they learn their lesson, and that may take a long time.

This story is more than a vivid narrative. Its message reverberates down through Scripture. It is recalled in Numbers 32, Deuteronomy 1:20–40 (cf. 8:2), the Psalms (95:10; 106:24ff.), the prophets (Amos 2:10; 5:25) and in the New Testament (1 Cor. 10; Heb. 3:7 – 4:13). Hebrews 3:12, 14 sums it up: 'Take care, brethren, lest there be in any of you an evil, unbelieving heart, leading you to fall away from the living God ... For we share in Christ, if only we hold our first confidence firm to the end.'

Additional note on the sources in Numbers 13 – 14

According to the usual source-critical theory the book of Numbers is compiled from two principal sources, JE, the earlier source and P, the later priestly source. The boundaries between these sources usually coincide with natural divisions of the material; thus, all the legal material in chapters 1 – 10 is P, while the narratives in 11 – 12 are JE. But in the spy story it is held that the two main sources are interwoven: two separate accounts have been combined to produce the present form of the story.

Gray[13] distinguished between the sources as follows: to P he assigned 13:1–17a, 21, 25, 26a, 32a; 14:1a, 2, 5–7, 10, 26–39a; to JE the rest, *viz.* 13:17b–20, 22–24, 26b–31, 32b–33; 14:1b, 3–4, 8–9, 11–25, 39b–45. However, Gray argued that 14:11–24, Moses' intercession, is really a secondary expansion of JE, but pre-P. Other commentators advocate similar analyses of the material, general differing by only a verse or two. However, de Vaulx[14] and McEvenue[15] hold that

---

12. Possibly to be identified with Khirbet el-Meshash, eight miles east of Beersheba.

13. Gray, pp. 129ff.

14. de Vaulx, pp. 171ff.

15. S. E. McEvenue, 'A Source-Critical Problem in Nm. 14:26–38', *Biblica*, 50, 1969, pp. 453–465.

14:30–33 is another secondary expansion of JE presupposed by P.

In support of this analysis it is urged that it explains the presence of doublets in the narrative, cf. 13:21 (P) with 13:22 (JE), 14:11ff. (JE) with 14:26f. (P), and certain contradictions within the narrative. According to JE (13:26b) the spies set out from Kadesh but in P they went from the wilderness of Paran (13:3, 26a). In JE (13:22–24) they spy out just the southern area round Hebron, but in P the whole land of Canaan (13:2, 17a, 21). In JE only Caleb dissents from the majority of the spies (13:30; 14:24), but according to P both Caleb and Joshua disagree and are spared to enter the land (14:6f., 38).

None of these arguments is entirely convincing. Repetition is a characteristic feature of biblical narrative, even within stories all assigned to one source. If Kadesh was on the borders of the wilderness of Paran, as suggested above, it would explain why the terms can be used interchangeably in the narrative. It is true that the material assigned to JE concentrates on the area round Hebron, while P insists that the spies visited the whole land. But they had a special interest in the Hebron area, because that was where the patriarchs were buried, and 13:29 (JE) does in fact hint that they went much further: the Jebusites in Jerusalem, and the Canaanites living beside the Mediterranean and Jordan are both mentioned. Finally, there were good reasons for Caleb to take the lead in opposing the majority of spies. Joshua, as Moses' assistant, would have been expected to disagree, and so did not speak up until it was obvious Caleb's remarks were going unheeded. In Deuteronomy 1:36, 38, generally regarded as pre-P, both Caleb and Joshua are associated as the only two of the exodus generation who would enter Canaan.

The arguments for this source analysis have most strength, when it is held that JE and P were independent sources. But McEvenue[16] has shown that, if JE and P are distinguished, there are so many points of similarity between the two versions of the spy story that the P version must be based on the JE version. This suggests that the contradictions between the two sources are only apparent; they

---

16. S. E. McEvenue, *The Narrative Style of the Priestly Writer* (Biblical Institute Press, 1971), pp. 92ff.

did not seem contradictory to the earlier writers. If so, these differences provide an inadequate basis for denying the unity of the present narratives.

However, other internal and external arguments favour the unity of the spy story as it stands. First, the earlier JE source is incomplete. It begins without saying who the spies were or even their number, or who sent them out or who they reported back to. It is clear that JE is presupposing material at present found only in P. If this were an isolated example, it would be possible to suppose that this shows merely that we do not have JE's story in its entirety. However, some of the speeches in JE also presuppose remarks found in P's speeches. For example, 14:7–9 echoes both 13:27–29, 32b–33 (JE) and 32a (P). As they stand, Moses' instruction to the spies (13:17–19), the narrator's description of their mission (13:21–26) and their own account of it (13:27–33) all go over the same points in the same order, though with elegant variation of wording. Yet source analysts split these three sections up in order to maintain the dubious distinctions between them.

Secondly, a comparison of the account in Numbers 13 – 14 with that in Deuteronomy 1 shows that the latter presupposes not only the material found in the JE account, but also that which is supposedly P or a gloss on JE. Deuteronomy mentions that there was one spy per tribe (1:23; cf. Num. 13:2), that both Joshua and Caleb were spared (1:36, 38; cf. Num. 14:6, 30, 38), and the worries about their little ones (1:39; cf. Num. 14:3, 31).

These observations do not of themselves demand that the source-critical analysis be abandoned. They can be squared with the source-critical theory, if Deuteronomy is dated after P, as a few scholars hold. But in view of the interrelationships between many parts of the story, it would seem safer to assume that it is a basic unity as it stands. Its present form may be the result of subsequent expansion by a later editor,[17] but it does not appear to be the product of the combination of two independent sources.

---

17. Criteria for distinguishing earlier and later elements are fairly questionable. But the comment in 13:16 about Hoshea's change of name may be a comment on the earlier source contained in 13:4–15.

B. Laws on offerings (chapter 15)

i. Meal, oil and wine accompanying sacrifices (15:1–16).

The abrupt transition from the spy story to the strange collection of cultic laws contained in this chapter baffles commentators. Why should they be placed here, when they would fit much more tidily after Leviticus 7 or after Numbers 29? Various allusions to the preceding episode may be noted (e.g. *the land* [2, 18], *Egypt* [41; cf. 14:3–4], *congregation* [24–25, etc.; cf. 14:1, etc.], *be forgiven* [25–26; cf. 14:19–20], *look* [39; cf. 13:18, 33], *eyes* [39; cf 13:33], *spy out/follow after* [Hebrew *tûr*, 39; cf. 13:2, etc.]). But these hardly account for the present position of these laws.

More striking is the careful arrangement of this group of laws. As is typical of the cultic laws in Leviticus, this chapter falls neatly into three sections, each beginning with *The LORD said to Moses, 'Say to the people of Israel'* (1f., 17f., 37f.), usually moving on to mention *the land* (2, 18), then a command to *do* or make something (Hebrew *'āśâ*, 3, 22ff., 28ff.) and concluding with the great formula recalling Israel's salvation from Egypt and her call to holiness (41; cf. Lev. 19:36f.; 20:26; 22:31–33; 23:43; 25:55).

It therefore seems likely that these laws have been placed here as a deliberate comment on the preceding narrative. The people have questioned the basic purpose of their journey, and in judgment God has declared the adults will die out in the wilderness. After a break of forty years their children will enter the promised land of Canaan. Chapter 14 closes with a defeat by the Canaanites at Hormah. A question mark hangs over the whole enterprise.

1–2. These laws reassert very emphatically that the LORD will bring his people into Canaan. They both explicitly look forward to this time (2, 18) and implicitly, by specifying that large amounts of flour, oil and wine must accompany animal sacrifice, guarantee Israel's entry into the land. If God insists that these things be offered, it is a pledge that Israel will eventually reach the land where they are freely available. These regulations also re-emphasize the role of sacrifice as the divinely appointed means of upholding the covenant and the importance of fulfilling the commandments. Though God's ultimate purposes will not be thwarted by disobedience, the individual and the congregation will still be judged for deliberate sin or even inadvertent mistakes that are not atoned for by sacrifice. This chapter, then, epitomizes and comments on some of the themes that dominate the book of Leviticus. Israel is to show forth her election by faithfully observing the moral and ritual law: in so doing they will become a truly holy people, and in a full sense the LORD will be their God (40f.). Their unbelief that was focused in the spy story did not nullify these covenant promises. Whole-hearted repentance and the offering of sacrifice can restore them to a position where they can fully experience God's blessing.

3–16 specify that every animal sacrifice that counts as *an offering by fire*[18] (3) must be accompanied by a cereal offering of flour and oil and a libation of oil. Both burnt offerings, a sacrifice in which the whole animal was burnt on the altar, and peace offerings, in which some of the animal was burnt and the rest shared between priest and worshipper, are termed offerings by fire which *make a pleasing odour to the LORD* (3). In Leviticus 1 – 3 this phrase simply applies to the burnt material: its aroma makes God well disposed towards the sinner who has brought it (cf. Gen. 8:21–22). Here the term also refers to the accompanying wine offerings. Though cereal offerings are mentioned in Leviticus as accompaniments of animal sacrifice (cf. chs. 8 – 9, 14), and a libation of wine is specified in the Nazirite law (Num. 6:15ff.), this is the first time that it has been made clear that they must accompany every burnt offering and peace offering. The insistence on a libation of wine is specially appropriate after the spies had brought back a huge cluster of grapes (13:23).

Animal	Cereal offering		Drink offering
	Flour	Oil	
Lamb	¹⁄₁₀ ephah (1.5 litres)	¼ hin (0.5 litre)	¼ hin (0.5 litre)
Ram	²⁄₁₀ ephah (3.0 litres)	⅓ hin (0.8 litre)	⅓ hin (0.8 litre)
Bull	³⁄₁₀ ephah (4.5 litres)	½ hin (1.0 litre)	½ hin (1.0 litre)

(There were 6 hins to an ephah, which is about 15 litres [25 pints].[19])

18. NEB translates Hebrew *'iššeh* as 'food offering', which may be preferable to RSV *offering by fire*; see Wenham, p. 56.

19. de Vaulx, *Ancient Israel*, p. 202.

There was a fixed tariff: the larger the animal, the larger the cereal offering and libation that had to accompany it. Canaanite and Greek sacrifices were also usually accompanied by cereal and drink offerings. The antiquity of the practice in Israel is proved by 1 Samuel 1:24; 10:3. A handful of each cereal offering was burnt: the rest was given to the priests and constituted an important source of income for them (Lev. 2:2f.; cf. 1 Cor. 9:13). The wine was simply poured out at the foot of the altar, and was probably viewed as complementing the animal's blood, which was also treated similarly. It was this act which completed the sacrifice (cf. Ecclus. 50:14–21).

The theological purpose of these additional offerings is not clear. In so far as they cover the main agricultural products of Canaan, it may be that they are intended to symbolize every aspect of life. The worshipper must symbolically offer his whole life and work to God. The New Testament sees Jesus as fulfilling the role of the sacrificial animals of the old covenant (e.g. Heb. 9:12ff.). The more valuable the animal, the larger the accompanying vegetable offerings. Early Christian commentators[20] asked what offerings could match the Lamb of God. They pointed to Paul's remarks about his sufferings, filling up Christ's afflictions, and his life being poured out as a libation (Col. 1:24; Phil. 2:17; 2 Tim. 4:6), a path which all Christ's disciples must follow, at least figuratively.

ii. First dough offering (15:17–21). This is another regulation that looks forward to the settlement in Canaan. When the Israelites arrive in the land and start to enjoy its crops, they must offer *the first of your dough*[21] (20–21, AV; cf. NEB), in the form of a cake, and give it to the priest. The word for *offering* (Hebrew *tĕrûmâ*, 19–20) is a technical term for a portion given to the priest (cf. Lev. 7:32; Num. 18:8). Alongside the regular tithe the Old Testament insists that the first-fruits be given to God. Thus, every first-born child belongs to God; first-born animals, the first-fruits of every crop

---

20. de Vaulx, p. 183.
21. This traditional Jewish understanding is as old as the LXX and is to be preferred to RSV *coarse meal*. The Hebrew term *'ărisōt* occurs only here and in Neh. 10:37; Ezek. 44:30.

must also be given to God (Exod. 22:29–30; 23:19). This means that they are given to the priest, who will offer them as a sacrifice, keep them for his own use, or allow them to be redeemed, i.e. exchange them for a cash payment. Here this principle of first-fruits is brought right into home life: when a housewife makes bread she must set aside a portion for the LORD. After the fall of the second temple this custom was still maintained: pious Jews would throw a handful of the dough into the fire as a sort of mini-sacrifice, thereby making every hearth an altar and every kitchen a house of God.

Jesus commented favourably on his contemporaries' punctilious observance of such laws as these (Matt. 23:23). Paul remarks on this custom: 'If the dough offered as first fruits is holy, so is the whole lump' (Rom. 11:16). The principle of the first-fruits applies just as much in the spiritual realm as in the material. The conversion of some Jews is a pledge 'that all Israel will be saved', just as the resurrection of Christ guarantees the resurrection of all believers (Rom. 11:26; 1 Cor. 15:20–23).

iii. Atonement for inadvertent sins (15:22–31). The dough law illustrates how demanding God's law is, and leads naturally into the next provision:[22] *suppose someone unintentionally fails to keep some of these regulations which the LORD has given Moses* (22, TEV). There follows a brief reminder of the provisions of Leviticus 4:1 – 5:13, dealing with sin offerings.[23] These might be better described as purification offerings, for the key feature in the ritual was the smearing of blood on the altar or on part of the tabernacle to purify it from sin.[24]

---

22. The heading *The LORD said to Moses* (17) shows that verses 17–36 are all one unit. See above on 15:1–6.

23. That this law presupposes Lev. 4 and not vice versa, see de Vaulx, p. 185, and D. Kellermann, 'Bemerkungen zum Sündopfergesetz in Nm. 15:22ff', *Wort und Geschichte: FS für K. Elliger* (Neukirchen, 1973), pp. 107–113; A. Toeg, 'A Halakhic Midrash in Nm. 15:22–31', *Tarbiz*, 43, 1973, pp. 1–20.

24. Cf. Wenham, pp. 88ff., and Additional note on Old Testament sacrifice, pp. 226ff.

The main differences between this law and those of Leviticus 4 may be ascribed to their different interests. The main concern of Leviticus 4 is the description of the sin-offering ritual. This section does not bother with the ritual, but concentrates on the sacrifices that ought to accompany the sin offering, the need for *strangers* (resident aliens) to sacrifice, and the impotence of sacrifice in cases of deliberate sin. Two cases of inadvertent sins which can be atoned for by sacrifice are cited first to emphasize that by contrast high-handed sins will not be forgiven but punished directly by God.

22–23. Sacrifice is necessary whenever one of the commandments is broken, whether by omission or commission. But it makes atonement only when the sin was committed *unwittingly* (24, 27, 28, 29; cf. 22, 25). The same Hebrew phrase (*bišgāgâ*) is used to distinguish manslaughter from murder in 35:11, 15. Murder is planned in advance, whereas manslaughter, as defined in Numbers 35:16–28, is committed by accident or in the heat of the moment.

24–26. The first example concerns an unwitting sin committed by the congregation,[25] i.e. a national sin. Leviticus 4:14 prescribes that a bull should be offered as a *sin offering*, whereas Numbers 15:24 stipulates a *bull as a burnt offering and a male goat* for a *sin offering*. In the case of an individual's sin Leviticus 4:28, 32 allows a goat or lamb to be offered, whereas Numbers 15:27 mentions only a goat. There is no obvious reason for the difference in the congregational offerings demanded by Leviticus and Numbers. Jewish commentators have held that Numbers is dealing with national idolatry, but it is difficult to see how this could happen *unwittingly without the knowledge of the congregation* (24). Nor is it likely that Leviticus 4 is dealing with sins of commission, whereas this chapter concerns sins of omission.[26] It seems simplest to suppose that the Leviticus rule is being modified slightly, as occurs with some other pentateuchal laws (cf. Exod. 13:2 and Num. 3:12f.; Lev. 7:34 and Deut. 18:3; Lev. 11:39f. Deut. 14:21).

27–31. However, the main thrust of the law comes in verses 30–

---

25. On this term, see on 10:3.
26. So Keil, p. 101.

31. Anyone who breaks the commandments with a *high hand* (cf. 33:3; Exod. 14:8, AV), that is deliberately and blatantly, *shall be cut off from among his people*: that is, suffer sudden death at the hand of God (cf. 9:13; Lev. 17:4, 9, etc.). It seems likely that the following story of the sabbath breaker illustrates what sinning with a high hand means (Num. 15:32–36). Leviticus 6:1–7 does allow sacrificial atonement in some cases of deliberate sin, if the sinner publicly confesses his fault, makes full restitution to the injured party and offers a guilt offering.

The New Testament contains similar dire warnings about the impossibility of forgiveness in cases of deliberate apostasy. 'If we sin deliberately after receiving the knowledge of the truth, there no longer remains a sacrifice for sins, but a fearful prospect of judgment …' (Heb. 10:26ff., referring to Deut. 17:2–6; cf. Mark 3:29; 1 John 1:7; 5:16).

iv. A sabbath breaker stoned (15:32–36). This incident illustrates how high-handed sinners were dealt with, when they were caught in the act. The penalty of cutting off (30–31) applied where they escaped human detection. The procedures followed in this case closely resemble Leviticus 24:10–23, describing the conviction and execution of a blasphemer. It was already recognized that sabbath breaking warranted the death penalty (Exod. 31:15; 35:2–3). Stoning was prescribed, a punishment which involved a large body of people, the *congregation* (36), thereby symbolizing the community's rejection of this offence. Since the sabbath was a sign of the covenant, its desecration was particularly serious (Deut. 5:15).

The death penalty[27] was exacted for several religious offences in the Old Testament, including idolatry, blasphemy, false prophecy as well as murder, some cases of incest and adultery. Hebrews 10:28–29 comments: 'A man who has violated the law of Moses dies without mercy at the testimony of two or three witnesses. How much worse punishment do you think will be deserved by the man who has spurned the Son of God?'

---

27. On the use of the death penalty in OT law, cf. B. N. Kaye and G. J. Wenham (eds.), *Law, Morality and the Bible* (IVP, 1978), pp. 38ff.

Why then was it necessary to ascertain God's will in this case? There are three possibilities. The traditional view is that it was necessary to discover how the man should be executed. Another suggestion is that the law laid down that kindling a fire on the sabbath merited the death penalty (Exod. 35:3) but did not cover the case of gathering firewood. The law in Numbers extends the Exodus rule somewhat lest the man should have gone on to start a fire.[28] The third possibility is a modification of the second view. By collecting sticks the man was demonstrating his clear intention of lighting a fire on the sabbath. His action prompted the query: Did premeditated preparation to break the law count as a high-handed sin and deserve the same penalty as actually breaking the law, or could it be overlooked? In favour of this view it may be noted that premeditation demonstrated in the preparations for committing a crime distinguishes murder from manslaughter, killing inadvertently, *bišgāgâ*, in Numbers 35:15ff. Intention to harm was also punishable when it issued in false testimony (Deut. 19:16–19).

v. Tassels on clothes (15:37–41). Prevention is better than cure. As a constant reminder of the commandments the Israelites must attach tassels to the corners of their clothing. Deuteronomy 22:12 specifies one at each corner of the square outer garment. Egyptian and Mesopotamian sculptures and paintings from the first and second millennia BC show garments with tassels hanging from them.[29] Whether these tassels were purely decorative (the wearers often appear to be nobles), or whether they had a religious function, perhaps serving as amulets to ward off evil spirits, is uncertain. But whatever their significance in other cultures, their use in Israel is made plain here. Like the *mĕzûzôt* little boxes containing verses of the law attached to the doorposts, or the *tĕpillîn* on the wrists, they were

---

28. J. Weingreen, 'The Case of the Woodgatherer', *VT*, 16, 1966, pp. 361ff.
29. See S. Bertman, 'Tasselled Garments in the Ancient East Mediterranean', *Biblical Archaeologist*, 24, 1961, pp. 119–128. B. Rothenberg, *Timna* (Thames and Hudson, 1972), pp. 123–124, notes that rock engravings at Timna from 13th century BC portray Midianites, or possibly Shosu bedouin, wearing tasselled garments. The Midianites were closely related to Israel (cf. Exod. 2 – 3; 18, etc.).

designed to promote constant meditation on the law of God (Deut. 6:6–9).

Each tassel must incorporate a blue thread. *Blue* or *violet* (NEB) distinguished royalty (Esth. 8:15) and divinity. The ark, God's throne, was wrapped in a blue cloth (Num. 4:6) and blue curtains adorned the tabernacle indicating that this tent was the palace of the King of kings (e.g. Exod. 26:31, 36). Blue was also used in the high priest's uniform (Exod. 28:31, 37, etc.). No doubt it had a similar significance in the layman's tassel. The blue thread reminded him that he belonged to 'a kingdom of priests and a holy nation' (Exod. 19:6). Like the high priest he was called to exhibit holiness not only in his outer garb, but in his whole way of life. *You shall be holy to your God* (40). These tassels were to act as reminders to be totally loyal to the LORD: verse 39 with its reference to *follow after* (Hebrew *tûr*), which in chapters 13 – 14 is translated 'spy out', alludes to the dangers inherent in following their own whims instead of the commandments. They also reminded the wearer of his redemption (verse 41).

This law has been considered of particular importance by the Jews (cf. Matt. 23:5). It forms part of the creed-like prayer, the Shema, recited every morning and evening.[30] Jewish prayer shawls have fringes attached to the corners. Our Lord wore fringes, i.e. tassels on his clothes, and the sick touched them to obtain healing (Matt. 9:20; 14:36). This Old Testament requirement finds no equivalent in the New Testament. Christians, however, have frequently taken to wearing various badges and signs of their faith; the most popular and significant has undoubtedly been the cross, a reminder to its owner to deny himself, take up his cross daily and follow Christ (Luke 9:23).

C. Prerogatives of the priests (chapters 16 – 18)

i. The rebellion of Korah, Dathan and Abiram (16:1–35). This narrative heads a longish section (chs. 16 – 19) demonstrating by story and law the centrality and indispensability of the priesthood. The punishment of the rebels in this chapter proves the authority

---

30. The full Shema consists of Deut. 6:4–9; 11:13–21; Num. 15:37–41.

of Moses and Aaron. The efficacy of Aaron's offering in stopping the plague and the budding of his rod demonstrate again the special role entrusted to the house of Levi (16:41 – 17:13). The rules about tithes and firstlings show how Israel was to acknowledge the ministry of the priests and Levites (ch. 18). Finally, the law on the red heifer once again emphasizes the priestly role in making atonement for the people (ch. 19). 'It is a complete theology of priesthood that is to be found in these chapters: its divine origin, its sacred character, its cultic role, but above all its expiatory function, for the theologies of sin and priesthood are intimately linked.'[31]

The section begins with a group of three stories establishing Aaron's role as high-priest: 16:1–35, the rebellion of Korah; 16:36–50, Aaron halts the plague; 17:1–13, Aaron's rod. The stories not only have the same theme, they have similar structures. The first two begin with the people protesting against Moses and Aaron and conclude with a divine judgment punishing the protesters and vindicating Aaron. The third inverts this sequence: God proposes a test of Aaron's standing and it ends with the people crying out for Moses. Most striking is the fact that each of these tests of Aaron's call takes two days.

There is no indication how long after the spies' return Korah mounted his rebellion. The events described here may have taken place at any time within the thirty-eight years the Israelites spent wandering in the wilderness near Kadesh. However, this story is explicitly related to the preceding law. The tassels every Israelite had to wear reminded them that they were called to be holy (15:40), that they belonged to 'a kingdom of priests and a holy nation' (Exod. 19:6). Korah, an archetypal heretic, affirms this truth to the exclusion of the other, the divine appointment of Aaron and Moses: *All the congregation are holy, every one of them ... why then do you exalt yourselves above the assembly of the LORD?* (16:3). Subsequent events demonstrate so frighteningly the dangers inherent in being called to be a holy nation that the survivors cry out for a priestly ministry that will act as mediator between them and God (17:13; cf. 18:5, 22; 19:20).

---

31. de Vaulx, p. 189.

1–2. The leaders of the revolt are listed in verse 1, Korah, a Levite of the Kohathite clan, and Dathan, Abiram and On of the tribe of Reuben (On is not mentioned again). According to 2:10ff. and 3:29, both Reubenites and the Kohathites were to encamp on the south side of the tabernacle.[32] The proximity of their tents explains their mutual involvement and their common fate. However, it is clear from 27:3 that members of other tribes were also involved in the revolt, referred to in verse 2 as *leaders of the congregation*. And though the Kohathites and Reubenites camped near each other and made common cause against Moses and Aaron, it seems that their objectives were rather different.

At least their complaints are mentioned separately (3, 13–14), and in a technique typical of biblical narrative the action is cut up into a number of scenes focusing first on one party and then on the other. But as they started out united in opposing Moses and Aaron, they die together as the earth opens its mouth and swallows them all up (24–33).

3–11. The target of Korah's complaint was Aaron's high priesthood. Though his remarks (3) sound as though he is advocating the priesthood of all Israel, it seems unlikely that he wished to abolish the prerogatives of the tribe of Levi altogether. Rather he frames his particular objection to the special status of the priestly family of Aaron in the most general terms so as to attract maximum support from other Israelites (3). At least this is how Moses takes Korah's complaint. He sees it as a demand for the priesthood and an attack on Aaron (10–11).

The dialogue between Moses and Korah is lively. Korah says *You have gone too far*, literally 'too much for you', *all ... are holy, you exalt yourselves* (3). Moses proposes that all who claim such a holy status should demonstrate it by undertaking a priestly task, the offering of incense. Since two of Aaron's sons had died for offering fire which the LORD had not commanded (Lev. 10:1–2) Korah's alacrity in

---

32. See diagram, p. 77. There is a textual problem in verse 1. The Hebrew reads *wayyiqqaḥ* 'he took'. RSV supplies 'men' as object. NEB emends to *wayyāqom*, literally 'he rose up', which it paraphrases 'challenged the authority of' Moses.

submitting to this test is striking. This will show *who is holy* and whom the LORD has chosen (6–7). Moses flings back at Korah his opening jibe, *You have gone too far, sons of Levi!* (7).

Moses then points out that the Levites are greatly privileged: *The God of Israel has separated you from the congregation of Israel, to bring you near to himself* (9). The Levites camped next to the tabernacle separating it off from the other tribes. What is more they had the duty of doing *service in the tabernacle*, that is dismantling, carrying and erecting the tabernacle. Though Moses does not make the point here, the Kohathites, of whom Korah was one, had the task of carrying the most sacred objects such as the ark (4:1–20). They were next in rank to the priests. But they want the priesthood itself.

12–15. The scene now switches to Dathan and Abiram, apparently grumbling in their tents, for when Moses summons them, they reply,[33] *We will not come up* (12). Exactly where they were being asked to go is not clear, presumably to where Moses was confronting Korah and his other supporters. The Reubenites' complaint is more traditional: they object to the divine programme of journeying to Canaan via the wilderness. Egypt, they say, was a real land of milk and honey, and Moses is incapable of bringing us to Canaan, which he says is a land of milk and honey (13–14; cf. 14:1–9). The acrimony of the occasion is again highlighted by the Reubenites throwing back Moses' expressions in his face. Moses said to Korah, *Is it too small a thing for you?* and then mentioned the privileges God conferred on the Levites (9). Dathan and Abiram use the same phrase to introduce their grievances about leaving the comforts of Egypt for death in the desert (13). Their truculent reply made Moses very angry, for it expressed their contempt for God's plan. It was the sort of unbelief that condemned the nation to die in the wilderness (cf. 14:2ff.). Maybe there is more to it. Perhaps, remembering the fate of Aaron's sons (Lev. 10:2), they were uneasy about Korah's audacious bid for the priesthood. Knowing the illegitimacy of his claim, they nevertheless wished to support him at a distance without endangering their own lives.

---

33. Note the concentric structure of their speech: A. come up (12); B. brought out; C. land of milk and honey (13); C^1. land of milk and honey; B^1. brought in; A^1. come up (14).

16–19. The grievances of both parties having been outlined, the story now relates how they were both judged in manners appropriate to their complaints. The Korahite faction, claiming the right to act as priests, are allowed to test their calling by offering incense, and their unholiness is proved by fire from the LORD consuming them. The Reubenites, who accused Moses of bringing them to die in the wilderness, do indeed meet their death there, just as the faithless spies did before them. Thus, as in the spy story, dramatic irony and retributive justice characterize the narrative.

To mark the change of scene and to indicate that the challenges of Korah and Dathan and Abiram were contemporary, Moses' instructions to Korah (6–7) are repeated with a little more detail in verses 16–17. The exact fulfilment of the command is noted in verse 18. This is often a cue for an announcement of divine blessing. Anticipating his own public vindication *Korah assembled all the congregation,* that is the representatives of all the nation (19). Sure enough, *the glory of the LORD appeared.*

20–24. But God announces judgment: he will destroy everyone except Moses and Aaron (21; cf. 14:10–12). Again their intercession saves the people (22; cf. 4; 12:11–13; 14:13–19). The *one man* referred to in verse 22 is Korah, the leader of this rebellion, unless it is a proverbial phrase meaning 'a few' (cf. Gen. 18:23–32). The congregation is told to separate itself from the tents of Korah, Dathan and Abiram. In view of his subsequent fate, it may be assumed that at this point Korah left his 250 supporters in the court of the tabernacle, and in defiance of Moses went and stood alongside Dathan and Abiram. As in the spy story immediate punishment is limited to those directly involved (cf. 14:37).

25–30. Moses announces that a novel and spectacular judgment, *the LORD creates something new,*[34] will overtake the rebels. The ground will open its mouth and swallow them up, so that they go down alive into Sheol (30). Sheol, the abode of the dead, is pictured as lying

---

34. NEB 'makes a great chasm'. The Hebrew word *bārā'* usually means 'to create'. That it means 'to cut or split' in this case has also been suggested by H. E. Hanson, *VT*, 22, 1972, pp. 353–359, cf. *bērē'*, Piel of *bārā'*, 'to hew', e.g. Josh. 17:15, 18, etc.

immediately under the surface of the ground, a concept also well known from Mesopotamian literature (cf. 1 Sam. 28:11; Isa. 14:15ff.; cf. Epic of Gilgamesh, tablet 12). This will prove conclusively *that the LORD has sent* Moses and *that it has not been of my own accord* (28), thereby refuting the accusations both of Korah (3) and of the Reubenites (13).

31–34. Exactly as Moses predicted, note the point by point fulfilment of verse 30 in verses 31–33, *the earth … swallowed them up* (32). Those who perished in this way were Dathan, Abiram and their families (27, 32), and *all the men that belonged to Korah*. From 26:10–11 we learn that this means Korah and his servants: his sons are noted as having survived the tragedy and were the ancestors of some of the temple singers (1 Chr. 6:33ff.). The company of Korah offering their incense in the tabernacle are not included, for their death is mentioned separately (35).

The nature of the catastrophe that overtook these men is unclear and theologically unimportant. If one looks for a natural phenomenon providentially timed (cf. the strong east wind of the exodus, Exod. 14:21, or the quails, Num. 11:31, or the damming of the Jordan, Josh. 3:16), the most likely explanation[35] is that Korah, Dathan and Abiram's tents were pitched on a *kewir*, that is a mud-flat hard on the surface and boggy underneath. If the crust of a *kewir* breaks up, those on it would be swallowed up in the mud much as described in our story. Such *kewirs* are found in the Arabah, which stretches southward from the Dead Sea to the Red Sea. No doubt sometime in their wanderings the Israelites would have camped in this area. Though such explanations are helpful in confirming the historicity of the exodus-wilderness traditions, they must be invoked with caution, especially in this case when the narrative stresses the uniqueness of the judgment (16:28–30). They must not obscure the point of the story: that the punishment was a heaven-sent vindication of the authority of Moses and Aaron.

35. Finally, almost as an afterthought, the death of Korah's supporters is mentioned. The writer felt no need to elaborate. If Aaron's

─────────────

35. G. Hort, 'The Death of Qorah', *Australian Biblical Review*, 7, 1959, pp. 2–26.

sons perished for offering incense that was not commanded (Lev. 10:1–2), how much less likely to escape were the followers of Korah, who were not even priests (cf. Jude 11).

ii. Aaron halts the plague (16:36–50 [Hebrew 17:1–15]). As a result of being offered to God, albeit irregularly, the censers had become holy. Eleazar, Aaron's son, was therefore instructed to gather them up, and make them into a bronze cover for the great altar of burnt offering.[36] This altar already had a bronze cover according to Exodus 38:2, and it is therefore uncertain how the two covers were related to each other. According to the LXX of Exodus 38:2, Bezalel actually made the first cover out of these censers. But since it is difficult to see how an altar made out of acacia wood could ever have been used without a bronze cover, modern commentators suggest that the bronze cover mentioned here must be either additional[37] to, or a replacement for, the first cover.[38]

36–40. The new bronze cover was given a specific function to be *a sign* and *a reminder to the people of Israel, so that no one who is not a priest ... should draw near to burn incense before the LORD* (38, 40). The importance of visual aids to prevent men sinning is an important theme in this section of Numbers. The tassels on garments (15:38–41) and Aaron's rod (17:10) also serve the same purpose (cf. Exod. 13:9; 31:13, 17; Deut. 6:8; 11:18; Josh. 4:7).

41–50. The disasters of the preceding day were quickly forgotten and the people started to murmur against Moses and Aaron again. Once more the glory of the LORD appears and God announces his intention of destroying the whole congregation (41–45; cf. 1–21). For the third time Aaron and Moses fall on their face in intercessory prayer (45; cf. 4, 22). Judgment again begins: a plague breaks out among the people. But this time it is stopped by Aaron offering

---

36. The differences between RSV and NEB in verse 38 reflect different emendations of the Hebrew. RSV omits *'et* at the beginning of the verse. NEB reads *waʿāśeh* instead of *wĕʿāśû*. With Gispen, I, p. 277, the MT may be retained and translated: 'And the censers of these men ... shall be made' (literally: 'they [impersonal] shall make them').

37. So Greenstone, p. 179.

38. So Gispen, I, p. 276.

incense in his censer (46), though not before many had died (49).[39]
Whereas Korah's illegitimate incense provoked God's wrath, the incense of the high priest offered at Moses' behest assuaged it (cf. Lev. 16:12–13). Thus for a second time Aaron's high priesthood is vindicated against its critics, and its practical value demonstrated.

iii. Aaron's rod (17:1–13 [Hebrew 17:16–28)]. This is the third in the group of three stories, proving the God-givenness of Aaron's priestly ministry (cf. 16:1–35, 36–50). As in the previous two, the demonstration takes two days. But there is a significant inversion in the structure of this incident compared with the first two. They begin with the people complaining and the LORD threatening to destroy them, and then comes the proof of Aaron's call. This story opens with God offering a test to show which tribe has been chosen, and ends with people crying out for mercy, *We perish, we are undone, we are all undone* (12). At last they understand, they need someone to draw near to God to make atonement for their sins on their behalf (13). Recognizing the necessity of the priesthood, they are now ready to pay for it and offer the tithes and first-fruits set out in the following chapter.

1–8. This test is quite simple and is in effect a symbolic re-enactment of the Korah scene.[40] The head of each tribe must write his name on a rod. The Hebrew word *maṭṭeh* means both 'rod' and 'tribe'. The rods (the twelve tribes plus Aaron's)[41] are to be deposited before the ark overnight in the *tent of the testimony* (7). In the morning Moses went in and collected the rods: only Aaron's had *sprouted ... produced blossoms* (*ṣîṣ*, the same Hebrew word is used for the high-priestly diadem in Exod. 28:36; Lev. 8:9) and *bore ripe almonds* (8). We are probably supposed to understand that some parts were in bud, others in bloom and others had fruited. Why it bore almonds is not stated, but it is probably significant. Almond blooms early with white blossom and its fruits were highly prized (Gen. 43:11). White

---

39. On large numbers see Additional note on pp. 68ff.
40. Cf. G. J. Wenham, 'Aaron's Rod', *ZAW*, 93 (1981).
41. This interpretation of verse 6 seems more likely than the alternative, namely that there were just twelve rods with the tribes of Joseph, i.e. Ephraim and Manasseh, sharing one rod between them.

in Scripture symbolizes purity, holiness and God himself (e.g. Isa. 1:18; Dan. 7:9; Rev. 20:11). Jeremiah associates the almond (*šāqed*) with watching (*šāqad*) (Jer. 1:11–12). All these qualities were personified by Aaron and the tribe of Levi. They were the holy tribe *par excellence*, who represented Israel before God and God to Israel, and they were responsible for watching over the people by instructing them in the statutes of the LORD (Lev. 10:11).

9–13. But in the presence of God the other rods had not sprouted at all. Again the message is clear. Only Aaron and the tribe he represents may approach God. If anyone else does he will die. *The people of Israel said ... 'We perish ... Every one who comes near to the tabernacle of the LORD shall die'* (12–13). Thus these three stories reiterate clearly and unequivocally God's choice of Aaron. He is the preeminently holy one. Only he can draw near to God. Only he can make atonement for Israel's sin. Israel must acknowledge his unique place in the scheme of salvation by not usurping his prerogatives and by supporting his ministry financially.

Aaron's high priesthood clearly prefigures that of our Lord, and Hebrews 4 – 10 explains how in every respect Christ's high priesthood surpasses that of the old covenant. In consequence of his atonement every believer has access to the presence of God (Heb. 10:19ff.). But one principle stressed in these stories still applies under the new covenant: while all God's people are called to be holy, a special authority belongs not just to Christ but to the apostles and their successors, the bishops and elders of the church (Titus 1:9; 1 Pet. 5:5). With that authority goes the grave responsibility of an exemplary standard of holy living (Acts 20:28; Titus 1:5 – 2:10; 1 Pet. 5:1–3).

Additional note on the source analysis of chapters 16 – 17

The story of Korah, Dathan and Abiram is another section where, according to the standard source-critical theory, the sources of Numbers are interwoven. In the spy story two sources, an early JE tradition and a later P tradition, were discerned. In these chapters there is said to be yet a third source present, a supplement to P (P_s, to distinguish it from Pg, the main priestly source).

The earliest source JE (16:1b, 2a, 12–15, 25, 26b, 27b–32a, 33–34) tells how the Reubenites, Dathan and Abiram, revolted against the civil authority of Moses and were punished for it by the ground swallowing them up. The P source (P = 16:1a, 2b, 3–7, 18–24, 26a, 27a, 35, 41 – 17:13) tells a quite different story of a layman, Korah (in the material assigned to Pg he is not called a Levite), who led a band of two hundred and fifty men protesting against the religious prerogatives of the tribe of Levi represented by Moses and Aaron. When they offered incense, they were killed by divine fire. Finally, the third source, P_s(P_s = 16:1a, 7b–11, 16–17, 32b, 36–40), which as we now have it is incomplete and only supplements Pg, tells how some of the Levites protested against Aaron's high priesthood and sought to open it up to the whole tribe of Levi.

Advocates of this view argue that it explains the frequent scene changes and repetitions within the narratives as we now have them. If one supposes that JE is earlier than Deuteronomy, but P later, this theory shows why Deuteronomy 11:6 mentions the death of Dathan and Abiram but not that of Korah.

Attractive as the source-critical hypothesis is at first blush, closer inspection reveals some difficulties. First, the argument from Deuteronomy can bear little weight. Other passages in it, both law and narrative,[42] imply knowledge of the P as well as the JE material in Numbers. Deuteronomy's failure to mention Korah may as easily be explained in terms of its author's intentions as by his ignorance. Psalm 106:16–18 refers both to the death of Dathan and Abiram and to the burning of Korah's supporters.

To justify their analysis source critics are forced to postulate that the sources have been modified by an editor. For example, it is held that 16:24, 27 have been altered from an original 'dwelling (i.e. tabernacle) of the LORD' into the present *dwelling of Korah, Dathan, and Abiram*, because these names occur in a P-context. Similarly, verse 32b is said to be an editorial or P_s addition because it is found in a JE context yet mentions Korah.

More decisive in my judgment is that the supposedly earlier sources assume what is mentioned only in the later accounts. Thus, Pg presupposes P_s, and JE presupposes Pg. The wording of 16:18 'Pg' clearly follows that of verse 17 (P_s), not of verses 6–7 (which

---

42. See Introduction, 4. Date and authorship, pp. 25 ff.

was the preceding section of Pg). Similarly, 16:21 (Pg) '*separate your-selves from among this congregation* …' is an allusion to 16:9 (P$_s$) just as verse 45 (Pg) alludes back to verse 37 (P$_s$). Similarly JE presupposes the material in Pg and P$_s$. In verse 12 Moses sends for Dathan and Abiram, evidently because they have been protesting against him. But this is not stated in the extant JE material: it only says *they rose up before Moses* (2). Similarly their jibe 'Is it a small thing' (13, JE) echoes Moses' remark (9, P$_s$). In verse 26 (JE) Moses warns the people to leave the tents of these wicked men. Their obedience is recorded in verse 27, which is Pg. It would have been expected that JE would also have mentioned it.

Finally, as it stands, the account of the death of Korah, Dathan and Abiram is very well integrated and dramatically told. I noted in the commentary how Moses turned Korah's charge 'You have gone too far' back on Korah (3, 7) and then how Dathan and Abiram did the same to Moses (9, 13). The story of Korah as it stands also coheres well with its two companion stories, Aaron's rod, assigned in its entirety to Pg, and Aaron stopping the plague, split between Pg and P$_s$. They constitute a trio of stories, a favourite device in the Pentateuch, each making the same point in a similar way: Aaron's vindication takes two days each time. The third one, Aaron's rod, symbolically re-enacts what happened in the first, Korah's rebellion. For these reasons it seems simplest to regard Numbers 16 – 17 as a unit. If it is based on more than one source, they are different from JE, Pg or P$_s$.

iv. Duties and privileges of the tribe of Levi (18:1–32). 1–7.
God's reply to the people's frightened cries (17:12–13) is given direct to Aaron. This is unusual (cf. 8, 20; Lev. 10:8): elsewhere Moses passes on God's instructions to Aaron (e.g. 6:23; 8:2). They are reminded (cf. 1:50–53; 3:5–10) that God has already provided what they are crying out for. It is the Levites' duty to guard the tent of meeting (3–4),[43] so that no unauthorized person may draw near and provoke God's wrath on the nation. But the Levites in their turn are precluded from undertaking specifically priestly jobs, such as entering the tent of meeting or officiating at the altar. It is the priests' task to

---

43. For this interpretation of *šāmar mišmeret*, RSV *attend the duties of*, see on 1:53.

guard against such trespass by the Levites, which would again provoke judgment (5, 7). Trespassers caught by the priests must be
executed (7).

Indeed, if mistakes are made and unauthorized persons usurp the
privileges of the priests or Levites, blame will fall on them for failing in their guard duty. *You and your sons and your father's house … shall
bear iniquity in connection with the sanctuary … with your priesthood* (1). The
priests and Levites thus act as spiritual lightning conductors,[44] taking upon themselves God's anger when individuals sin so that the
people as a whole is spared. In this context (cf. 17:2, 6) *your father's
house* probably means the tribe of Levi, not the Kohathite clan or the
family of Aaron's father Amram (Exod. 6:20). Thus the priesthood
is a gift, not just to the priests but to all Israel (7).[45]

8–20. In recognition of their altar service, the priests are to receive
parts of the sacrifices, first-fruits of the harvest and first-born animals. Most of these rights have already been mentioned elsewhere
in the Pentateuch (cf. Lev. 6:14 – 7:36; 27:6–33). They are reminded
that members of the priests' families may eat from these offerings
as long as they are 'clean', i.e. not suffering from skin diseases, bodily discharges or contact with the dead (cf. 5:2; Lev. 7:19–21; 22:2–
9). These sacrificial dues compensate for the priests' lack of inheritance. Their inheritance is God himself, who provides for their
needs through his people's gifts (20).

Two groups of priestly perquisites are listed here. First, those sacrifices to which they had sole right, save for a token portion burnt
on the altar: the cereal offering, the sin offering and the guilt offering (Lev. 2; 4:1 – 6:7; 6:14 – 7:7). These were *most holy* (9) and could
be eaten only by priests, *every male may eat of it* (10).

The other group of offerings are simply described as holy (17–
18) and could be eaten by any members of the priest's family as long
as they were cultically clean (11, 19). These comprise the parts of the
peace offerings assigned to the priest: the *offering*, i.e. the right thigh
of the animal, and *the wave offerings*[46], i.e. the breast (11; cf. Lev. 3;

---

44. Cf. J. Milgrom, *Studies in Levitical Terminology*, p. 31.
45. So Gispen, I, p. 292, understands *I give your priesthood as a gift.*
46. On the technical terms *offering* and *wave offering*, see above on 6:20.

7:31–34). The priests and their families are also entitled to the first-fruits of the harvest (13; cf. Exod. 22:29; 23:16, 19; Lev. 2:14; 23:10; Deut. 26:1–4). They also receive *every devoted thing*, that is things dedicated to God by a binding oath, usually in war (14; cf. Lev. 27:28f.; Josh. 6:18ff.; 1 Sam. 15:21). All first-born animals belong to the priests; the priests must sacrifice them in the normal manner and then they and their families may eat them (16–19). Unclean animals (cf. Lev. 11) and human first-born which cannot be sacrificed must be redeemed: that is, their owner must make a cash payment to the priest instead of giving him his animal or child. The redemption fee for first-born children is fixed at five shekels, that is about six months' pay (15–16). The binding and permanent nature of these obligations is underlined by calling them a *covenant of salt*, that is to say, this covenant is indestructible, like salt (19; cf. 2 Chr. 13:5; Exod. 13:2; 22:29f.; 34:19f.; Lev. 27:26–27, 6).

21–24. The above regulations about priestly dues are little more than a systematization of earlier rules found elsewhere in the Pentateuch. The assignment of the tithe to the tribe of Levi is something new. Tithing, giving a tenth of one's agricultural produce, was an ancient institution in the Near East.[47] Both Abraham and Jacob gave tithes (Gen. 14:20; 28:22). Leviticus 27:30–33 regulates the redemption of tithes, evidently presupposing their existence, but it does not state who would receive them. This law, looking forward to the settlement in Canaan when tithing would become possible, lays it down that the Levites are to receive them.

The tithe is a payment *in return for their service in the tent of meeting* (21, 31), i.e. their work of dismantling, carrying and erecting the tabernacle. It is a recognition of the dangers inherent in their occupation: by dealing with such holy things they may be subject to divine judgment, and they protect the people from that risk (22–23). Finally, the tithe compensates the Levites for their lack of inheritance in the land: whereas the other tribes had large tracts of land assigned to them to settle in, the Levites were given only forty-eight villages, scattered throughout the land (24; 34:16–35:8; Josh. 13–21).

---

47. Cf. J. Milgrom, *Cult and Conscience*, pp. 55–62; M. Weinfeld, *Encyclopedia Judaica*, 15, pp. 1156–1162.

25–32. But the Levites are to treat the tithes they receive just like a farmer's income: they are to give a tenth of their tithes to the priests, in fact the best part of the tithe must be passed on (29). Once they have done that, they can eat the rest of the tithe when and where they like without any blame being attached to them (31–32).

The tithes, firstlings and sacrificial offerings which the priests and Levites received would have constituted a huge income for them if the nation had been faithful in paying them (cf. Mal. 3:10; Hag. 1). As this passage makes plain, these payments were an acknowledgment of the enormous importance of the ministry of the tribe of Levi, representing the nation to God and God to the nation. Through their mediation the people were saved from the danger of extermination. Similarly, Jesus and Paul expected those who heard the gospel to recognize its worth by paying its ministers adequately (Matt. 10:9–10; 1 Cor. 9:3–10; 16:2; cf. Matt. 23:23).

D. Laws on cleansing (chapter 19)

Theologically there were three important social divisions in Israel, the priests, the Levites and the ordinary people. Chapter 18 dealt with the responsibilities and privileges of the first two groups, how they were to guard the tabernacle against unauthorized persons trespassing. But even if laymen avoided blatant trespass like Korah's, they could still pollute the tabernacle through being unclean close to the tent. For this reason those who were unclean had earlier been expelled from the camp (5:2–4; 12:14; Lev. 13:45–46). The most serious and obvious type of human uncleanness was that caused by death. Anyone who touched a corpse or a human bone or a grave, or entered the tent of a dead man, became unclean (14–16). Furthermore, this uncleanness was contagious: anything the unclean man touched would itself become unclean and infect others (22; cf. Lev. 15). Thus the death of someone in the camp could pollute all those in it, and this would *defile the tabernacle of the LORD* (13, 20) unless preventive measures were taken. Whenever the holy came in contact with the unclean, sudden death was the result (13, 20; cf. Lev. 7:21; 22:3; cf. Isa. 6:3, 5).

Chapter 18 was concerned with the appointment of the priests and Levites as custodians of the tabernacle to prevent such divine judgment falling on the nation. This chapter deals with the provision of a means to cure the uncleanness of death. Leviticus prescribes two methods of dealing with uncleanness: either washing in water and waiting till evening (11:28, 39–40; 15:16–18), or in more serious cases waiting seven days and then offering a sacrifice (14:10ff.; 15:13ff., 28ff.). Offering a sacrifice was a difficult and expensive procedure, which would have greatly added to the distress of family and friends when someone died. This chapter provides an alternative remedy which marked the seriousness of the pollution caused by death, yet dealt with it without the cost and inconvenience of sacrifice. Instead, those who have come in contact with the dead can be treated with a concoction of water that contains all the ingredients of a sin offering.

To many modern people rites such as the one described here look like mumbo-jumbo, sheer magic that shows how primitive and unsophisticated the men of the Old Testament were. But it is now recognized by anthropologists that, whether the rituals are found in Africa or in ancient texts, their practitioners are not acting in ignorance. They are not doing something magical; rather, such ceremonies, just like ours, express the deepest truths about life as the society sees them.

For serious uncleanness sin offerings were an essential part of the process of expiation. The standard procedure with a sin offering was to sprinkle some of the animal's blood over the altar or over part of the tabernacle to cleanse it from sin. Some parts of the animal were burnt on the main altar, but most of it was burnt outside the camp (Lev. 4:1–21). In the case of the red heifer we do not have a proper sacrifice, in that the slaughtering of the animal takes place outside the camp, not by the altar; and though the animal is burnt, the word used, *śārap*, denotes a non-sacrificial burning.[48] What is important here is producing ash with purificatory properties. It is for this reason that the blood is burnt (5), something without parallel elsewhere in the Old Testament. Blood is the most potent cleansing and sanctifying agent in the Bible (cf. Heb. 9:22).

---

48. Hebrew *hiqṭîr*, literally 'turn into incense', is used of burning on the altar.

For the same reason other traditional cleansing agents are also thrown into the fire to fortify the ash: cedarwood, hyssop (marjoram, *Origanum maru*, is meant), and scarlet stuff were also used in the cleansing of the leper (Lev. 14:4, cf. Ps. 51:7). Presumably, similar reasons lay behind the insistence on a red heifer. Normally the animal's colour did not matter. This one had to be red to resemble blood. *Heifer* (RSV) is more accurately rendered 'cow' by the NEB. However, if it had never been used for ploughing or pulling a cart (2), it must have been relatively young, hence the traditional English translation.

When the ash had been prepared, it was collected and kept outside the camp ready to be mixed with water when required. It thus acted as an instant sin offering[49] (9, NEB). When someone came in contact with a corpse, some of the ash was mixed with fresh water, and the liquid was sprinkled over him, using a sprig of marjoram (18). This had to be done twice, on the third and the seventh day after contact (12, 19). Failure to undergo this ritual led to the unclean person being cut off, that is suffering a sudden and premature death (13, 20).[50]

Both those who prepare the ash and those who sprinkle the water containing it become unclean, though not as seriously as the man who has touched the corpse. All they need to do is to wash and wait till evening (7–10, 21). Though perplexing at first sight, this is quite consonant with the ash being regarded as a cleanser like blood. Sacrificial blood is cleansing when correctly used, but garments or vessels accidentally splashed with it must be washed or destroyed (Lev. 6:27–28). Similarly, it is the discharge of blood associated with menstruation and childbirth that makes them occasions for uncleanness (Lev. 12; 15:19ff.).

Balak compared Israel to an ox (22:4; cf. Isa. 1:3). Hosea twice likens Israel to a heifer (Hos. 4:16; 10:11). For the New Testament our Lord is the personification of the ideal Israel, and it was therefore natural for Hebrews 9:13–14 to compare the blood of

49. Cf. J. Milgrom, 'The Paradox of the Red Cow', *VT*, 31, 1981, pp. 62–72.
50. Cf. above on 9:13.

Christ to the ashes of the heifer. As the men of the old covenant had in this ritual an ever-ready means of bodily purification, so we are reminded that 'the blood of Jesus cleanses us from all sin' (1 John 1:7).

4. FROM KADESH TO THE PLAINS OF MOAB (20:1 – 22:1)

The brief notice of the death of Miriam (20:1) introduces the third and last travel narrative in Exodus-Numbers. The first deals with the journey from the Red Sea to Sinai (Exod. 13 – 19); the second covers that from Sinai to Kadesh (Num. 11 – 12), while this final one summarizes the journeyings from Kadesh to Transjordan (Num. 20 – 21). As was noted in the Introduction,[1] certain motifs occur in all three travelogues, e.g. battles with enemies (Exod. 14; 17:8–16; Num. 14:45; 21:1–35), complaints about the lack of food and water and its miraculous provision (Exod. 16 – 17; Num. 11; 20:2–13), the need for faith (Exod. 14:31; Num. 14:11; 20:12), the role of Moses, Aaron and Miriam (Exod. 15:20–21; Num. 12; 20:1).

But the narratives each develop quite differently. The first begins with the defeat of the Egyptians, and Moses and Miriam singing songs of triumph by the Red Sea (Exod. 15), and the people

---

1. See above, pp. 16ff.

believing in the Lord and his servant Moses (14:31). Then the mood
changes with the complaints of the people about the lack of food
and water. The second journey begins well with the cloud of fire
leading the advance to the promised land (Num. 10:11ff.). But
grumbles from the people and from Miriam and then the disheart-
ening report of the spies lead to the postponement of the conquest,
and finally a defeat by the Canaanites at Hormah. But the third journey proceeds quite differently. It begins in gloom and ends on a note
of subdued but real jubilation. Chapter 20 records the deaths of
Miriam and Aaron, and Moses' unbelief that shut him out of
Canaan. But this is followed in chapter 21, by victory at Hormah,
where years earlier Israel had been defeated (cf. 14:45), and further
victories over Sihon, king of Heshbon, and Og, king of Bashan, are
accompanied by short songs of celebration (21:14–15, 17–18, 27–30).
These three victories and their songs recall the first and greatest victory over Egypt by the Red Sea that Moses and Miriam had hailed
in Exodus 15. Thus this final travel narrative inverts the patterns
found in the earlier two; whereas they recount triumphs that turned
into tragedy, this tells of tragedy that ends in triumph and a re-
awakened hope of entry into the promised land.

i. **The death of Miriam (20:1).** Miriam, Moses' sister, was the
leading female protagonist in the story of the exodus, and it is
therefore appropriate that her death should be recalled (Exod. 2:4–
9; 15:20–21; Num. 12). It also serves as a reminder of the divine sentence that none of the generation who came out of Egypt would enter Canaan, and foreshadows the similar fate that was to befall her
brothers, Aaron and Moses (20:12, 24–29; Deut. 34). It has often
been noted that the central woman in the New Testament was also
called Miriam, usually abbreviated to Maria or Mary.[2]

The wilderness of Zin is adjacent to Kadesh and covers much of the
northern Negeb. *In the first month*, though there is no textual evidence
for any omission, it seems likely that the year has been omitted. According to 33:38, Aaron died in the fortieth year after the exodus
from Egypt (cf. 20:22–29). It therefore seems likely that the tribes

2. R. le Déaut, 'Miryam, soeur de Moïse et Marie, mère du Messie', *Biblica*,
45, 1964, pp. 198–219.

re-assembled in Kadesh after their period of wandering earlier in the same year.

ii. Meribah (20:2–13). This is another classic murmuring story in which the people complain about the lack of food, and Moses and Aaron provide it at God's behest (cf. Exod. 15:22 – 17:7; Num. 11:4–35; 21:5–18). Particularly remarkable, though, is this story's similarity with that recorded in Exodus 17:1–7, the first occasion when Israel complained about a total lack of water. Both times *the people contended with Moses*, and asked *Why did you bring us up out of Egypt?* Both times Moses is told to take a rod and use it to bring water out of the rock. Both places are called as a result of the incident *Meribah* (13).

On these grounds it has been suggested that the Exodus and Numbers accounts are really duplicate versions of the same incident. But it seems unlikely that the writer of Numbers understood the story in this way for several reasons.

First, Exodus 17 mentions only Moses, but Numbers 20 both Moses and Aaron. Secondly, the Numbers story presupposes the account in chapter 17 of Aaron's budding rod. 20:3 clearly alludes to 17:12–13, and the instruction to take the rod *from before the Lord* (20:8f.) refers back to 17:9–10. But the most obvious difference between the two accounts is that in the first Moses is commanded to strike the rock, whereas this action constitutes the essence of his disobedience in the second account.

Though both the context (verses 1 and 14) and Deuteronomy 32:51 associate these events with Kadesh, this poses problems for the usual identification of Kadesh-barnea with Ain Qudeirat, which has very strong springs. It may be that we are dealing with a different Kadesh from that mentioned in 13:26 (Meribah-kadesh has been identified with Ain Qadeis which, though near to Ain Qudeirat, has less abundant springs), perhaps coupled with a freak disturbance in supplies.[3]

---

3. M. Harel, *Masei Sinai*, p. 217, identifies Kadesh-barnea with Ain Qudeirat and Meribah-kadesh with Ain Qadeis. Harel suggests the possibility of the wells drying up after several dry seasons, p. 217.
   Y. Aharoni, *Encyclopedia Miqrait*, 7, pp. 39–42 suggests Kadesh-barnea refers to the whole group of wells and Ain Qadeis is the only one to preserve the old name Kadesh.

More puzzling is why Moses' behaviour on this occasion should
have been regarded as damnable, whereas at Rephidim he had acted
similarly with impunity. Verse 12 says *Because you did not believe in me*,
but some commentators find it difficult to see how Moses' action
could be construed as unbelief. The key to the problem is to be
found in a comparison of God's instructions to Moses with their
execution. Very often narratives in the Pentatench appear pedantic
and repetitious as they record the precise fulfilment of divine commands (cf. verses 25–26 with 27–28). But here there is a marked di-
vergence between what was commanded and what was done. Moses
was instructed to *take the rod, assemble the congregation* and speak to *the
rock* (8), but in the event he *took the rod, gathered the assembly*, spoke to
them instead of to the rock, and then *struck the rock* (9–11). Though
this brought forth water, it was not produced in the divinely intended
way, and counted as rebelling against God's command (24) and unbelief. Whereas Christian theologians, following Paul's supposed
distinction, often contrast faith with obedience, this dichotomy is unknown to the Old Testament. Faith is the correct response to God's
word, whether it is a word of promise or a word of command. Psalm
119:66 can say 'I *believe* in thy *commandments*'. The opposite of faith
is rebellion or disobedience (e.g. Deut. 9:23; 2 Kgs 17:14). Thus
Moses' failure to carry out the Lord's instructions precisely was as
much an act of unbelief as the people's failure to trust God's promises instead of the spies' pessimistic reports (Num. 14:11). Both were
punished by exclusion from the land of promise. Because Aaron
helped Moses (8, 10), he received the same sentence (12).

Moses' unbelief was compounded by his anger, expressed in his
remarks to the people (10), 'he spoke words that were rash' (Ps.
106:33), and by his striking the rock twice (11). De Vaulx[4] suggests
that there was an element of sacrilege in striking the rock, for it symbolized God. The people were gathered in a solemn assembly (10)
before it as though before the ark or tent of meeting, and Moses was
told to *speak* to it (8, NEB). An additional argument in favour of this
suggestion is that elsewhere God is often likened to a rock (e.g.
Pss. 18:2; 31:3; 42:9, etc.). This understanding of the rock closely

4. de Vaulx, p. 223.

corresponds to that of the targums, and of Paul, who says 'they drank from the supernatural Rock which followed them, and the Rock was Christ' (1 Cor. 10:4).

In disobeying instructions and showing no respect for the symbol of God's presence, Moses failed to *sanctify* God; that means he did not acknowledge publicly his purity and unapproachability. When unholy men approach God, he shows *himself holy* by immediate or delayed judgment (13; cf. Lev. 10:3). Whereas Aaron's sons died on the spot for offering incense that was not commanded, Moses and Aaron received a lighter sentence: they would not be allowed to lead the people *into the land which I have given them* (12). Nevertheless, this was enough to vindicate God's holiness (13). This last phrase he *showed himself holy* (*wayyiqqādēš*) is evidently a play on the word Kadesh (*qādēš*, 'holy person' or 'holy place'), in the vicinity of which this episode took place.

The death of Miriam followed by the death sentence passed on her brothers makes this one of the most tragic sections of Numbers. Yet these verses stand as a reminder of the holiness of God and the sinfulness of men (cf. 1 Cor. 10:4–12), and the need for faithful obedience (Heb. 3:7 – 4:13). In Jesus there is one through whom we can receive 'rivers of living water' (John 7:38; cf. 4:10–15) enabling us to enter the rest promised to the people of God (Heb. 4).

iii. Encounter with Edom (20:14–21). The entry to the promised land began quietly with a request by Israel to pass through the territory of Edom. When their request was refused they skirted Edom instead (21:4; cf. Deut. 2:1–8). Despite the clarity of the biblical statements, it is difficult to know exactly which route the Israelites took from Kadesh to the land of Moab. This is because the location of the places mentioned is uncertain. In verse 16, Kadesh is said to be *on the edge of* Edomite *territory*, which implies that the territory of the Edomites extended west of the Arabah into the northern Negeb, if this Kadesh is the same as Kadesh-barnea. But if Meribah-kadesh were to be located elsewhere (see above on 2–13) such an extension of Edomite territory would not be required. Certainly their territorial heartland was to be found in the mountains east of the Arabah in the mountains running south from the Dead Sea to the Gulf of Aqabah. It was through these eastern mountains that 'the King's Highway', probably to be identified with the trade route from Damascus to Arabia, passed (verse 17; cf. 21:22). Deuteronomy 2:8 and Judges 11:15ff. appear also to picture the Israelites skirting the eastern border of Edom to reach the wilderness of Moab. For these reasons it may be easier to suppose that the Kadesh from which Moses *sent messengers to the king of Edom* (verse 14) should be distinguished from Kadesh-barnea and lay further to the east, than to maintain that Edomite control extended as far west as Kadesh-barnea.

The main thrust of this paragraph is to demonstrate Israel's irenic approach to its neighbours. Though the inhabitants of Canaan itself, i.e. the area west of the Jordan, were dealt with ruthlessly, those on the east were treated more courteously (cf. Deut. 20:10–18). Edom in particular was handled gently, because he was Israel's *brother* (14; Deut. 23:7). According to Genesis 27:30; 36:1, the Edomites were descended from Esau, the brother of Jacob (Israel, Gen. 32:28).

The request was couched in the form of a diplomatic letter that closely conformed to the conventions of oriental scribal practice, known from the archives of Mari, Babylon, Alalakh and El-Amarna. It consists of several standard parts. First, a mention of the recipient, *King of Edom* (14). Second, the formula *Thus says*. Third, a mention of the sender Israel and his rank, *Your brother*; 'your servant' is the more common phrase in diplomatic correspondence, but here a different phrase was preferred. Fourth, there is mention of Israel's present predicament and their motives in making their request (15). Finally, the request itself (17).

All that Israel requested from Edom was the right of passage along the main highway, but this was refused with a show of strength, perhaps recalling the previous occasion when Esau had confronted his brother with force (Gen. 32:6ff.). Both times the confrontation was resolved harmoniously, unlike some of the bitter battles in later times (1 Kgs 11:15–16; 2 Kgs 14:7; Ps. 137:7; Obad.).

iv. The death of Aaron (20:22–29). Clinically, without a hint of emotion until verse 29, the death of Israel's first high priest is recorded. This low-key description emphasizes the inevitability of the judgment on Aaron (24; cf. 12) for his disobedience at Meribah; its contrast with some of the early phases in Aaron's career heightens the pathos surrounding his death (cf. Exod. 7ff; 24; 32; Lev. 8 – 10).

22–23. *Mount Hor.* A tradition as early as Josephus[5] identifies
Mount Hor with Jebel Nebi Harun (Mount of the Prophet Aaron),
a mountain near Petra. However, most modern scholars reject this
identification, preferring to locate Mount Hor somewhere to the
north-east of Kadesh-barnea. It is argued that since Petra lies within
the territory of Edom, Mount Hor cannot be Jebel Harun, because
it is said to be *on the border of the land of Edom* (23). However, as the
boundaries of Edom at this period are most uncertain, the objections to the traditional identification are not cogent. Deuteronomy
10:6 states that Aaron died and was buried at Moserah, apparently
the same place as Moseroth (Num. 33:31), seven stopping-places before Mount Hor (33:38). Since we are not certain where either
Moserah or Mount Hor was located, it is idle to speculate on the relationship between these remarks.

24. *Gathered to his people.* This is the usual phrase to describe the
death of a righteous man in a ripe old age. It is used of Abraham,
Ishmael, Isaac, Jacob and Moses (Gen. 25:8, 17; 35:29; 49:33; Num.
31:2). By contrast it is a fearful mark of divine judgment to be left
unburied and not 'be gathered' (Jer. 8:2; 25:33; Ezek. 29:5). But the
phrase is more than a figure of speech: it describes a central Old Testament conviction about life after death, that in Sheol, the place of
the dead, people will be reunited with other members of their family. As David said when Bathsheba's baby died, 'I shall go to him, but
he will not return to me' (2 Sam. 12:23). Thus, though both Aaron
and Moses die outside the promised land, because of their sin at
Meribah, that is the limit of their punishment. In death they are on
a par with the patriarchs and other saints of the old covenant.

25–29. The retirement of Aaron as high priest was a moment of
vital significance in the life of Israel which had to be symbolized in
the ritual stripping of Aaron's high-priestly vestments and the in-
vestiture of his son, Eleazar. The high priest was the supreme
mediator between God and Israel: the dignity of his office was expressed in the magnificence of his vestments. In a real sense the life
of the nation was contingent on his carrying out his duties faithfully.
Thus the death of a high priest marked the end of an era, and

5. *Antiquities* iv.4.7.

Numbers 35 implies it made atonement for some sins. At least manslaughterers, who had accidentally killed someone and had been punished by confinement within a city of refuge, were released when the high priest died (Num. 35:28). On the death of the person who represents God to Israel and embodies in his office the life of the nation, those who have killed their fellow Israelites, albeit unintentionally, may go free and enjoy their lives again.

The New Testament sees Aaron as prefiguring the priestly work of our Lord. But whereas the Old Testament priesthood was imperfect in its atoning efficacy, Christ's death, resurrection and heavenly intercession are fully and finally effective in making the Aaronic high priesthood obsolete (Heb. 4:14 – 10:18, esp. 7:23–27).

v. Victory at Hormah (21:1–3). This brief notice records Israel's first victory over the Canaanites and heralds the dawn of a new era. The long delay in the fulfilment of the promises is nearly over. It was at Hormah that an abortive attempt was made to enter Canaan after the spies returned from their mission (14:45). It was there nearly forty years later that they triumphed for the first time, a pledge of the conquest of the land that was soon to begin (cf. Eph. 1:13–14).

1. Arad was a large town in the northern Negeb, about 17 miles (27 km) south of Hebron. If it were certain that the Israelites fought the king of Arad after they left Mount Hor, this would be the clearest clue to the location of Mount Hor that the text provides. But it is widely supposed by scholars of all shades of opinion that this incident is placed here for topical rather than chronological reasons.[6] Against this it may be noted that Numbers 33:37–41 presupposes the same route as 21:4. It therefore seems probable that the battle took place somewhere in the northern Negeb or Arabah, but the description in 21:1–3 is really too brief to build an itinerary on. We do not know how far the forces of Arad travelled to intercept the Israelites *by the way of Atharim.* Here, AV 'the way of the spies' follows the interpretation of Atharim adopted by most of the early versions except LXX, which understands Atharim to be an alternative spelling of *tārîm,* 'spies'. The RSV and NEB follow the LXX in supposing that Atharim is an otherwise unknown place-name.

---

6. Keil, p. 127.

Excavations at Tell Arad[7] have demonstrated that it was an important city in the Early Bronze Age and in the period of the Israelite monarchy. But no remains of the Middle or Late Bronze Age have been found at this site, and it therefore seems likely that the Arad of the conquest period must be identified with one of the other sites in the vicinity, and that its name was later attached to Tell Arad. One suggestion is that Arad was the name of the region, and that the king of Arad had his capital at Hormah, to be identified with Tell el-Milh, 7½ miles (12 km) southwest of Tell Arad. However, Joshua 12:14 distinguishes Arad from Hormah. Another possibility is that Canaanite Arad should be identified with Tell el-Milh and that Hormah is Khirbet el-Meshash, 3½ miles (6 km) to the west of Tell el-Milh. Both sites have Middle Bronze Age fortifications, which would be compatible with a fifteenth-century date for the exodus and conquest, but not with the more usual thirteenth-century dating.[8]

Other battles in this area are mentioned in Joshua 12:14 and Judges 1:16–17. It would seem that initially the Canaanites were defeated by Moses, and then by Joshua, but they returned and were only finally driven out at a later stage of the settlement mentioned in Judges. This is more obviously the case at Hazor, which was taken by Joshua (11:10–14), but then reoccupied by Jabin, king of Canaan, who was driven out only after the campaign led by Deborah and Barak (Judg. 4)

2–3. *I will utterly destroy their cities.* Like many other place-names mentioned in Numbers, e.g. Taberah (11:3), Kibroth-hattaavah (11:34), Meribah (20:13), the name Hormah, 'destruction', recalls the most significant feature of the events there. Israel vowed to annihilate the Canaanites. This policy is endorsed by Deuteronomy (e.g. chs. 7 and 9) and the book of Joshua shows how it was partially carried out.

Deuteronomy justifies this treatment of the Canaanites as a preventive against apostasy (7:4). Brutal as it seems to us, it is of a piece with the rest of Israel's penal code, which insists on the death

---

7. 'Arad', in M. Avi-Yonah, *Encyclopedia of Archaeological Excavations in the Holy Land* I (OUP, 1975), pp. 74–89.

8. J. J. Bimson, *Redating the Exodus and Conquest*, pp. 203–205.

penalty for a wide range of religious offences. Fidelity to the LORD
and the purity of the faith ranked highest of the values in Israel's eth-
ical and religious system.[9]

vi. The copper serpent (21:4–9). 'As Moses lifted up the serpent
in the wilderness, so must the Son of man be lifted up' (John 3:14).
Our Lord's use of this story as a type of his crucifixion has made it
one of the most familiar parts of the book of Numbers. But despite
its familiarity some writers have questioned the historicity of this incident, suggesting that it is a fictitious explanation of the origin of
the bronze serpent in the temple destroyed by Hezekiah (2 Kgs 18:4).
More fundamental is the question why this means was appointed to
cure snake-bites. Why did not God use a miracle without resort to
a potentially misleading symbol?

From excavations at Timna about 15 miles (25 km) north of Eilat
has come remarkable confirmation of the biblical story, or at least
of its origin in the wilderness period.[10] At the foot of one of the Pil-
lars of Solomon in Timna, Rothenberg found a temple of the
Egyptian god, Hathor, used in the 13th century BC. When abandoned
by the Egyptians about 1150 BC, it was taken over by the Midianites
who covered it with curtains to make a tent shrine, somewhat like
the tabernacle. Inside this tent temple in the holy place was found
a copper snake 5 in. (12 cm) long.[11]

4. How this archaeological evidence should be interpreted
depends on one's presuppositions, but that there must be a
connection with the biblical story is plain. For verse 4 states, *From
Mount Hor they set out by the way to the Red Sea, to go around the land of
Edom.* Whether Mount Hor is to be located near Petra or near
Kadesh-barnea, it seems clear that the Israelites were heading
south down the Arabah towards Timna. Furthermore, Moses
had married a Midianite and greatly valued the advice of his father-

---

9. Cf. J. W. Wenham, *The Goodness of God* (IVP, 1974), pp. 119ff.
10. See B. Rothenberg, *Timna* (Thames and Hudson, 1972), pp. 129ff.
11. Other copper serpents have been found at a variety of sites in the Near
East, but none so close to the site of a biblical tradition as this. Cf. K. R.
Joines, 'The Bronze Serpent in the Israelite Cult', *JBL*, 87, 1968, pp.
245–256, esp. 245f.

in-law (Exod. 2:16ff.; 18; Num. 10:29–32). Thus, it may be that Moses owed the idea of the tabernacle and the copper serpent to his Midianite relatives. Alternatively, it may be that the Midianite tent-temple and copper serpents were imitations of the Mosaic ones which had been seen in this area at least a century prior to the erection of the Midianite tent in 1150 BC. Whichever hypothesis is adopted, it seems likely that the story of the brazen serpent is based on a historical incident, and is not merely the retrojection of a later writer's imagination.

5–6. This is the last recorded occasion that Israel grumbled about their food (cf. 11:4ff.; Exod. 16) and yearned for the delicacies of Egypt. They describe the manna as *worthless food*. The term *worthless* (*qĕlōqēl*) is found only here and may be derived from *qillēl*, to 'despise' or *qal*, 'light', hence the AV rendering. Whichever translation is preferred, it is a disparaging comment on the bread of heaven (Pss. 78:24–25; 105:40; cf. John 6:31). As on the previous occasion, it provoked God's anger (cf. 11:33), this time in the form of *fiery serpents*, whose bite was lethal. It seems likely that the inflammation caused by this bite prompted them to be called *fiery*.[12]

7–9. As an antidote to the snake-bites Moses was instructed to make a snake,[13] and he decided to make it out of 'copper'. Though the English versions generally translate *nĕḥōšet* as brass or *bronze* (i.e. copper alloys), it certainly can mean the pure metal (Deut. 8:9). In the light of the discoveries at Timna, 'copper' seems the best translation here. But why make a serpent at all, and why make it out of copper?

The text is not explicit, but various explanations have been offered. Among Israel's neighbours the serpent seems to have been a

---

12. The Hebrew word *śārāp* (fiery) is probably related to *śārāp*, 'to burn'. The seraphim of Isa. 6:2, 6, though homonymous with this word, were winged creatures not snakes. D. J. Wiseman (cf. *TB*, 23, 1972, pp. 108–110) suggests *śārāp* means 'poisonous'.

13. Here the Hebrew word *śārāp* stands alone, apparently designating the species of snake involved (cf. Deut. 8:15). The NEB, following some of the ancient versions, has clarified the term by paraphrasing, 'serpent of bronze'.

symbol of life and fertility, and in Egypt model serpents were worn to ward off serpent-bites.[14] But neither of these explanations seems very appropriate here. In Israel snakes were unclean and personified sin (Lev. 11:41–42; Gen. 3). Here, too, the serpent is a cure for those bitten, not a protection against bites. I suggest that the clue to the symbolism should be sought in the general principles underlying the sacrifices and purificatory rites in the Old Testament. Animals are killed, so that sinful men who deserve to die may live. Blood which pollutes when it is spilled can be used to sanctify and purify men and articles. The ashes of a dead heifer cleanse those who suffer from the impurity caused by death. In all these rituals there is an inversion: normally polluting substances or actions may in a ritual context have the opposite effect and serve to purify. In the case of the copper serpent similar principles operate. Those inflamed and dying through the bite of living snakes were restored to life by a dead reddish-coloured snake. It may be that copper was chosen not only because its hue matched the inflammation caused by the bites,[15] but because red is the colour that symbolizes atonement and purification.[16]

Finally it should be noted that in every sacrifice (e.g. Lev. 1 – 4) the worshipper had to lay his hand on the animal's head. In purification rituals the worshipper had to be sprinkled with the purifying liquid (Lev. 14; Num. 19, etc.). Without physical contact the sacrifice or cleansing ritual was ineffective. In the case of the copper serpent there is a similar insistence on the affected person appropriating the healing power of God through looking at the snake set up on the pole. The importance of seeing the copper snake is brought out by the command to *set it on a pole* (8–9) and the twice-repeated comment *everyone who … sees it shall live*. In other words, contact between the saving symbol and the affected person was still required, but in the special circumstances here described visual contact was all that was necessary.

If this is the right way to interpret the story of the copper snake,

---

14. See K. R. Joines, *JBL*, 87, pp. 251f.

15. Luther's suggestion quoted by Keil, pp. 140f.

16. Cf. the reddish materials used for the water of purification in ch. 19, red heifer, cedar wood and scarlet cord. There may also be a play on words: the snake's (*nḥš*) bite (*nšk*) was cured by copper *nḥšt*.

it is clear how our Lord could use it as an apt picture of his own saving ministry. Men dying in sin are saved by the dead body of a man
suspended on the cross. Just as physical contact was impossible between those bitten by snakes and the copper snake, so sinners are unable to touch the life-giving body of Christ. Yet in both situations the
sufferers must appropriate God's healing power themselves: by looking at the copper snake or 'believing in the Son of man' (John 3:15).

vii. Journey round Moab (21:10–20). The tempo of advance
quickens as Israel approaches the promised land. Extracts from the
travel log interspersed with fragments of old poems convey the sense
of elation as the goal of their wanderings comes into sight. Their route
took them east of the territory of Moab, which covered the fertile high
ground on the eastern shore of the Dead Sea, through the drier area
between Moab and the desert, the arid part of the Dead Sea valley.

It seems probable that the last section of the itinerary (14–20) anticipates the outcome of the battles with Sihon and Og described in
verses 21–35, for it involved passing through the territory of the
Amorites. This is confirmed by the fuller account in Deuteronomy
2 – 3. Again, it is impossible to locate precisely many of the places
mentioned here, but the mention of Zered and Arnon, rivers which
flow into the Dead Sea from the east, give a clue to their approxi-
mate locations (see map, p. 256).

14–15. This is the only mention of *the Book of the Wars of the
Lord*, but, like the Book of Jashar (Josh. 10:13; 2 Sam. 1:18), it is generally assumed to be a collection of ancient popular songs. It may
be that the song of the well (17–18) also comes from the same
source. The variation in the English translations of verses 14–15
highlights the problems of the Hebrew text. The RSV gives a literal
rendering of the Hebrew. It takes Waheb and Suphah to be place-
names. Most commentators suggest that a verb has been omitted at
the beginning of the quotation, so that it originally read 'We passed
through Waheb …' or 'We took Waheb'.

A more recent suggestion involves minor emendations of the
consonantal text. Christensen[17] translates the poem as follows:

17. D. L. Christensen, 'Num. 21:14–15 and the Book of the Wars of
    Yahweh', *CBQ*, 36, 1974, pp. 359–360.

The LORD came in[18] a whirlwind;
He came[19] to the branch wadis[20] of the Arnon.
He marched[21] through the wadis;
He marched,[22] he turned aside to the seat of Ar.
He leaned toward the border of Moab.

This reinterpretation of these difficult lines produces poetry with a clear metre and an authentic archaic ring about it (cf. Deut. 33; Judg. 5; Ps. 68). They picture God as the divine warrior sweeping through the territory of Moab ready for the great battles in Transjordan that anticipated the conquest of Canaan. As such they would make a fine opening to a poem called 'The Book of the Wars of the LORD'. Though this re-interpretation of the Hebrew text is attractive, like all new readings based on conjectural emendation, its validity is ultimately undemonstrable.

17–18. In contrast to the last poetic fragment, the song of the well poses few textual problems.[23] The RSV renders the second half of 18b literally, *And from the wilderness they went on to Mattanah*: the NEB presupposes unnecessary emendations.[24] The song itself was probably

---

18. Apart from the occasional omission of the definite article and conjunction *waw* following the theories of F. M. Cross about early poetry, the only major change is in the first line. For '*et wāhēb* (Waheb) read '*ātā yahweh*, 'The LORD came'.

19. Reading '*ātā* (he came) for '*et* (definite object marker).

20. Understanding final *m* as enclitic.

21. Reading with Samaritan text, '*āśar*, 'he marched' (cf. Deut. 33:2) for '*ešed*, 'slope of'.

22. Repointing '*ǎšer*, 'which' as '*āśar*, 'he marched'.

23. For a discussion of its scansion, see D. N. Freedman, *ZAW*, 72, 1960, pp. 105–106.

24. It omits *w*, 'and', before 'wilderness', and reinterprets Mattanah as 'a gift'. Then in v. 20 it alters 'from Mattanah' into 'from Beer'. The Septuagint reading 'from Beer to Mattanah' in 18b makes for greater continuity in the itinerary (cf. 16a), but the MT reading 'from the wilderness to Mattanah' is more difficult and therefore should probably be preferred.

sung to encourage those digging the well, and expressed their joy at
their repeated experience of God's life-giving supply of water (cf.
20:2–13; Exod. 15:22ff.; 17:1ff.; John 4:10–15; 7:37–38; 1 Cor. 10:4).
    viii. Victory over Sihon and Og (21:21 – 22:1). The narrative
now explains in detail what happened when Israel arrived at the border of the Amorite kingdom (cf. 13).
    21–23. As with Edom, they sent messengers requesting the right
of passage (21–22; cf. 20:14–17). As before, their request was rejected
and opposed by force. Whereas before Israel had skirted their op-
ponents, this time they had to join battle as the kingdom of Sihon
blocked their only route to the Jordan. It covered the area east of the
Dead Sea from the Arnon in the south to the Jabbok in the north
(24, see map, p. 256). Its capital was Heshbon, traditionally identified
with Hesban.[25] But the battle took place at Jahaz, possibly Hirbet
Libb,[26] between Madaba and Diban (23).
    24–26. The Amorites were defeated and Israel *took possession of his
land* (24). The settlement referred to in the following verse did
not occur immediately, as chapter 32 makes plain. 24b mentions that
the Israelites did not invade the territory of the Ammonites, because
its *border was strongly defended* (TEV). The RSV follows the LXX and Vulgate reading *ya'zēr* for *'az*, 'strong'. But this seems unnecessary.

---

25. However, recent excavations at Tell Hesban have discovered nothing
     earlier than Iron 1, i.e. contemporary with the Israelite monarchy. It is,
     therefore, impossible to identify Tell Hesban with Sihon's capital. In the
     neighbourhood of Tell Hesban there are some fifteen sites with traces
     of Middle and Late Bronze Age settlement, though only two, Tell Jalul
     and Tell el Umeiri, were large enough to count as towns. It is possible
     that, as at Arad (see above on 21:1), the old name Heshbon was later
     adopted by the newer settlement at Tell Hesban. For reports of the
     excavations, see R. S. Boraas and L. T. Geraty, et al., 'The Fifth
     Campaign at Tell Hesban', *Andrews University Seminary Studies*, 16, 1978,
     pp. 1–303, particularly pp. 201–213, R. Ibach, 'Expanded Archaeological
     Survey of the Heshban Region'. Shorter reports on earlier excavations
     are also to be found in *AUSS*.
26. According to J. Simons, *The Geographical and Topographical Texts of the OT*
     (Brill, 1959), p. 262.

Deuteronomy 2:19 gives an additional reason for the Israelites restraint against the Ammonites: like the Moabites they were descended from Lot and, therefore, remote relations of Israel and, like Israel, their territory had been given to them by God (cf. Deut. 2:9; Gen. 19:37–38).

27–30 is the so-called song of Heshbon, a very old poem apparently composed by Amorite bards to celebrate Sihon's defeat of Moab.[27] It is probably inserted here to justify Israel's right to hold the land. It appears that at one time Moab had occupied the land lying between the Arnon and the Jabbok, but Sihon had defeated Moab, as this song recalls. Now, Israel had conquered Sihon. Thus Israel showed itself superior to Moab as well as to the Amorites, and therefore Moab had no right to claim it back from Israel. The argument is spelt out more fully in Judges 11:12–28, where the Ammonites lay claim to this stretch of land.

27. The song begins by a call to rebuild Heshbon, consequent on Sihon's overthrow of Moabite overlordship.[28]

28. Heshbon, Sihon's base, was the source of a fire that burnt up

---

27. This is the traditional Jewish view, which has recently returned to scholarly favour, e.g. Gispen, II, pp. 43ff; de Vaulx, p. 246; P. D. Hanson, 'The Song of Heshbon and David's *Nir*', *HTR*, 61, 1968, pp. 297–320. The alternative hypotheses that it is an Israelite song taunting the Amorites after the defeat, or celebrating the Israelite victory over Moab in the 9th century are problematic. The chief difficulties with the first theory are that it demands a rapid change of subject that the text gives no hint of, an over-subtle use of irony, and finally, that it appears to suggest an advance from north to south whereas the Israelites came in the opposite direction. The second theory is contradicted by the references to Sihon who is always described as an Amorite, and presupposes that the Elohist, the notional author of this section generally dated in the 9th century, had forgotten the real origin of the song very quickly.

28. D. N. Freedman, *ZAW*, 72, 1960, p. 106 followed by Hanson, *HTR*, 61, 1968, p. 301 and D. K. Stuart, *Studies in Early Hebrew Meter* (Scholars Press, 1976), p. 93 repoint *tikkônēn* as *tikkōnanna* (Niphal with *nun energicum*). It makes no difference to the sense.

the cities[29] of Moab and devoured[30] the high places of the Arnon.
29. This verse laments the fate of the Moabites, who worshipped
Chemosh (1 Kgs 11:33). Sihon has taken prisoner many young
people from Moab. These two verses are quoted by Jeremiah 48:45–
46 in his prophecy against Moab. **30.** The variety of translations of this verse underline its difficulty.
AV gives a literal rendering of the Hebrew: *We have shot at them;
Heshbon is perished even unto Dibon, and we have laid them waste even unto
Nophah, which reacheth unto Medeba.* The poem evidently concludes by
listing the towns captured from the Amorites; all except Nophah are
well-known. Although the Hebrew is accepted by a few commentators,[31] it is a patently unpoetic conclusion to an otherwise well-
constructed piece of verse. Something is clearly awry in the text as
it stands, but none of the proposed reconstructions is entirely
convincing.[32]

29. Reading *'ārĕ* instead of MT *'ār*, see Hanson, p. 301, Stuart, p. 93. In early
Hebrew both would have been spelt the same way, *'r*. Ar is a city well
south of the Arnon, whereas all the other places captured by Sihon
were north of the Arnon.

30. So TEV, and probably NEB 'swept', reading with LXX *bālĕ'â* instead of MT
bā'ălê (RSV *lords of*).

31. E.g. Greenstone, p. 232; Gispen, II, pp. 51–52.

32. RSV and TEV adopt the LXX reading instead of *wannîrām*, 'we shot at
them', and read *wĕnînam*, 'and their descendants'. NEB reinterprets the
Hebrew; *nîr* means 'lamp', hence NEB 'embers'. Probably the best
solution is that of the Targums, Vulgate and Rashi, p. 105, taking *nîr* as
'dominion'. Hanson has provided a strong philological defence of this
rendering. He further (p. 304) suggests that through haplography with
'ābad, *'b* has been omitted, and the line originally read *nîr mô'ab 'ābad*,
'the dominion of Moab has perished'. Following Stuart, p. 95, the case
endings have been omitted.

In the second half of the verse TEV takes *wannaššîm*, 'we laid waste', as
a place-name, and leaves the last words unaltered. RSV and NEB retain
'we laid waste' and emend the following words. *Nōpaḥ* is taken as a
verbal form *nāpĕḥú*, 'to blow'. BHS mentions *nāpĕḥú*, 'they blew' or
hinnāpeḥ, 'is blown'. Then *'ăšer*, 'which' is altered to *'ēš*, 'fire', by omitting

31–35. The story concludes with a brief mention of the victory over Og, king of Bashan (Northern Transjordan), in a battle at Edrei (modern Dera). Jazer may be Hirbet jazzir[33] (see map, p. 256). Deuteronomy 3:1–11 gives a fuller account of the conquest of Bashan. Later writers looked back on these encounters as great victories (e.g. Josh. 2:10; Neh. 9:22; Pss. 135:11; 136:19–20). We do not know the size of the forces involved, but these conquests were symbolically and historically most significant. These Transjordanian territories were the first to be settled by the Israelite tribes (cf. chapter 32), and their settlement was an assurance that the promised land of Canaan would also be conquered and settled by Israel.

---

r as suggested by the dot over this letter in the MT. The LXX and Samaritan version also read '*ēš*. Hanson, p. 306, conjectures that the original reading was *našammū bamōt kamuš nōpḥa 'adê mēdabā'*, 'deserted are the high places of Chemosh, from Nophah as far as Medeba'.

33. According to J. Simons, *Geographical and Topographical Texts*, p. 119.

5. ISRAEL IN THE PLAINS OF MOAB
(22:2 – 36:13)

For the third time on their journey from Egypt to Canaan the people of Israel encamp for an apparently lengthy period. Their encampment at the foot of the mountains of Moab resembles their situation at Sinai. Once again the revelations and events during their period of waiting bear a marked resemblance to those at their earlier stopping-places, Sinai and Kadesh.[1] It is the record of these events that makes up the fifth and longest section of the book of Numbers.

The section begins with Balaam, a Mesopotamian prophet, declaring that the patriarchal promises are being fulfilled in the history of Israel (chs. 22 – 24). This has analogies in the allusions to God's promises at the beginning of the Sinai and Kadesh sections (Exod. 19; Num. 13). As before, this is followed by a great apostasy with atonement made by the priests or Levites (ch. 25; cf. Exod. 32;

---

1. See Introduction, 2. Structure, pp. 16ff.

Num. 14; 16 – 18). Chapter 26 records another census (cf. chs. 1 – 4). The section ends with more laws about worship and the land, important themes in the earlier legislation, which serve here as an implicit promise that Israel will shortly enter into its inheritance (chs. 28 – 29; 33 – 36; cf. Lev. 1 – 7; 23; 25; Num. 15).

A. Balaam and Balak (chapters 22 – 24)

The charming naïvety of these stories disguises a brilliance of literary composition and a profundity of theological reflection. The narrative is at once both very funny and deadly serious. The stupidity and stubbornness of the human characters, Balaam and Balak, is accentuated by the behaviour of the ass. This animal, proverbial for its dullness and obstinacy, is shown to have more spiritual insight than the super-prophet from Mesopotamia whom Balak is prepared to hire at enormous expense to curse Israel. Yet this numb-skulled, money-grubbing, heathen seer is inspired by the Spirit of God with a vision of Israel's future destiny truly messianic in its dimensions. The drama, irony and paradoxes of this story fascinate and perplex the reader. Was Balaam a sinner or a saint? Why did God change his mind about letting Balaam go? What did Balaam really foretell in his visions? What is the point of including these stories in Numbers? It is convenient to consider some of these general points before beginning the detailed exegesis.

The clearest structural device in these chapters is the use of threefold repetition noted in the narrative itself (22:28, 32, 33). Not only does the ass try to avoid the angel of the LORD three times (22:23, 25, 27); Balaam arranges for three sets of sacrifices to be offered before attempting to curse Israel (23:1, 14, 29), and before arriving in Moab he has three encounters with God (22:12, 20, 22–35). Thus the drama falls into six main acts in two sets of three (22:7–14, 15–20, 21–35, 41 – 23:12, 13–26, 27 – 24:25); in every one there is the insistence that Balaam say only what the LORD permits him to say (22:12, 20, 35; 23:3, 12, 17, 26; 24:2, 13). There are further correspondences between the first three acts and the last three. In the first, second, fourth and fifth acts Balaam seeks the LORD on his own initiative (22:8, 19; 23:3, 15), in the third and sixth God meets him unbidden (22:22; 24:1–2). The third and sixth acts also match each other in being considerably longer than the preceding pair.

Act three consists of three short scenes dealing with the ass, while act six contains two long and three short oracles by Balaam instead of the one long oracle of acts four and five. Within each act there are many allusions and parallels to others in the series, which help to maintain the tension and keep the listener's interest.[2] Some of these will be noted in the commentary. Finally, the whole narrative is staged so as to cover three pairs of consecutive days, with gaps of unspecified length between each pair. This is a similar arrangement to that found in chapters 16 – 17. The events on days 1–2 are related in 22:2–14, days 3–4 in 22:15–35, days 5–6 in 22:36 – 24:25. Admittedly it is not explicitly stated that all the oracles in chapters 23 – 24 were given on a single day, just as the time taken by the messengers is not recorded in 22:7, 15, but the phrase 'in the morning' (22:41) recalls 22:13 and 21 which clearly describe schematized two-day sequences. These interlocking patterns make the usual source-critical analyses unlikely.[3]

---

2. J. Licht, *Storytelling in the Bible* (Magnes, 1978), pp. 69–74.

3. Usually the material is allocated to the sources J and E, but there is considerable hesitation about which verses should be assigned to which source, cf. Gray, pp. 309ff.; Noth, p. 171; W. Gross, *Bileam: Literar- und form-kritische Untersuchung der Prosa in Num 22–24* (Kösel, 1974). It is more confidently asserted that the story of the ass (22:22–35) must be from a different source from the rest of the material, for in verse 20 Balaam has been given permission to go to Balak, whereas in verse 22 we read of God's anger at Balaam's departure.

Such an argument betrays a lack of appreciation of our narrator's dramatic skill. On the one hand the episode serves to underline verse 20 in a very emphatic fashion. Balaam may go, but he will risk his life if he says anything but what God tells him. On the other it prepares the reader to accept the validity of Balaam's oracles despite his foreign background. If God can open a donkey's eyes to an angel and enable it to speak, how much more easily can the Spirit of God enlighten heathen Balaam and put true words into his mouth (22:28, 38; 23:5, 12, 16; 24:2).

The arrangement of the narrative may be tabulated as follows:

22:2–14		Days 1–2
	2–6	Introduction
	7–14	Balaam's first encounter with God
22:15–35		Days 3–4
	15–20	Balaam's second encounter
	21–35	Balaam's third encounter
		22–23 Ass sees angel (1)
		24–25 Ass sees angel (2)
		26–35 Ass sees angel (3)
22:36 – 24:25		Days 5–6
	22:36–40	Introduction
	22:41 – 23:12	First blessing of Israel
	23:13–26	Second blessing of Israel
	23:27 – 24:25	Third blessing of Israel
		3–9 Blessing 3
		15–19 Blessing 4
		20–24 Three curses

What can be said about Balaam's character? More precisely, how did the writer of Numbers 22–24 view Balaam? On first reading, Balaam appears to be portrayed in a very positive light. Despite

---

Assigning verses 22–35 to a separate source from the rest of the narrative destroys the integrated triadic patterning of the narrative and also overlooks the linguistic echoes and allusions that connect it with its surrounding context.

pressing financial inducements to curse Israel, he steadfastly insists
on listening to God and blesses them comprehensively, much to the
annoyance of his sponsor (22:18; 24:10–13). On these grounds
Coats has argued that 'The Balaam story presents Balaam ... as a
saint who intended from the beginning to do nothing other than
obey Yahweh's word'.[4]

But other passages of Scripture paint Balaam in a very different
light, as an opponent of Israel who would have cursed Israel had not
God intervened, a man who preferred money to serving God (31:8–
16; Deut. 23:4–5; 2 Pet. 2:15; Jude 11; Rev. 2:14). So great is the contrast between Num. 22 – 24 and these passages that it has been suggested that they represent an alternative tradition about Balaam, or
that the early positive evaluation of the man was later replaced by
this negative view.

Though such theories about rival traditions or sources appear to
eliminate the problem, they in fact merely alter its shape. It is universally agreed that the author of Deuteronomy must have known
the material in Numbers 22 – 24. If the picture of Balaam in Numbers 22 – 24 is so unequivocally positive, how can Deuteronomy have
misunderstood it? Similar questions arise with the editor of Numbers. Did he not realize the conflict between chapters 22 – 24 (JE)
and 31:8–16 (P$_s$)? How can the earliest interpreters of Numbers 22
– 24 have failed to recognize Balaam's faith in Yahweh and his
altruism, if that were patent in the stories described here?

The deeds of Balaam which many commentators construe so
positively might have a more sinister meaning. The constant harp-
ing on money matters might suggest that Balaam's apparent indifference was really an oblique demand for a huge fee (cf. Gen. 23:11–
15). The repeated statements that Balaam will declare only the word
that God puts in his mouth may be intended to emphasize the inspiration of his oracles rather than the holiness of his character.

It must be remembered that biblical writers rarely comment explicitly on the characters of the actors. 'The narrator's emotional and
moral values are as a rule conveyed indirectly, by the implicit tenor

---

4. G. W. Coats, 'Balaam: Sinner or Saint?', *Biblical Research*, 18, 1973,
   pp. 21–29, quotation from p. 22.

of the stories.'[5] If one searches for such oblique clues to the narrator's evaluation of Balaam in these chapters, two stand out. First, Balaam is offered 'fees for divination' (22:7) and resorts to 'omens' (24:1), abominable practices that were not permitted in Israel (23:23; Deut. 18:10; 1 Sam. 15:23; 2 Kgs 17:17). Second, the conduct of the ass prefigures that of Balaam.[6] Just as Balaam drives on his ass until brought up short by the angel of the LORD, so Balak will push Balaam to curse Israel until he is stopped by his encounter with God. As God opens the ass's mouth, so he will put his words in Balaam's to declare his will. This parallelism between Balaam and his ass suggests that the ability to declare God's word is not necessarily a sign of Balaam's holiness, only that God can use anyone to be his spokesman.

Throughout the Bible, prophecy and other ecstatic spiritual gifts are regarded as signs of inspiration, but not necessarily of holiness or of a right standing with God. False prophets may accurately foretell the future (Deut. 13:1–5). Though condemned to lose his throne, Saul still prophesied (1 Sam. 19:23–24). Caiaphas prophesied the death of Christ (John 11:51–52). Jewish exorcists cast out demons in Jesus' name without believing in him (Mark 9:38–39; Acts 9:13–16). The Corinthian church was long on ecstatic spiritual experience but short on love, holiness and sound doctrine (1 Cor. 1 – 15). Our Lord warned that on the last day neither prophecy, exorcism nor miracles would guarantee entry to the kingdom of heaven, only 'he who does the will of my Father who is in heaven' (Matt. 7:21–23).

These considerations at least leave open the possibility that the author of Numbers 22 – 24 did not intend to portray Balaam as a saint. He regarded Balaam as a man inspired by the Spirit to declare God's will, but that does not necessarily mean that he thought Balaam a good man or a true believer in Yahweh. There are at least hints in these chapters that he had a poor opinion of Balaam's character. And, since the earliest interpretations of these stories found elsewhere in the Old Testament take this negative line, there is a strong case for supposing that this is the author's understanding too.

---

5. J. Licht, *Storytelling in the Bible*, p. 32.

6. D. Daube, *Ancient Hebrew Fables* (OUP, 1973), p. 15.

The theological importance of the Balaam episode is revealed by the length and detail in which the events are described. The repeated insistence in the narrative that Balaam will say only what God tells him focuses our attention on the oracles. What did the Spirit have to announce through Balaam? In general terms, he announced that Israel was blessed, meaning they enjoyed and would continue to enjoy God's protection and consequent prosperity. But in fact these oracles are much more specific: they reaffirm the promises made to the patriarchs.

In Genesis 12:1–3, and subsequent passages, Abraham was promised three things: land, descendants and a covenant relationship. Balaam's first oracle mentions Israel's special relationship with God and her great population (23:8; cf. Gen. 12:3. Num. 22:17; cf. Gen. 13:16; 12:2–3). The second oracle concentrates on Israel's covenant relationship (cf. Gen. 12:2–3). The third vision describes how Israel will shortly enjoy peace and prosperity in the promised land. The fourth vision describes an Israelite king, a much rarer element in the patriarchal promises (cf. Gen. 17:6, 16; 35:11). The eloquent restatement of the old promises is most appropriate at this juncture. Israel, camping beside the Jordan, the eastern border of Canaan, is reminded that her promised home is not the territory of Sihon and Og which they have just conquered, but lies to the west. The extraordinary means through which the heathen prophet is led to make these predictions is a sign of their divine origin and a guarantee of their ultimate fulfilment. The people should, therefore, take courage despite the daunting prospect of the struggles ahead of them.

i. Balak sends for Balaam (22:1–6). 1. The account of the war against the Amorites is concluded (21:21–35) and the scene set for the next episode. The war against Og of Bashan had taken them into northern Transjordan. Now they returned and encamped in the Jordan valley, a little north of the Dead Sea, across the river from Jericho.

2–4. Israel had skirted the kingdoms of Edom and Moab on their way north from the wilderness (20:21; 21:13); but now Balak, king of Moab, consulted with the Midianites, tribesmen who lived both in Sinai and in the deserts east of the Jordan (4; cf. Exod. 2:15ff.; Judg. 6). They sent a joint delegation to seek help from Balaam (4, 7).

5. Balaam lived in *Pethor*, generally identified with Pitru of Assyrian inscriptions, a town on the Euphrates, called here *the River*, some 12 miles (20 km) south of Carchemish. *In the land of Amaw*, or more literally 'the land of the Amavites' (NEB). The Hebrew actually reads 'the land of the children of his people' (AV). Modern translations have altered just one vowel (*'ammô* to *'ammaw*) to produce the place name Amaw, mentioned only here in the Bible. But it is also mentioned in a 15th century BC inscription from Alalakh, and therefore must be somewhere in northern Syria.[7]

6. It is widely supposed that, since Balaam lived in northern Mesopotamia, he was a *bārû*, a priest-diviner, using the usual tricks of his trade such as dreams and omens to predict the future. But neither Balak nor the Bible was particularly interested in this: Balak wanted a man who could pronounce a powerful curse on his enemies which would thereby lead to their defeat (6). That blessings or curses properly pronounced can be really effective runs through biblical thought (cf. Gen. 27; 48:14ff.; Judg. 17:1ff.; Matt. 21:18ff.).

ii. Balaam's first encounter with God (22:7–14). In traditional manner Balaam seeks God's will at night. Quite unequivocally he is told *You shall not go with them; You shall not curse the people, for they are blessed* (12). Balaam is thus trapped between the demands of Balak and the commands of God. It is this conflict that sustains the whole drama that follows.

iii. Balaam's second encounter with God (22:15–20). The tension increases. Princes are again sent to plead with Balaam *more in number and more honourable* (15). Large fees are discussed (17–18). But Balaam insists on discovering God's will in a night vision. This one is recounted more briefly, and rather surprisingly concludes with a modification of the previous policy. Balaam may go, but he may say and do only what God permits (20). The listener or reader is meant to be surprised and to ask himself why this apparent change of mind on God's part? Will Balaam really be allowed to curse Israel after all? The next scene answers such questions beyond all ambiguity.

---

7. W. F. Albright, *BASOR*, 118, 1950, p. 16, n. 13, located Amaw between Aleppo and Carchemish. This would fit in well with Num. 22:5, but W. Gross, *Bileam*, pp. 109ff. points out that this is unproved.

iv. Balaam's third encounter with God (22:21–35). Up to this point Balaam has been portrayed as a man of great spiritual stature, who can meet with God when he wants and whose words have tremendous effects on the fate of nations. Here his spiritual blindness and powerlessness are disclosed. He cannot see the angel of the LORD standing in his path, though his donkey can. Furthermore, he sees no significance in her behaviour, though strange actions by animals were often regarded as omens in Mesopotamia.[8] As a specialist in this sort of divination, he ought to have realized the deity had a message for him. Instead, he beats his donkey viciously three times, an ungodly act in itself (Prov. 12:10).

Then to our astonishment the ass speaks (28–30). Such a thing would have seemed just as unlikely to the ancient Israelite as it does to us. It is immaterial to the story whether the donkey really spoke, or whether Balaam just imagined it talking. The Old Testament certainly sees inspiration as a supernatural phenomenon caused by the Spirit of God. Thus if men were able to utter God's words, why should not the same be true of animals? This is the real point of the episode. The donkey's acts and words anticipate the problems Balaam is about to face. The ass was caught three times between the angel's sword and Balaam's stick. Soon Balaam will find himself trapped three times between Balak's demands and God's prohibitions. Through his third encounter with God, Balaam was reminded that God wields a sword and that disobedience means death.[9] So he

---

8. See R. Largement, 'Les Oracles de Bile'am et la mantique suméro-akkadienne', *Travaux de l'institut catholique de Paris*, 10, 1964, pp. 37–50.

9. Verses 32–33. English versions with the ancient versions insert *lĕkâ*, 'to you', *I have come out to withstand you,* but the MT omission of the phrase is likely to be original. In the following clause, *your way is perverse before me,* RSV represents an emendation of *hadderek* 'the way' > *darkĕkā*. NEB 'you made straight for me' emends *yaraṭ* to *yāraṭṭa. yaraṭ* is generally connected with Arabic *warrata*, 'be precipitate', whence the very different translations. Probably the MT can be retained and given the sense of RSV.

If she had not: the Hebrew word *'ûlay* is everywhere else translated 'perhaps'. Either the sense is unique here, or *'ûlay* is a corruption of *lûlê*, 'unless, if not'.

goes on his way fully committed to declaring God's words rather than submitting to Balak's wishes (35).

v. Balak welcomes Balaam (22:36–40). Balak's pleasure at Balaam's arrival is demonstrated by his journey to meet him at the Moabite border. The Arnon formed the northern border of Moab. *The extremity of the boundary* means the eastern end of the Arnon (see map, p. 256). Neither *the city of Moab* (NEB 'Ar[10] of Moab') (36) nor *Kiriath-huzoth* (39) can be precisely located. The first was on the north-eastern border, the second somewhere in northern Moab. Balak celebrated by holding a large feast in Balaam's honour: sacrificial meals were a regular means of fêting holy men (cf. 1 Sam. 9:12ff.; 16:2ff.).

Balak chides Balaam for not coming more quickly and assures him that he will give a very large fee (37). But Balaam has learnt his lesson from the ass. 'Although I have come to you now, am I able to say anything? The word that God puts in my mouth, that must I speak' (38; cf. 35).

vi. Balaam's first oracle (22:41 – 23:12). 41. Balak conducts Balaam to various vantage-points from where he can glimpse the camp of Israel. None of the places mentioned can be precisely located, but since Israel was encamped in the Jordan valley, north of the Dead Sea, it seems likely that all the places mentioned were beyond the northern border of Moab, the Arnon river. *Bamoth-baal*, literally 'the high places of Baal', is presumably identical with Bamoth (21:19–20) and was in the vicinity of Heshbon and Dibon, according to Joshua 13:17 (cf. Num. 21:25–26).

23:1–2. Following the traditional methods of oriental diviners, Balaam tells Balak to *build ... seven altars* and offer *seven bulls and seven rams*. A Babylonian tablet describes a similar procedure: 'At dawn [cf. 'in the morning', 22:41], in the presence of Ea, Shamash and Marduk [Babylonian deities], you must set up seven altars, place seven incense burners of cypress and pour out the blood of seven sheep'.[11] Sometimes the ritual was even more elaborate and needed to be

---

10. NEB and TEV 'Ar' represents a slight emendation *'îr* > *'ār*, but it lacks support in the versions.

11. R. Largement, art. cit., p. 46.

repeated eight times. When this had been done the diviner presented himself before the deity and reminded him of the offerings (cf. 23:4). In Israel seven was also a sacred number. Sevenfold sprinkling was required in rites of purification (Lev. 8:11; 14:7, 16; 16:14, 19, etc.). Creation took seven days (Gen. 1:1 – 2:3). The seventh month of the year was full of religious festivals (Num. 29). The seventh year and the fiftieth year ($7 \times 7 + 1$) were also of special significance (Lev. 25). Seven or fourteen lambs were offered at the major festivals (Num. 28:19, 27; 29:4, 13, 17ff.). The choice of bulls and rams also enhanced the prestige of Balaam's offerings, for they were the most valued sacrificial beasts of ancient Israel (Lev. 4:1–21; 5:14 – 6:7). They were offered as burnt offerings, a sacrifice in which the entire animal was burnt on the altar (Lev. 1). Unlike the other sacrifices, neither offerer nor priest had any share in eating a burnt offering: it was all given to God. By selecting fourteen of the most valuable animals and offering them in this way, Balaam and Balak were evidently doing their utmost to secure a favourable response from God.

3–6. The religious atmosphere is further heightened by Balaam. He tells Balak: *Stand beside your burnt offering.* The verb used here (*hityaṣṣeb*) echoes 22:22 and suggests a patient waiting for God, possibly in prayer (cf. Exod. 14:13; 1 Sam. 12:7, 16). Balaam himself goes to a *bare height*,[12] where he evidently hoped to meet with God. Some commentators surmise that such places were considered especially favourable for divination. Balaam's hopes were realized, *God met Balaam.* Once again the narrator underlines the inspiration of the oracle he is about to deliver, *the LORD put a word in Balaam's mouth* (23:5; cf. 22:20, 28, 35, 38).

Balaam's oracles are poetic in form, as the printing in modern translations indicates. The archaic Hebrew spelling of these poems and their metre prove the early date of their composition.[13] The most

12. *šĕpî* elsewhere is always plural (e.g. Isa. 41:18; Jer. 3:2, 21; 4:11) and the versions translate in various ways. NEB, 'forthwith', adopts an interpretation of the LXX and Vulgate.

13. The basic modern treatment is W. F. Albright, 'The Oracles of Balaam', *JBL*, 63, 1944, pp. 207–233; see also D. Vetter, *Seherspruch and Segensschilderung* (Stuttgart, 1974), and D. K. Stuart, *Studies in Early Hebrew*

obvious feature of Hebrew poetry, quite clear even in translation, is its use of parallelism. Notice how the first line parallels the second line, (*Balak//king of Moab: from Aram//from the eastern mountains*) and the third parallels the fourth and so on.

7–8. Balaam begins by summarizing how he, a Mesopotamian seer, comes to be prophesying about Israel. He has been brought by Balak from *Aram*, short for Aram-Naharaim, that is north-eastern Syria or northern Mesopotamia. *Eastern mountains* is an ancient Canaanite expression designating the mountains of eastern Syria. He was summoned to *curse Jacob* and *denounce Israel*. Here Jacob is just an alternative name for Israel (cf. 10, 21, 23; 24:5, 17; cf. Gen. 32:28). Cursing was a very solemn business in the ancient world and often thought to be automatically effective: the words themselves contained the power to affect those who heard them and disregarded them (cf. Deut. 27:15ff.; 1 Sam. 14:24ff.). But Balaam, as a man inspired, cannot just curse whom he likes. He must express God's thoughts. *How can I curse whom God has not cursed?*

9. Through the Spirit Balaam is able to appreciate Israel's peculiar character. Because God has chosen her, she is different from the other nations. Therefore she lives apart from them and is conscious of her distinctiveness, *not reckoning itself among the nations.* Here Balaam alludes to a fundamental principle of Old Testament theology: God's choice of Israel to be his own people (cf. Exod. 19:5–6; Deut. 7:6ff.; Rom. 9). This was much more than an abstract theological idea. The consciousness of their election was expressed and fostered in numerous laws, most obviously the prohibitions on intermarriage with foreigners and on using mixtures, and the dietary laws (e.g. Deut. 7:3; 22:9–11; 14:1ff.).

10. Proof of their election is the fulfilment of the promises to the patriarchs. *Who can count the dust of Jacob?* is a clear allusion to Genesis 13:16: 'I will make your descendants as the dust of the earth; so

---

Meter, pp. 109–119. Albright, p. 226, thought the content of the poems pointed to their composition about 1200 BC and their orthography to their being written down no later than 900 BC. Most recent writers agree that these poems are among the earliest in the Bible but the exact date of composition is still a matter of debate.

that if one can count the dust of the earth, your descendants also can be counted.' *Let me die the death of the righteous, and let my end be like his* could be construed as an example of Genesis 12:3: Balaam, a non-Israelite, prays to be as blessed as the children of Abraham. *Number the fourth part of Israel* stands in parallel with *count the dust of Jacob* and presupposes a slight emendation of the text.[14]

11–12. Balaam's affirmation of Israel's unique place in God's providence was not what Balak wanted. In comparison with the subsequent oracles, this first one is quite obscure in detailing the way in which God is helping Israel; but it revealed clearly enough that the LORD was backing Israel, not Moab. This enraged Balak. Balaam reminded him of the terms under which he had accepted employment: *Must I not take heed to speak what the LORD puts in my mouth?* (12; cf. 5; 22:38).

vii. Balaam's second oracle (23:13–26). 13–18. Undeterred by the initial setback, Balak insists on trying again. Perhaps another set of sacrifices at another site will produce different results (13–14; cf. 22:41 – 23:3). He chooses the *field of Zophim* (literally 'watchmen') on the *top of Pisgah*. The name suggests it was a watchpost for observing troop movements in the Jordan valley. At least Balaam could see some of the Israelites from there. On another peak of the Pisgah range, Mount Nebo, Moses had a vision of the whole land of Canaan that Israel was to occupy (Deut. 34). The whole rigmarole of sacrifice and sign-seeking is repeated and once again *the LORD met Balaam, and put a word in his mouth.*

19–20. This word like the first begins with a criticism of Balak's theological assumptions: *God is … not a man that he should change his*

---

14. Hebrew *mispār 'et-rōbaʿ* is literally 'a number, the fourth part'. It is peculiar having two nouns in apposition with the definite object marker *'et* between them. Modern English versions therefore redivide the Hebrew *mî sāpar 'et-rōbaʿ*, 'who has counted the quarter …?' Maybe *'et* should also be omitted as it is unusual in poetry and adds nothing to the sense. NEB adopts a further emendation *'et-ribĕbôt*, 'thousands', in the text and in the margin notes another possibility, *trbʿt*, 'sands', cf. Akkadian *turbuʾttu* (dust). The last suggestion is preferred by Albright, p. 213, n. 28, and Vetter, p. 11.

mind (19, NEB; cf. 1 Sam. 15:29). He cannot be manipulated by magic
or dictated to by seers, even those of the stature of Balaam. *He has
blessed, and I cannot revoke it* (20; cf. 8). Consequently Israel will suffer
no misfortunes or troubles (21). An equally possible rendering of the
Hebrew is offered by NEB: *He has discovered no iniquity in
Jacob … no mischief in Israel.* In his vision Balaam sees God's ideal for
the nation: it must be free from sin, so that God may dwell among
them.

21. *The* LORD *their God is with them.* Here Balaam goes much further than in his first vision. Israel is not merely blessed, but enjoys
the very presence of God walking among them. The LORD is Israel's
king and they acclaim his presence in their worship: *the shout of a king
is among them.* Shout (*tĕrû'â*) often denotes the sound of a trumpet
blown in war or at religious festivals (e.g. Lev. 23:24; Num. 10:5–6;
1 Sam. 4:6), and the word here may allude to such occasions. The notion of the LORD as king is fundamental in the Pentateuch. It is as
Israel's sovereign that the LORD made a covenant with her and gave
her the law. But he was no distant emperor: he lived and reigned
among them. The tabernacle was set up to be a portable palace, with
the ark as God's throne. The camp in the wilderness was organized
on the model of the Egyptian army with the companies encamped
in square formation around the royal tent at the centre.

22–23a. The exodus from Egypt is the supreme demonstration
that God cared for Israel. Balaam likens God's support for his
people to *the horns of the wild ox.* This is the interpretation of NEB and
TEV, 'He fights for them like a wild ox', and is preferable to RSV which
compares Israel itself to the horns of the wild ox.[15] With such divine intervention *enchantment* and *divination* such as Balaam practised
are powerless against Israel (RSV, TEV) or are redundant within Israel
(NEB). Again the Hebrew is ambiguous; *bĕ* normally means 'in', but
the context favours 'against' here.

---

15. The Hebrew is ambiguous. Literally it may be translated 'Like the horns
of the wild ox (he) is to him/or he has'. The wild ox (Heb. *rĕ'ēm*),
probably *bos primigenius*, is also mentioned in 24:8; Deut. 33:17; Job 39:9–
10; Pss. 22:21; 29:6; 92:10; Isa. 34:7. It is probably identical with
Akkadian *rímu*, Ugaritic *r'um*. See *Encyclopedia Miqrait* 7, pp. 296–297.

23b–24. *Now*[16] *it shall be said of Israel, 'What has God wrought!'*
Israel's future victories will be a vivid proof of God's power in the
world, just as the exodus was a few years earlier. They will be talked
about by the surrounding nations with trepidation (cf. Josh. 2:9–11).
Balaam concludes his second oracle by comparing Israel's policy of
total annihilation of its enemies to a lion devouring its prey.

25–26. In other words, Balak's plan is hopeless. The magician is
unable to thwart God's purposes. Balak hoped with the aid of spiritual power to defeat Israel and drive them out of his land (22:6).
Balaam declares that just what Balak fears will happen: Israel will
destroy its enemies and nothing can stop them. Balak responds,
Neither curse them at all, nor bless them at all; it would be better to say
nothing than bless Israel so comprehensively. But Balaam insists he
must say what God tells him (26).

viii. Balaam's third oracle (23:27 – 24:13). 27–28. Third time
lucky is Balak's motto. Unpersuaded by Balaam's last message that
the LORD would not change his mind, he takes Balaam to another
place, *the top of Peor, that overlooks the desert.* Again the site cannot be
exactly identified, but since chapter 25 locates the Israelite camp near
Peor, it may be surmised that Peor is somewhere near the north-
eastern shore of the Dead Sea. This time Balaam could see the whole
camp of Israel (24:2), not just part of them (23:13).

29 – 24:2. The same sacrifices are offered as on the previous two
occasions (29–30; cf. 1–2, 14). But this time Balaam dispenses with
divination, looking *for omens* (24:1 cf. 23:3–4, 15–16), because he
realized *that it pleased the LORD to bless Israel.* Previously God had put
a word in Balaam's mouth (23:5, 16); this time *the Spirit of God came
upon him* (24:2). This is probably not just a stylistic variation on the
earlier phrase. It suggests that this time Balaam fell into an ecstatic
trance as he saw the vision[17] (cf. 1 Sam. 10:6, 10; 1 Kgs 22:10–22).

---

16. Metrically *kāʿēt*, 'now' (cf. Judg. 13:23; 21:22) fits better than the much-
    favoured revocalization *kî ʿattā*, 'for now', though the latter phrase
    would be more common in Hebrew. See D. K. Stuart, *Studies in Hebrew
    Meter*, p. 112.
17. Cf. Keil, p. 186, 'The former (utterances) were communicated to him …
    without his being thrown into an ecstatic state; he heard the voice of

This is supported by Balaam's own description of his state in the opening lines of his next two oracles.

3–4. His *eye is opened*,[18] he *hears the words of God, sees the vision of the Almighty* and he *falls down* with his *eyes uncovered* (cf. verses 15–16). Whereas the first two oracles are theological statements about God's relationship to Israel and what he has done for them already, the subsequent oracles include visionary predictions of Israel's future settlement in Canaan, the rise of the monarchy and victories over specific foes.

5–6. Balaam compares Israel's future settlements in Canaan to strong trees growing by life-giving streams of water, *Like valleys that stretch afar.* On the basis of Arabic, NEB/TEV reinterpret *naḥal* (*valley*, RSV, wadi, bourne, a river that flows in the rainy season) as palm-tree. This seems unnecessary and obscures the gradual build-up in this verse – wadis, *gardens, aloes, planted by the LORD, cedar trees* (the king of the trees; cf. Judg. 9:15). Commentators more concerned with scientific accuracy than poetic imagery have been worried by the final clause, *like cedar trees beside the waters.* Cedars do not grow by rivers, so why should Balaam liken Israel to one here? Cedars' strength is unsurpassed without a river running nearby, but Israel will be even stronger, 'like a cedar by a river'.

7a. *Water shall flow from his buckets, and his seed shall be in many waters.* Here the image is of a man with two pails hanging from his shoulders and overflowing with water. Again water is being used as symbolic of great fruitfulness. Though the reference could again be to the fertility of the land, resulting from the abundance of rain, it more probably refers to a growing population as the result of sexual intercourse (cf. Prov. 5:15–19). Though Israel may already be too many to count, Balaam declares they will multiply yet further (cf. Gen. 17:5–6).

God within him telling him what to say. But this time, like the prophets in their prophesyings, he was placed by the Spirit of God in a state of ecstatic sight; so that, with his eyes closed as in clairvoyance, he saw the substance of the revelation from God with his inward mental eye, which had been opened by the Spirit of God.'

18. *śětum* (open) occurs only here and in 24:15 and alternative meanings and emendations have been proposed. But none is obviously superior.

7b–8. Three times God promised the patriarchs that 'kings would come forth from them' (Gen. 17:6, 16; 35:11). Here Balaam first broaches the topic of Israel's future king, a theme he develops more fully in the following oracle, in quite a cryptic fashion, *His king shall be higher than Agag.* Saul, the first king of Israel, defeated Agag, the king of the Amalekites (1 Sam. 15:8), and this word of Balak would appear to be a straightforward prophecy of the eventual defeat of Israel's oldest enemy (cf. Exod. 17:14–16). The defeat of Amalek was also, of course, a guarantee that Israel's king would triumph over all his foes[19] (cf. 23:22–24).

9–13. This magnificent prophecy ends with another obvious allusion to the promises made to the patriarchs: *Blessed be every one who blesses you, and cursed be every one who curses you* (9; cf. Gen. 12:3; 27:29). But Balak remained unconvinced of his hired seer's inspiration and angrily told him to go home without payment (12). Balaam insists he has only done what he promised: to declare God's word, however much he was paid (24:13; cf. 22:18). And before Balak can send him home, he falls into another trance declaring in yet greater detail how Moab and her neighbours will be affected by the great king of Israel. Thus the last four oracles (24:15–24) really continue the third (verses 3–9).

ix. Balaam's fourth oracle (24:14–19). Formally this oracle and the shorter ones following it are expansions and developments of the third oracle describing more fully the feats of Israel's future king (cf. 7).

14–16. Like the third oracle these later ones were delivered in an ecstatic visionary trance (15–16; cf. 3–4). But whereas the third oracle is talking about the future rather indefinitely, Balaam's final speeches are explicitly said to concern the distant future: *in the latter days* (14). Though this phrase may simply mean 'in future' (e.g. Jer. 23:20), it can also mean 'the final days', whatever the period that constitutes the particular prophet's time horizon (Isa. 2:2; Dan. 8:19). That Balaam evidently senses a gap between his vision and its fulfilment is suggested by verse 17: *I see him, but not now; I behold him, but not nigh.* Thus, though these predictions were fulfilled for the first

---

19. RSV; cf. TEV, *pierce them through with his arrows* (8) involves no emendation. NEB however reads *ḥālāṣaw*, 'limbs', for *ḥiṣṣaw*, 'arrows'.

time, partially at any rate, some three hundred years after Balaam in the reign of David, traditional Jewish and Christian interpreters have seen another and fuller realization of these prophecies in the Messiah. And this is characteristic of many messianic passages in the Old Testament. On one level they are but expressions of hope for a good and righteous king. But on another plane, they must be looking for something more, for no real king ever came up to the ideals expressed (e.g. Ps. 72; Isa. 11, etc.). In interpreting these last words of Balaam both perspectives must be respected. Primarily they refer to royal triumphs in the period of the early monarchy, but these victories prefigure the greater conquests of Christ at his first and second advents.

17. *A star shall come forth out of Jacob.* Astrological imagery must have come naturally to a Babylonian diviner such as Balaam. That stars could be used metaphorically for kings is suggested by Isaiah 14:12, where the king of Babylon is called 'Day Star', and Revelation 22:16, which calls Jesus 'the off-spring of David, the bright morning star'. That a king is meant here is confirmed by the second line of the couplet: *a sceptre shall rise out of Israel,* a sceptre being part of the royal insignia (Ps. 45:6; Amos 1:5, 8; cf. Gen. 49:10). The NEB translation, 'a comet', makes a nice parallel to 'a star', but since 'staff, or 'sceptre', the usual meaning of *šēbeṭ*, fits the context well, there is little reason to abandon it here.

This king of Israel will conquer the neighbouring countries, Moab, Shut, Edom, Seir, Amalek and the Kenites: *He shall crush the forehead of Moab* and the skull of all the sons of Shut. 'The skull of' (*qdqd*) is the reading of the Samaritan version and of Jeremiah 48:45, which quotes this passage. Graphically it is very little different from the MT Hebrew (*qrqr*), 'break down'. The root *qrqr* is much rarer than *qdqd* (possibly in Isa. 22:5) and as the more difficult reading is preferred by most English versions. 'Shut': the Hebrew reads *šēt* which is normally rendered 'Seth' in English (e.g. Gen. 5:3). However, the 'sons of Seth' would be roughly equivalent to 'sons of Adam', i.e. all mankind. It would be strange for a king to be at odds with all men. Furthermore, the parallelism between 'Moab' in the first line of the couplet and 'sons of Shut' in the second line implies they must be comparable entities, either neighbouring peoples or two names for Moab, cf. Jacob/Israel, Edom/Seir (17–18). The Šutu are mentioned in the Egyptian execration texts (c. 1900 BC) as living somewhere in Palestine, and it seems easiest to take this remark to refer to them. But this tribe's home was forgotten even in Jeremiah's time, who, therefore, paraphrases 'sons of tumult' (*šā'ôn*, probably connected with *šē't*). This interpretation is adopted by NEB. The mention of this tribe of Shut is a pointer to the antiquity of this oracle.

18–19. With a slight rearrangement of the Hebrew text, these verses may be rendered:

> 18 Edom shall be dispossessed,
>   and Seir shall be dispossessed,
>   when Israel does valiantly.
> 19 Jacob shall rule his enemies,
>   and destroy the survivors from Ir.

This translation involving a slight rearrangement of the Hebrew text is adopted in other modern studies of this passage,[20] though not recent English translations. In the Hebrew text (cf. RSV) 'his enemies' stands in line 2 (18b) making this line too long, whereas line 4 (19a) is too short in the Hebrew. Moving 'his enemies' from line 2 to line 4 is quite a trivial change: the *m* prefixed to Jacob (meaning 'from') is instead attached to the previous word as a suffix (enclitic *m*). In the last line I take Ir to be a name of a Moabite town, rather than the common noun spelt the same way meaning 'city' (cf. 22:36).

Balaam's vision next concentrates on the Edomites who lived in Mount Seir (Deut. 2); this explains the parallelism Edom/Seir in verse 18. The Edomites were the immediate neighbours of Moab living to the south of them. In the final verse of his vision, however, Balaam probably reverts to the fate of Moab. Balak had met Balaam at Ir-Moab or City of Moab (22:36), and Ir in this verse could be an abbreviation of this longer term. With spine-chilling drama he declares that every inhabitant of Ir will perish. This prediction of Moab's total defeat at the hand of a future Israelite king is an appropriate point for Balaam to end. He had been called in so that through his curse Balak, king of Moab, might defeat Israel; Balaam

---

20. de Vaulx, p. 292; Stuart, op. cit., pp. 115f.; Vetter, op. cit., p. 44.

declares that the reverse will be the case: Moab will be destroyed by a coming king of Israel.

x. Balaam's three final words (24:20–25). Yet rather unexpectedly Balaam does not end here. He adds three short, cryptic oracles dealing with the fate of other nations. It is difficult to know why they are included, except that they bring up the total of oracles to the mystic number seven and, like the oracles of doom against foreign nations in the later prophets, they serve as a back-handed encouragement to Israel. If Israel's enemies are destroyed, her future will be secure.

20. The first of these short sayings about other nations is cast in proverbial form and concerns the tribe of Amalek. They lived in the Sinai peninsula and were implacable foes of Israel (cf. Exod. 17:8–16; Num. 14:43–45; Judg. 6:3, 33, etc.). They considered themselves *the first of the nations*, either because of their antiquity (they are termed Meluhha in third-millennium inscriptions) or because of their quality (cf. 1 Sam. 15:21; Amos 6:1). But in sharp contrast 'his end' (literally 'his last') will be 'utter destruction' (NEB).[21] In fact both Saul and David defeated the Amalekites (1 Sam. 15:18; 30:17) and they were finally destroyed in Hezekiah's time (1 Chr. 4:43).

21–22. The second saying deals with the Kenites who lived in the dry hilly country south-west of the Dead Sea, quite close to the Amalekites (cf. 1 Sam. 15:6; 27:10; 30:29). But unlike the Amalekites they were on good terms with Israel, Hobab, Moses' brother-in-law, being a Kenite (Judg. 1:16; 4:11). The RSV gives a literal translation of the Hebrew, and it may be retained with one or two possible inconsequential changes.[22] Two things are odd about this oracle though. First, why is a nation on good terms with Israel picked out for doom? Second, how could Asshur, generally identified with

---

21. No textual emendation is necessary here or in verse 24; *'ōbēd* (destruction) is a participle, 'perishing', acting as an abstract noun; cf. P. Wernberg-Moeller, *ZAW*, 71, 1959, p. 55.

22. Possibly move Kain from 22a and add it to 21c after 'dwelling place' to make the lines of more equal length. For *'ad māh*, 'how long?' (22) read *'ad* and enclitic *m* meaning 'while', so Albright, *JBL*, 63, p. 222 followed by de Vaulx, p. 294; Vetter, op. cit., pp. 49f.

Assyria (cf. TEV), take the Kenites captive without simultaneously desolating Israel and Judah? And if Assyria is meant, does the oracle not spell doom for Israel as well as Qain? To avoid any mention of Assyria, NEB revocalizes the Hebrew of verse 22b. A better solution is that offered by de Vaulx, who says Asshur is not the well-known empire of northern Mesopotamia, but a small tribe that lived in northern Sinai, mentioned in several places in the Old Testament (Gen. 25:3, 18; 2 Sam. 2:9; Ps. 83:8). This word then foretells that the Kenites will be subdued by their neighbours, the tribe of Asshur. But they in their turn will meet their match, as the final saying foretells (verse 24), probably at the hands of the Philistines.

23–25. The third and final saying of this group is the longest and the most problematic. As traditionally understood (see RSV) it refers to ship-borne invaders from the west (Kittim may be a town in Cyprus) attacking Assyria and Mesopotamia (Eber). This could be a prediction of Alexander the Great's conquests in the fourth century BC or those of Rome in the first century BC. However, it seems more likely that the reference is really to the invasion of the sea-peoples, who swept through the coastal plain of Canaan and attacked Egypt c. 1200 BC. The best-known of the sea peoples were the Philistines, who have given their name to Palestine. On this reading of the text, Balaam foretells that the Philistines will defeat Asshur (see 22) and Eber, presumably neighbours of Asshur. It could be a name for some of the Israelites (Eber//Hebrew, cf. 1 Sam. 4:9). But the Philistines in turn will be doomed. *He also shall come to destruction* (24). It was, of course, one of David's greatest achievements to defeat the Philistines.

This interpretation of the text can stand without resort to textual emendation, but several quite plausible suggestions have been made which makes the description of the sea peoples even clearer.

Alas, who shall live when God does this?

But ships shall come from Kittim (23b–24a) can be reinterpreted as 'The isles shall assemble in the North, ships from the farthest sea'. Though the meaning is radically different, the textual changes involved are quite small, and have won wide acceptance.[23]

---

23. All that needs to be done is to rewrite the text in archaic spelling (i.e. omit vowel letters), reinterpret *ḥyh* as 'assemble' instead of 'live', and

The last four oracles of Balaam (24:15–24) are on this interpretation all looking forward to the time of the early monarchy,
specially to the reign of David, when the Moabites, Edomites,
Amalekites and Philistines were all subdued by Israel (e.g. 2 Sam. 8).
But the subjugation of these nations was only temporary: whenever
the kingdoms of Israel and Judah were weak, their fortunes revived
and they attacked the Hebrew kingdoms again. Thus many of the
later prophets contain oracles directed against Moab, Edom and
Philistia (e.g. Amos 1:6 – 2:3; Isa. 14:28 – 16:14; Jer. 47 – 49). Sometimes indeed they quote the prophecies of Balaam (e.g. Jer. 48:45//
Num. 24:17; Dan. 11:30//Num. 24:24). And the great royal Psalm 110
contains enough verbal parallels with Numbers 24:15–19 to make it
probable that the psalmist knew Balaam's oracle and was consciously
alluding to it.[24] This re-use of the prophecies by later writers shows
that they realized that they had been only partially fulfilled.

So quite naturally in early Jewish literature the prophecies of
Balaam were often interpreted messianically. For example the Dead
Sea scrolls (c. 1st century BC) take the star and the sceptre as the messiahs of Aaron and Israel, i.e. the priestly and kingly messiahs. Rabbi
Akiba, hailing the leader of the second Jewish revolt (AD 132–135)
as the messiah, called him Bar-Kocheba, i.e. Son of the star. Similarly the foreign nation oracles were given an eschatological
interpretation. Targum Onkelos (cf. Dan. 11:30) takes 24:24
as a description of the Romans attacking Mesopotamia, while

----

change *d* into *r* in one word. Consonantally the new interpretation is:

'*ym yhy msm'l wsym myrkt ym*

and the old:

'*y m yhy mśm 'l wsym myd ktym*.

Vowel signs, as opposed to vowel letters, were not inserted in the
Hebrew Bible till c. AD 900. For a fuller discussion see Albright, *JBL*, 63,
1944, pp. 222–223; de Vaulx, p. 296; Vetter, pp. 49–50. The emendation
is partially adopted by NEB.

24. de Vaulx, p. 292 notes the following: *nĕ'ūm* 'oracle' (24:15//110:1), *rādâ*
'rule' (24:19//110:2), *māḫāṣ*, crush (24:17//110:6). Also 'sceptre',
'heads', though different Hebrew words are used (24:17//110:2;
24:17//110:6), and the general theme of victory over enemies.

Josephus[25] identified Asshur with the Seleucid empire of Antiochus Epiphanes.

The New Testament does not cite the prophecies of Balaam explicitly, but there are probable allusions to it in Luke 1:78; Revelation 2:26–28; 22:16 and, of course, Christ's birth was announced by a star (Matt. 2:1–10). If the primary fulfilment of Balaam's prophecies was in the rise of David and the defeat of his foes, a further fulfilment may surely be seen in Jesus, the son of David, who has conquered sin and death, and now reigns 'until he has put all his enemies under his feet' (1 Cor. 15:25).

As de Vaulx writes, 'All Christian commentators see in this oracle (24:15–19) the announcement of the Christ. The sole disagreement is between those holding to a literal messianic prophecy and those holding to a typological one. It is best to avoid the dilemma: the allusions to David are too obvious for it to have a direct and exclusive messianic sense; while the typological is a little too external to the text. We have here a very good example of the fuller sense, a really literal sense hidden in the text, which is only discovered gradually through the meditation of successive generations.'[26]

B. National apostasy (chapter 25)

The Bible startles its readers by the way it juxtaposes the brightest of revelations and the darkest of sins. The lawgiving at Sinai was followed by the making of the golden calf (Exod. 20 – 32), the ordination of Aaron by the disobedience of his sons (Lev. 8 – 10), the covenant with David by the Bathsheba affair (2 Sam. 7 – 12), Palm Sunday by Good Friday. Here we have another classic example of this pattern, the wonderful prophecies of Balaam are succeeded by the great apostasy at Peor. In this way Scripture tries to bring home to us the full wonder of God's grace in face of man's incorrigible propensity to sin.

The basic reason for mentioning the sin of Peor at this point is that the narrative of Numbers is arranged more or less

25. *Antiquities* xiii.6.7.
26. de Vaulx, p. 294.

chronologically. However, many more things happened on the way from Egypt to Canaan than are actually recorded, and it is always right to ask why a particular incident is included. I noted that there are certain parallels between the journey from Egypt to Sinai and the journey from Kadesh to the plains of Moab. There are also clear parallels between the events at Sinai and those in the plains of Moab. In both the revelation of God is followed by a flouting of basic covenant principles; there is a census, and laws about sacrifice and the festivals are given. Not only do the incidents of the golden calf and Baal-peor (Exod. 32; Num. 25) correspond in the overall arrangement of the books, there are several internal correspondences. Both episodes involve the worship of other gods (Exod. 32:8; Num. 25:2). Both times God's wrath is appeased by the immediate slaughter of those involved (Exod. 32:26–28; Num. 25:7–8). As a result the tribe of Levi is set apart for divine service in the first case, while in the second Phinehas is promised an eternal priesthood (Exod. 32:29; Num. 25:11–13). There is another interesting point of comparison between the stories. At Sinai the people did not know what was going on between God and Moses (Exod. 32:1). Similarly in the plains of Moab, the Israelites cannot have known what Balaam was predicting for them. In both cases they must have learnt subsequently what happened. These repetitions are more than just a literary device, they enshrine theological truth. God's character does not change with changing circumstances. The older generation who had witnessed the exodus and Sinai had died out. The new generation who were to conquer Canaan had to learn the same lessons over again.

As with many biblical narratives, the story of the sin of Baal-peor falls into three sections, each centred on a word from God. Verses 1–9 describe the sin, the ensuing plague and how it was stopped, not through carrying out the divine sentence in verse 4, but by Phinehas slaying two blatant sinners. Verses 10–15 explain why Phinehas' action was so meritorious. Priests, such as Phinehas, were God's representatives among Israel and were to symbolize God's character in their life and behaviour. Phinehas had done just that. His anger mirrored the divine anger and as a reward he and his family are guaranteed a perpetual priesthood. Finally, verses 16–18 pronounce

God's judgment on the Midianites for seducing the Israelites from total loyalty to the LORD.

1–2. *Shittim* (literally 'acacias'). This last encampment of Israel before they crossed the Jordan, is called Abel-shittim in 33:49 (cf. Josh. 2:1; 3:1). Though the exact location is uncertain, recent writers usually identify it with Tell el-Hammam where the Wadi Kefrein enters the Jordan valley. *Play the harlot* has both a physical and a spiritual sense. Sacred prostitution was a common feature of Canaanite religion; through it some of the Israelites were allured to participate in pagan sacrifices and *bowed down to their gods*. In so doing they broke both the first and second commandments, 'You shall have no other gods before me ... You shall not bow down to them or serve them' (Exod. 20:3, 5).

The daughters of Moab. The woman slain by Phinehas was a Midianite (6, 15, 17–18). Midianites and Moabites are closely associated in the Balaam story (22:4, 7), so it is unnecessary to suppose for this reason that verses 1–5 are from a different source from verses 6–18. The Midianites were a mobile group (cf. Judg. 6) who evidently at this time were worshipping at the same shrine as the Moabites.

3. This shrine was dedicated to Baal of Peor and may well be identical with the place where Balaam delivered his final prophecies (cf. 23:28). Baal was the great Canaanite fertility god, whose worship Israel always found very alluring (e.g. Judg. 2:13; 1 Kgs 18; 2 Kgs 17:16; Jer. 2:8, etc.). By participating in this cult Israel had *yoked* or coupled *himself to Baal of Peor* (3). In so doing they flagrantly repudiated the essential heart of the covenant, total and exclusive allegiance to the LORD, and a severe plague broke out killing twenty-four thousand people (9; cf. Exod. 32:35).

4–5. To stop such a plague atonement had to be made (cf. 16:45–50; 2 Sam. 24:15–25), and an exemplary punishment was therefore called for: *Take all the chiefs of the people, and hang them in the sun before the LORD.* The tribal chieftains, and maybe leaders of sub-groups within the tribes, were to be executed. Under biblical law human judges could sentence only those directly involved in a crime (cf. Deut. 24:16). In this case the whole nation, corporately though not individually, was involved in the offence, therefore representatives of all Israel had to atone for it. An additional reason for punishing the chiefs of the people was that they should have restrained their followers.

However, in verse 5 Moses tells the judges to punish only the active participants in the Baal cult, apparently tacitly dropping God's demand that the chiefs be put to death. Keil[27] indeed argues that verse 5 correctly interprets 'hang them' (4): 'them' refers to the Baal worshippers, not the chiefs, he claims. However, this is not the natural interpretation of the Hebrew, and most commentators suppose the death of the chiefs is being called for.

The mode of execution is also a little uncertain. RSV *hang* follows the Vulgate. The targums suggest that the men were to be stoned and then 'hung up'. The Septuagint says 'make an example of', but in 2 Samuel 21:6, 9, 13, the only other passage where this Hebrew verb is used (*hôqaʿ*) translates 'hang in the sun'. NEB 'hurl them down' is based on an Arabic root and has little to commend it. Where such a mode of execution is specified in the Bible other terms are used (2 Chr. 25:12). The various translations, and particularly 2 Samuel 21:6–13, suggest that an aggravated form of death penalty was intended, probably involving a refusal to bury the victims. Those sentenced to death were normally buried promptly. But in really heinous cases it was customary in the ancient Near East to impale their dead bodies on a stake or hang them up after execution. This served as a public warning and prevented the criminal's spirit resting in the underworld. Within the holy land such practices were forbidden, as they would have caused its pollution, but here in Transjordan such considerations would not have applied (Deut. 21:22–23; cf. 21:1–9; Josh. 10:26–27). At any rate, whatever the precise nature of the death sentence, it was designed to underline the seriousness of the flagrant breach of the covenant stipulations.[28]

---

27. Keil, p. 205.
28. For further discussion, see G. E. Mendenhall, *The Tenth Generation* (John Hopkins UP, 1973), pp. 113ff. R. Polzin, '*HWQY*' and Covenantal Institutions in Early Israel', *HTR*, 62, 1969, pp. 227–240. Polzin suggests that *hôqaʿ* means carrying out the covenant curse of dismemberment of covenant breakers (cf. Gen. 15:10). This is possible but not proven. Lev. 17:4 says that worshippers of foreign gods will be 'cut off', normally interpreted to mean sudden death at the hands of God. Note that on this occasion idolatry is followed by a deadly plague.

6. It is not surprising that Moses watered down God's sentence somewhat. The chiefs of the people had an authority comparable to modern cabinet ministers, and it is hardly likely that they would have acceded to a demand for their own execution, even if it would have brought national salvation. Gispen[29] suggests that it was the refusal to implement God's sentence in verse 4 that brought on the serious plague (8–9). At any rate there developed a national crisis, obliquely referred to here with the people *weeping at the door of the tent of meeting*. This was further aggravated by Zimri, son of a minor chieftain, bringing a Midianite girl right into the camp. Up to this point intercourse with foreign girls had taken place outside the camp. Now under the nose of Moses and the other people, Zimri showed his contempt for the covenant and the divine sentence pronounced against leaders like his father.

7–9. It is within this context that Phinehas' bloody and brutal act must be viewed. *He took a spear in his hand and went after the man of Israel into the inner room, and pierced both of them, the man of Israel and the woman, through her body. Thus the plague was stayed from the people of Israel.* The 'inner room' (Hebrew *qubbâ*) occurs only here and its exact meaning is uncertain: it probably means 'the tent' or 'part of the tent' where the couple were having intercourse.[30] *Her body* is literally 'her stomach' (cf. Deut. 18:3). As in 5:21, the idea is that of mirroring punishment. She led astray an Israelite man with her body and therefore she is pierced through the organ of his downfall. The description of the crime may be intended to suggest that Phinehas slew them in the very act of intercourse.

10–15. We are shocked that a priest should behave in this way, and even more so that his behaviour is regarded as supremely meritorious. Of course, the priests and Levites were responsible for guarding the tabernacle against illegitimate entry, and had the duty of killing

I have suggested that 'cutting off' may involve unpleasant consequences in the after-life as well as sudden death, Wenham, p. 242. This would fit in with non-burial probably envisaged here.

29. Gispen, II, p. 147.
30. S. C. Reif, 'What Enraged Phinehas?', *JBL*, 90, 1971, pp. 200–206, suggests a cult shrine is meant, but this seems unlikely.

trespassers (chs. 3 – 4). Here, however, Phinehas kills a sinner in the camp, not a would-be trespasser into the sanctuary. Nevertheless, this is quite compatible with the biblical doctrine of priesthood. The priest represents God before men. Therefore, his body must be unblemished, to symbolize the perfection of God. His wife and children must be of exemplary character, so that they do not tarnish the priest's reputation (Lev. 21). The priest, in his life and acts, must personify, even incarnate, the character of God. This is precisely what Phinehas did: *he was jealous with my jealousy among them, so that I did not consume the people of Israel in my jealousy.* In other words, because Phinehas executed the sinner, expressing so clearly and visibly God's own anger through his deed, that anger was turned away. *He made atonement for the people.* To make atonement (*kipper*) is the usual phrase to describe the effect of sacrifice (e.g. Lev. 1:4; 4:20; 5:16). In normal circumstances the animal died in place of the guilty man. Here the sinners themselves are put to death and consequently animal sacrifice is unnecessary.

Not only does the priest represent God to the people, he represents the people before God. He should be the ideal Israelite. The whole nation was called to be a kingdom of priests and a holy nation (Exod. 19:6); the priest was expected to show true holiness in his life. This idea of the priest representing the people to God explains the covenant of peace made with him. Israel had broken the covenant by worshipping foreign gods. Phinehas had restored that covenant by his deed, and is therefore rewarded with *the covenant of a perpetual priesthood* a reward that mirrors the sin atoned for. This covenant with Phinehas is probably a guarantee that the high priesthood would always remain in his family (1 Chr. 6:4ff.).

16–18. Finally Moses urges the people to continue the fight against the Midianites. Further encounters are recorded in chapter 31 and Judges 6 – 8. Indeed Isaiah 9:4 likens the victories of the messiah to Gideon's triumphs over Midian. Jewish tradition has made much of Phinehas' zeal: Ecclesiasticus 45:23f. ranks him next in honour to Moses and Aaron, while the Pseudo-Jonathan targum says his deed was accompanied by twelve miracles. Some Christian commentators have seen Phinehas as a type of Christ. In that he embodied the ideal of Israelite priesthood this is surely legitimate: our Lord was angry more than once with sin (e.g. Mark 3:5; 11:15ff.). Yet there is another side to it: whereas it was Phinehas' spear that

pierced the sinners that made atonement for Israel, it was the nails
and spear that pierced Jesus that made atonement for the sins of the
whole world. For Paul, the main point of the story is that Christians
should beware of the dangers of immorality. Like the other stories
of judgment from the wilderness, 'these things are warnings for us'
(1 Cor. 10:6–8).

C. Census (chapter 26)

Nearly forty years after the last census (chs. 1 – 4) in the wilderness
of Sinai another is called for in the plains of Moab (26:63–64). Both
censuses had a military purpose: to record all those men aged twenty
or over who were fit for military service (26:2; cf. 1:3). Since a campaign against Midian has just been announced (25:16–18), and the
conquest of Canaan is imminent, a military census is appropriate
here. However, there was a more important reason for this census:
to determine the relative size of the tribes so that they should each
receive a proportionate share of territory in the promised land
(26:52–56). This chapter thus looks forward and backward: backward
to those events which have determined the growth of Israel's population in the past, and forward to the implications of this growth for
the settlement in the land.

If this census list is compared with those in chapters 1 and 3, there
are two obvious differences. First, chapters 1 and 3 just give the
total number of men in each tribe: chapter 26 gives these totals and
also lists the families or clans that make up each tribe. The second point
of difference is in the census figures themselves: the number belonging
to each tribe and to all Israel varies from the first census. The additional
material about the clans of Israel is probably taken from Genesis 46:8–
27, which lists all the sons and grandsons of Jacob. Jacob's grandsons
were the ancestors of the various families that made up the tribes of
Israel. For example, Reuben's sons, Hanoch, Pallu, Hezron and Carmi,
all had clans named after them (26:5–6; cf. Gen. 46:9). These extra details about the clans and their forefathers serve as reminders that the
cause of the great multiplication of the children of Israel was the oft-
repeated promise to the patriarchs that their descendants would
become a great nation (e.g. Gen. 12:2; 26:24; 46:3).

Working against the fulfilment of these promises was the

faithless disobedience of various members of the family. Dathan and Abiram (9–11; cf. ch. 16), Er and Onan (19; cf. Gen. 38:2–9), Nadab and Abihu (61; cf. Lev. 10:1–3), and finally the whole generation who came out of Egypt (64–65; cf. chs. 13 – 14) are mentioned. Yet despite these great setbacks, the total population of Israel after the years of wandering is almost the same as it was at Sinai – 601,730 (26:51) as opposed to 603,550 (1:46) – and the people are on the verge of entering the promised land (26:52–56). In this way this table of census returns develops one of the great themes of the book of Numbers: God's promises to the patriarchs may be delayed by human sin, but they are not ultimately frustrated by it (cf. Rom. 11).

A comparison of the tribal totals in chapters 1 and 26 shows that most of the tribes increased in size during the wilderness wanderings, but four show a slight decline: Reuben (46,500 – 43,730), Gad (45,650 – 40,500), Ephraim (40,500 – 32,500), Naphtali (53,400 – 45,400), and Simeon, a catastrophic fall (59,300 – 22,200). It may be that the fall in Reuben and Simeon's population should be linked with these tribes' support for Dathan and Abiram (ch. 16) and Zimri (ch. 25), but it is hard to identify any factor that would account for the decline of the other tribes.[31]

4. *(Take a census of the people) from twenty years old.* The words in brackets are missing from the Hebrew and must be understood on the basis of verse 2. Verse 4 recapitulates verse 2 more succinctly. This is better than the textual emendation proposed by NEB and TEV. Comparison of this list of Jacob's grandsons with that in Genesis 46:9–24 discloses a number of slight differences, e.g. Simeon's sons according to Genesis 46:10 are Jemuel, Jamin, Ohad, Jachin, Zohar and Shaul, but according to Numbers 26:12, Nemuel, Jamin, Jachin, Zerah and Shaul. Ohad is omitted from Numbers, presumably because he did not found a family, while Jemuel/Nemuel, Zohar/Zerah probably represent variant spellings. Other differences between the lists can be explained in similar fashion.

33. Daughters are rarely mentioned in biblical genealogies, but Zelophehad's lack of sons posed a legal problem where the inheritance of land was concerned. The solution to this question created

---

31. On the large numbers, see Additional note, pp. 68ff.

precedents which are discussed more fully in chapters 27 and 36.

52–56. The land is to be divided among the tribes according to their different sizes: the bigger tribes are to receive the larger inheritances. But to avoid any dissension the precise allocation was decided by lot, generally recognized as a sure way of discovering God's will (Prov. 16:33; 18:18). The use of the lot to determine the distribution of land is attested in the Near East from pre-Mosaic to modern times. The carrying out of these directions is described in Joshua 15ff.

57–62. As in 3:14ff. the census of the Levites is recorded separately, there because the Levites are engaged in religious duties not military ones, here because the Levites have no tribal territory assigned to them (62), only forty-eight villages scattered through the inheritances belonging to the secular tribes (35:1–8). In both cases the Levite census covered all males aged one month or over, whereas the other tribal lists began with men aged twenty years (26:62; cf. 3:15). During the wilderness wanderings the number of Levites increased from 22,000 to 23,000 (3:39; 26:62).

63–65. From Sinai to the plains of Moab there had been a complete turnover in population; only Caleb and Joshua survived of the previous generation (65). Under the latter this new people of God would enter their inheritance.

Through the ministry of a greater Joshua (Jesus is Greek for Joshua), the people of God in every generation are invited to enter into God's rest (Heb. 4:1–13).

D. Laws about land, offerings and vows (chapters 27 – 30)

i. The daughters of Zelophehad (27:1–11). Chapter 27 tells of further preparations for the entry to Canaan. First of all a problem raised by the daughters of Zelophehad is discussed. Zelophehad's name will be forgotten if his daughters do not receive an inheritance in the land. What should be done about it? Since Zelophehad's case was far from unique, God's decision set important precedents for the whole settlement programme and it is recorded here. Yet more crucial for the future of the nation was the leadership question: who was to succeed Moses and bring Israel into the promised land, since his disobedience at Meribah-kadesh had barred him from this honour?

The second half of the chapter tells how Joshua was publicly appointed Moses' successor. Both these topics are adumbrated in the preceding chapter (cf. 26:33, 64–65).

From a legal point of view the case of the daughters of Zelophehad is extremely interesting. It shows how many of the laws in the Bible came to be enacted. When a problem arose without previous precedent, it was referred to Moses, who then sought the LORD's direction. The decision then became a precedent for future similar cases (cf. 15:32–36; Lev. 24:10–23). It seems likely that many of the case laws in the Old Testament originated in a similar way.

The case is also interesting for the light it sheds on the rules of inheritance in biblical times. It shows that in Hebrew law, as in Mesopotamian law, daughters did not usually have a share in the family estate.[32] A father's property was divided between his sons after his death, the eldest son receiving twice as much as his brothers (Deut. 21:15–17). Daughters were treated quite differently: they received a very substantial wedding present from their fathers, called a dowry. Typically this consisted of clothes, jewellery, money and furniture, but richer fathers gave their daughters slave-girls, land or even cities (Gen. 29:24, 29; Judg. 1:13–15 ; 1 Kgs 9:16). Having married off his daughter and given her a dowry, a father had no further financial responsibility for her. She became a member of her husband's family and her sons inherited his estate. By this patrilineal system land was kept within the family, a fundamental principle of biblical law, which also underlies the jubilee legislation in Leviticus 25 (cf. 1 Kgs 21:3).

However, Zelophehad had no sons, and therefore under traditional law his inheritance would on his death be transferred to his nearest male relative. By that means the land would be kept within the family. The surviving male relatives are listed in order of closeness in verses 9–10, brothers, uncles, others. The same order is found in Leviticus 25:48–49. His daughters challenged this accepted practice pleading that it would lead to their father's name being forgotten (4). Their plea was accepted: if a man has no son, but only daughters, they may inherit from him. In other cases the traditional

32. For fuller discussion, see Z. Ben-Barak, 'Inheritance by Daughters in the Ancient Near East', *JSS*, 25, 1980, pp. 22–33.

rules apply (verses 8–11). Allowing daughters to inherit, where there were no sons in a family, created another problem though. When they married, they would take the family land with them, thus destroying their father's estate. To deal with this, chapter 36 brings in additional rules governing the marriage of heiresses.

3. Though Korah's rebellion was mentioned in the previous chapter (26:9–11), it is not immediately apparent why Zelophehad's daughters mention it here. Most probably it indicates that those found guilty of serious religious offences were not only put to death but that their property was confiscated as well.[33] It was on this basis that Jezebel trumped up a charge of blasphemy against Naboth to obtain possession of his vineyard (1 Kgs 21:7ff.; cf. Dan. 3:29).

For his own sin. Probably this refers to the sin of the whole nation in refusing to enter the promised land and therefore sentenced to die in the wilderness. Zelophehad is acknowledged as at least tacitly having supported the sceptical spies (chs. 13 – 14; cf. 26:64–65).

The strangest aspect of this law is its timing. Why should these women have been worrying about inheritances when as yet none of the promised land had been conquered? Their problem was a hypothetical one. The usual critical view is that the story represents a reading back of a post-settlement problem into pre-conquest times. The ascription of the decision to God, mediated by Moses, gave the legal innovation greater authority. Though such an explanation is possible, it overlooks the fact that half of the tribe of Manasseh, to which Zelophehad belonged, did settle in northern Transjordan in the territory of Sihon and Og, whose defeat is recorded in chapter 21. Though the tribes of Reuben, Gad and Manasseh make the proposal that they should settle in Transjordan only in chapter 32, this episode suggests that the womenfolk at any rate were already thinking along these lines. Alternatively Calvin's suggestion[34] has much to commend it: the request of Zelophehad's daughters showed their faith in the divine promises. Moses arranged another census to make sure the as-yet-unconquered land would be divided equitably among the tribes. They respond by requesting a

---

33. So J. Weingreen, *VT*, 16, 1966, pp. 521–522; de Vaulx, pp. 319–320.
34. Calvin, IV, p. 256.

portion in that land, thereby demonstrating that they have no truck with the unbelief that damned their father's generation. Because of their piety their action is recorded for posterity (cf. Matt. 26:6–13).

ii. Joshua appointed to succeed Moses (27:12–23). In the gospels our Lord's predictions about his death form a sombre background to the growing success of his mission. In Numbers there is a similar interplay between the promise of the land and the warning that Moses will never enter it. The closer Israel comes to Canaan, the nearer draws the death of their founding father.

12–15. His sister, Miriam, and his brother, Aaron, have already been gathered to their people (13; cf. 20:1–29); now Moses is advised that his time has come (12). He is to *go up into this mountain of Abarim* (Deut. 34:1 is more specific, Mount Nebo), *and see the land which I have given to the people of Israel* (12). Lest this should awaken fresh hope that he might enter Canaan after all, Moses is reminded of his sin at Meribah-kadesh (14; cf. 20:2–13).

16–17. Moses therefore prays that God will be merciful to his people and provide for their future well-being by appointing someone to lead them in battle (cf. Josh. 14:11; 1 Sam. 18:13, 16, etc.) *God of the spirits of all flesh.* The only other passage where this phrase is used is 16:22, where Moses pleads that the whole nation should not suffer for Korah's sin. God, as the giver of all life, must be specially concerned with the continued existence of his chosen people, Israel. *Sheep which have no shepherd* (cf. 1 Kgs 22:17; Ezek. 34:5; Matt. 9:36). Kings and other leaders are often likened to shepherds in the prophets and in other oriental texts (e.g. Isa. 40:11; 44:28; Ezek. 34).

18–23. Joshua is therefore commissioned as Moses' successor. He was ideally suited to the job, having been for many years Moses' assistant (11:28; Exod. 17:9ff.; 24:13; 32:17) and one of the spies who had actually visited Canaan (13:8; 14:6). But the narrative makes clear that his leadership will not be of the same type as that of Moses: *You shall invest him with some of your authority* (20). Whereas God spoke to Moses face to face (12:6–8), Joshua will be instructed by Eleazar the priest, who will use the Urim and Thummim, the sacred lot, to discover God's will (cf. Exod. 28:30: 1 Sam. 14:41[LXX]; 28:6). Thus the days of Moses are quite different from the succeeding period. Then God's will was made known directly through Moses, a prophetic mediator; later generations had to rely on the priests, the authoritative teachers of the law (Lev. 10:10–11). When guidance was required on political or military questions not covered by the law, the priests could use the Urim and Thummim as a sort of oracle.

Despite the difference in authority between Moses and Joshua, there was a real continuity between them expressed symbolically by the laying on of Moses' hands (18, 23). In this symbolic gesture Joshua was identified with Moses and made his representative for the future. Through the imposition of hands either blessings or sins were transferred, and the one on whom hands were laid became the substitute or representative of the other man. Thus Jacob placed his hands on his grandsons' heads to bless them (Gen. 48:14); the people placed their hands on the blasphemer's head to transfer their guilt incurred through hearing blasphemy to the blasphemer (Lev. 24:14); and all worshippers placed a hand on the head of the sacrificial animal to indicate it was taking their place in dying for their sin (Lev. 1:4, etc.). But the closest parallel to the imposition of hands on Joshua is the ordination of the Levites (8:10ff.), when the Israelites appointed them as their substitutes in place of their first-born children. Laying on of hands continued in New Testament times to ordain people to church offices (Acts 6:6; 13:3; 1 Tim. 4:14; Heb. 6:2).

Joshua's appointment as Moses' successor was, as it were, publicly announced by the laying on of his hands. It was later confirmed by God himself appearing in the pillar of cloud in the court of the tabernacle (Deut. 31:14–15, 23). Further revelations to Joshua followed the death of Moses (Josh. 1:1–9; 5:13–15), but we are told that it was the crossing of the Jordan that really convinced the people that Joshua was God's chosen successor to Moses (Josh. 4:14). Thus the ceremony recorded here inaugurates a co-regency, when Moses and Joshua were joint leaders of the people, a transition period that was terminated by the death of Moses on Mount Nebo, recorded in Deuteronomy 34.

iii. Calendar of public sacrifices (28:1 – 29:40). Sacrifice is the heart of biblical worship and many chapters of the Pentateuch are devoted to describing and prescribing its form and occasion. Some of the material discussed here has already been mentioned. For example, in connection with the construction of the altar of burnt offering in Exodus 29:38–41 the daily morning and evening sacrifices are mentioned. Leviticus 1 – 7 describes how the different sacrifices are to be performed. Leviticus 23 lists the different festivals, concentrating on those aspects of each festival that are of most concern to laymen, obligatory rest days, fasts, and living in booths. Numbers 15 prescribes what cereal offerings and libations should accompany animal sacrifices.

Now Numbers 28 – 29 overlaps with these earlier regulations to some extent, and it has been suggested that it is based on them.[35] But in reality the central concern of these chapters is quite different: it prescribes the type and number of sacrifices that must be offered on every day of the year by the priests for the nation as a whole. Whereas in Leviticus lay obligations are paramount, in Numbers 28 – 29 the priestly sacrificial duties are the prime concern. These chapters list the minimum number of sacrifices that can be offered in a year; sacrifices initiated by laymen due to sin, impurity, vows or any other reason are additional to those listed here (29:39).

But why should these laws about sacrifice come here? To the Western mind it would have seemed much more logical to have grouped them with other laws dealing with the festivals and sacrifices. Modern commentators have no answer to this problem, generally contenting themselves with the observation that Numbers does mix law and narrative in an incomprehensible way. Knobel[36] observed that the time was ripe for such a law to be given because Israel would soon be in a position to carry out the programme of sacrifices when they entered Canaan. Rosenmüller[37] suggested that the section is placed here because the people would soon acquire enough cattle from the Midianites to carry out these laws (ch. 31). There is probably truth in both these suggestions. I noted above that

35. The lateness of this section of Numbers is widely asserted by critical commentators. But L. R. Fisher has argued that Numbers 28 – 29 resembles a ritual calendar from Ugarit (c. 14th century BC) more closely than do other biblical texts and therefore could be early. *HTR*, 63, 1970, pp. 485–501. Cf. *Ras Shamra Parallels*, II (Pontifical Biblical Institute, 1975), pp. 143ff. B. A. Levine, *JAOS*, 85, 1965, pp. 315–318 also notes the archival character of Num. 28 – 29.

36. Quoted by Keil, p. 216.

37. Quoted by Gray, p. 403.

chapter 15, the laws about the cereal offerings and libations, was placed immediately after the spy episode as a promise that, notwithstanding the people's doubts and God's judgment, they would eventually inherit the land flowing with milk and honey. Here again the giving of these laws acts as a strong reaffirmation of the promise to Joshua and the rest of the people. Every year in future the priests will have to sacrifice 113 bulls, 32 rams and 1086 lambs and offer more than a ton of flour and a thousand bottles of oil and wine.[38] Clearly Israel is destined to be a prosperous agricultural community. These laws about sacrifices then contribute to the note of triumph that grows ever louder as the border of Canaan is reached. And like the other narratives and laws that fall in the closing chapters of Numbers, they serve to make Israel's experiences in the plains of Moab comparable with Sinai, for most of Israel's other laws on sacrifice were revealed there (cf. 28:6).

The sacrifices are arranged according to their frequency: first come the daily burnt offerings (28:2–8); second, the weekly sabbath offering (28:9–10); third, the monthly offerings (28:11–15); finally, the once-yearly offerings arranged in chronological sequence (28:16 – 29:38).

It should be noted that these figures are cumulative. Thus on the sabbath, both the daily sacrifice of two lambs and the sabbath sacrifice of two lambs were offered (28:10). On the first day of the seventh month, the daily sacrifice of two lambs, the usual first-day sacrifice of two bulls, one ram, seven lambs, and the special first-of-the-seventh-month sacrifice of one bull, one ram and seven lambs were offered. I have put these cumulative totals in brackets. Every burnt offering had to be accompanied by the appropriate cereal and libation offerings: a bull by a cereal offering made with three-tenths of an ephah of flour and ½ hin of oil, a ram by one made of two-tenths of an ephah of flour and a third hin of oil, a

---

38. The number of animals is specified in Num. 28 – 29. For the calculation, see A. F. Rainey, *Biblica*, 51, 1970, p. 492. I have calculated the volume of cereal offerings and libations on the basis of the tariff in Num. 15. The volume of flour is 149 ephahs, of oil 339 hins, of wine 339 hins. On the volume of the ephah and hin, see de Vaux, *Ancient Israel*, p. 202.

Occasion	Burnt offering			Sin offering
	Bulls	Rams	Lambs	Goat
Every day (28:3–8)	—	—	2	—
Sabbath (28:9–10)	—	—	2(4)	—
1st of month (28:11–15)	2	1	7 (9)	1
Unleavened bread, i.e. 15–21 of 1st month (28:17–25)	2	1	7 (9)	1
Pentecost: Feast of Weeks (28:26–31)	2	1	7 (9)	1
1st of 7th month (29:1–6)	1 (3)	1 (2)	7 (16)	1
Day of Atonement (29:7–11)	1	1	7 (9)	1 (2)
Tabernacles 1st day	13	2	14 (16)	1
(29:12–38) 2nd day	12	2	14 (16)	1
3rd day	11	2	14 (16)	1
4th day	10	2	14 (16)	1
5th day	9	2	14 (16)	1
6th day	8	2	14 (16)	1
7th day	7	2	14 (16)	1
8th day	1	1	7 (9)	1

lamb by one-tenth ephah of flour and ¼ hin of oil. The corresponding drink offerings of wine were a half, a third and a quarter hin (28:12–14; cf. 15:4–10).

The daily sacrifices consisted of two burnt offerings: *one lamb … in the morning, the other lamb … in the evening* (4, 8). This last phrase, *in the evening*, literally 'between the evenings', is used for the time when the passover lambs had to be slain (cf. 9:3; Lev. 23:5) and probably means late afternoon. On sabbaths and festivals, when additional sacrifices were appointed, they were offered in the time between the regular morning and evening sacrifices. 28:23 suggests they were presented immediately after the morning sacrifice. A sin offering of a goat was required on all festivals apart from the sabbath, and this would probably have been offered before the additional burnt offerings (cf. 6:16; Lev. 9; 16, etc.). Numbers 28 – 29 is concerned with the quantity of the sacrifices, not their timing.[39]

Within this scheme of sacrifices the number seven is very prominent. Not just in the number of lambs[40] (7 or 14) each day of the festivals, but in the duration of the great festivals of unleavened bread and tabernacles. Over and above the weekly sabbath, there are seven additional days in the year on which work is not permitted (28:18, 25, 26; 29:1, 7, 12, 35). Just as the seventh day of the week is hallowed by rest and worship, so is the seventh month of the year by three very important festivals. It begins with a holy convocation on the 1st day (nowadays the Jewish new year, *Rosh hashana*, lasts two days). The day of atonement, when fasting and other penitential exercises were obligatory (29:7, cf. Lev. 16:29–31), falls on the 10th day. Finally, the greatest of the festivals, the feast of tabernacles, lasts from the 15th to the 22nd of the month (cf. Lev. 23:39–43). Socially and spiritually the seventh month (September–October) is the most appropriate season for a long break. By then all the harvests should be complete and the people begin to hope that the long rainless summer (April to October) will soon end. Unless the rain arrived promptly the following year's crops would be poor. In this situation the Israelite farmer had time for spiritual concerns. On the first day of the month and particularly on the day of atonement, he was encouraged to review his past and repent of all those sins that might impede God's future blessing. Then at the feast of tabernacles they compared their present prosperity to the nation's former plight: for a whole week they lived in booths as a reminder of what it had been like living in tents in the wilderness (Lev. 23:39–43). The lavish sacrifices offered by the priests during this week expressed the nation's gratitude for the gift of the land and for the harvest just completed. It was probably at this period that many families went to

---

39. Cf. A. F. Rainey, 'The Order of Sacrifice in OT Ritual Texts', *Biblica*, 51, 1970, pp. 485–498; B. A. Levine, 'The Descriptive Tabernacle Texts of the Pentateuch', *JAOS*, 85, 1965, pp. 307–318.

40. The total of bulls offered on days 1–7 of the feast of the tabernacles is 70.

the national shrine to offer their personal gifts and make vows to
God (cf. 1 Sam. 1).

But the idea of giving the seventh time-period to God is not ex-
hausted by the celebrations of the seventh month. The seventh year
was a sabbatical year, in which the land was left untilled, slaves released and debts remitted (Exod. 23:10–11; Deut. 15:1–18). And in
the fiftieth year (50 = 7 × 7 + 1), the year of jubilee, land that had
been sold in the previous forty-nine years reverted to its original
owners (Lev. 25). These recurrent celebrations of the seventh helped
to underline the importance of the sabbath and Israel's status as
the holy covenant people of God, of which the sabbath was an important sign (Exod. 31:13–17). The weekly sabbath being so frequent could be taken for granted, but the sabbatical month and
years broke the routine and kept them aware of the symbolism
involved.

28:1–8. The daily sacrifices. The New Testament views all the
old covenant sacrifices as types of the death of Christ. The different sacrifices bring out different aspects of the significance of his
death. Lambs sacrificed every morning and evening were the
most typical victim, so Jesus is called 'the Lamb of God, who takes
away the sin of the world' (John 1:29). Indeed he died at the time of
the evening sacrifice. His death made animal sacrifice obsolete,
and in fact temple sacrifices ceased just forty years later when the
temple fell in AD 70. But Jewish and Christian commentators
have always regarded the daily burnt offerings as a model of worship for all time. Prayer should be offered at least every morning and
evening: indeed, the whole of life is to be dedicated to God through
repeated acts of praise and thanksgiving (cf. Rom. 12:1; 1 Thess.
5:16–18).

Offerings by fire (2; NEB, TEV, 'food-offerings'). The term refers to
sacrifices burnt on the altar, the priestly portions (Lev. 2:3) and the
shewbread (Lev. 24:7). But the etymology and precise meaning of
'iššeh are uncertain.[41] That the term seems to be explained here and
in Leviticus 3:11, 16 by the common word for 'bread' or *food (leḥem)*,
suggests that food-offering may be the best translation. That the

41. Wenham, p. 56.

sacrifices all consisted of choice food items does not mean the Israelites thought God literally needed feeding. Rather sacrifice was an
acknowledgment that all life came from God and belonged to him
(Ps. 50:8–15).

My pleasing (NEB 'soothing') *odour* (2). Basic to the whole sacrificial
scheme is the concept of atonement. Sacrifices appease the wrath
of God provoked by human sin (Gen. 8:21; cf. 6:5–7). But only
animals *without blemish* were good enough for this purpose (3; cf. Lev.
22:18–22; Mal. 1:13–14).

Continual burnt offering (3, 6), *cereal offering* (5, 8), *drink offering*
(7, 8), see Additional note on Old Testament sacrifice (p. 226).

9–10. The sabbath sacrifices. The layman hallowed the sabbath
day (Saturday) by resting from his normal work, thereby imitating his
creator and recalling his redemption (Exod. 20:8–11; Deut. 5:12–15).
The priests marked the sabbath by offering two extra lambs as a
burnt offering after the usual morning sacrifice. The church has likewise celebrated its redemption by joining together once a week to eat
the Lord's Supper (Acts 20:7; 1 Cor. 16:2).

11–15. The new moon sacrifices. The importance of the new
moon festival is shown by the number of extra sacrifices required,
as many as at the festivals of unleavened bread and weeks (18–31),
and by its frequent mention elsewhere in the Old Testament. It was
an opportunity for family worship (1 Sam. 20:5–6; 2 Kgs 4:23) and
all trading ceased (Amos 8:5). Like the other Old Testament festivals
it prefigured the new age inaugurated by Christ (Col. 2:16–17; cf. Isa.
66:23). *Sin offering* (15). See Additional note on Old Testament sacrifice (p. 226).

16–25. The festival of unleavened bread, the first of the great
national festivals, fell in the first month of the year, Nisan
(March/April). Immediately following passover, it commemorated
the exodus from Egypt (Exod. 12 – 13). As usual in Numbers 28 –
29 the main focus of interest is on the priests' obligations: the days
of rest and convocation, a national gathering for worship, are but
mentioned in passing, and the passover lambs eaten by every Israelite
family are not mentioned at all.

Jesus died at passover time and usually the feasts of passover and
unleavened bread overlap with Holy Week and Easter. The New
Testament makes full use of the passover imagery to explain the

significance of our Lord's death. He called it his exodus that he was to accomplish at Jerusalem (Luke 9:31). John points out that, like the passover lamb, none of his bones was broken (John 19:36), while Paul says Christians must be as ruthless in expelling sin from their lives as the Jews are in throwing out leaven prior to passover (1 Cor. 5:7–8).

26–31. The second national feast, the *feast of weeks*, also called here *the day of the first fruits*, celebrated the conclusion of the barley harvest (cf. Exod. 23:16; Lev. 23:15–21; Deut. 16:9–12). Being seven weeks (50 days) after the feast of unleavened bread, it was called Pentecost in Greek and corresponds to Whitsun (Acts 2:1). The same number of sacrifices was required as at new moons and on the days of unleavened bread.[42]

29:1–39. The seventh month. Besides the usual additional sacrifices for a new moon, extra burnt offerings were required on the first day of the seventh month to mark the holy character of this month. The trumpet was also blown, and still is during synagogue worship on this day (29:1; cf. Lev. 23:24–25).

The first ten days of the seventh month are a penitential season that culminate in the day of atonement, whose distinctive ceremonies are more fully described in Leviticus 16 and 23:26–32. Here the quantity of extra sacrifices is again the chief concern (7–11).

During the feast of tabernacles more bulls and rams, the most valuable sacrificial animals, were sacrificed than in the whole of the rest of the year. In this way the priests expressed liturgically the joy of the whole nation for all God's mercies both spiritual and temporal (12–38; cf. Deut. 16:13–15). For a description of their dwelling in booths see Leviticus 23:39–43; Nehemiah 8:13–18. Solomon dedicated the temple in the seventh month at this feast with a vast number of sacrifices (1 Kgs 8; cf. 2 Chr. 5 – 7).

---

42. Lev. 23:16–19 mentions various other sacrifices that were required, and reverses the numbers of rams and bulls for the burnt offering (cf. 23:18 with Num. 28:27).

Additional note on Old Testament sacrifice

If ritual is the key to understanding a society's deepest values,[43] then the sacrifices of the Old Testament are of prime importance in any evaluation of biblical religion. Their cost and frequency demonstrate that in the sacrificial system we are at the very heart of ancient Israel's system of social and religious beliefs. Yet paradoxically, because sacrifice was basic to their world-view, it is the more difficult for us to interpret. For them its significance was so self-evident, that the meaning of the rites did not need to be explained; consequently few texts give us anything more than hints as to the meaning of sacrifice. The rituals of the different types of animal sacrifice are fully described in the Old Testament and though the occasions for the different rituals are also specified, the exact theological difference between them, why one should be offered on one occasion rather than another, is somewhat uncertain. In this brief note[44] I shall try to sum up the basic features of Old Testament sacrifice, its characteristic rituals, the occasions for its use, and its religious significance.

a. Animal sacrifice

1. The rites. Four main types of sacrifice are described in Leviticus 1 – 7, the burnt offering, the sin offering, the guilt offering and the peace offering. They are distinguished by the type of animal offered and, more important, by the different rituals employed.

However, there was a common core to all these rites. The worshipper brought the animal to the tabernacle, laid his hand on its head, killed it, skinned it and chopped it up. The priest sprinkled the blood over the altar, and then burnt part of the animal on the altar.

The differences between the rites concerned the disposal of the flesh, how much could be eaten by the priests and how much by the worshipper and his family, and in the handling of the blood. With the burnt offering the whole beast was burnt and no-one had any flesh to eat. With the sin and guilt offerings some of the flesh was

---

43. Cf. the discussion of ritual in chapter 5, pp. 93ff. and in Introduction, 6, pp. 30ff.
44. For a fuller discussion see Wenham, pp. 47ff.

burnt and some was eaten by the priests. However, in the case of the peace offering some of the flesh was burnt, some eaten by the priests, and some by the worshipper. The sin offering was distinguished from the guilt offering in the disposal of the blood. Some of the sin-offering blood was smeared on the altar or other parts of the tabernacle, whereas the blood of the guilt offering was poured out at the foot of the altar in the normal way.

2. *The occasions.* The burnt offering was the commonest sacrifice both in the official worship of the tabernacle and temple (see Num. 28 – 29) and in acts of private devotion offered by individuals. Though it could be offered by itself (Judg. 11:31), it seems more usually to have accompanied other sacrifices such as the sin offering (Lev. 5:7; 12:8) or the guilt offering (Lev. 14:21–31; Num. 6:11–12).

The sin offering was a regular, though less important, ingredient of regular worship (see Num. 28 – 29). It could also be offered by individuals after they had recovered from some long-term uncleanness (e.g. Lev. 5:2ff.; 15).

The guilt offering was not part of the normal round of official sacrifices. It was reserved for serious sins, such as sacrilege, the abuse of oaths, adultery with a slave girl, or breach of the Nazirite vow (Lev. 5:14 – 6:7; 19:20–22; Num. 6:9–12). Former 'lepers'[45] also had to offer a guilt offering, probably because their affliction was suspected of being the result of serious sin (Lev. 14:12; cf. 2 Kgs 5:27; 2 Chr. 26:19–20).

The only festival for which the peace offering is specifically prescribed is the feast of weeks (Pentecost) (Lev. 23:19), though the passover lambs may be classed as a sort of peace offering. However, at great events like the ratification of the covenant and the dedication of the tabernacle and temple, peace offerings were offered in great numbers (Exod. 24:5; Num. 7; 1 Kgs 8:63). Since peace offerings were the only type of sacrifice in which the layman had a share of the meat, it made these occasions very festive and joyful. Individuals could also offer peace offerings whenever they liked: these were called freewill offerings (according to Lev. 17, anyone who wanted to eat meat had to offer the animal as a peace offering. Deut.

---

45. On this term see above on 5:2, p. 87.

12:15ff. relaxes this rule for those who lived far from the altar). Peace offerings were also expected when one made or completed a vow (Lev. 8:22; 9:22; Num. 6:14; 1 Sam. 1:11, 24).

3. The significance. Owing to the sparsity of data the interpretation of the sacrifices remains controversial, but the following seems the most probable view. Every sacrifice began with the worshipper placing his hand on the animal's head. In this gesture he identified himself with the animal, or maybe transferred his sins to the animal. 'The plain implication is that, in some metaphysical sense, the victim is a vicarious substitution for the donor himself.'[46] Thus in giving the animal to God, the worshipper is reminded that he should die for his sins had the animal not taken his place. The animal is a ransom payment (*kōper*) which atones (*kipper*) for the worshipper's sin.

The burnt offering which is wholly consumed in the altar fire represents these truths more starkly and simply. The animal given in its totality to God pictures at once the total annihilation the sinner deserves and the total consecration God expects from his followers.

The sin offering[47] (*ḥaṭṭā't*) pictures another aspect of atonement. Sin causes uncleanness, polluting both the individual concerned and the tabernacle. By smearing the blood of the sin offering on parts of the altar and tabernacle the sanctuary is cleansed so that God can continue to dwell among his people. *Ḥaṭṭā't* can be translated 'sin' or 'purification', and it is probably the latter sense that is central in references to this sacrifice, which would, therefore, be better termed the 'purification offering'.

The guilt offering (*'āšām*) introduces another analogy for sin: it is a debt that has to be repaid. Elsewhere *'āšām* may be translated 'reparation', and the significance of this sacrifice is better brought out by the translation 'reparation offering'.

The peace offering (*šĕlamîm*) was offered when an individual was seeking, or already enjoying, peace (*šalôm*) with God. Thus it was

---

46. E. R. Leach, *Culture and Communication* (CUP, 1976), p. 89.

47. On this interpretation of the sin and guilt offerings, see J. Milgrom, *Cult and Conscience* (Brill, 1976), and 'Sacrifices and Offerings, OT', *IDBS*, pp. 763–771; Wenham, pp. 86ff.

thought particularly appropriate to offer it when one made a vow and
was seeking a blessing, or on those occasions where God's goodwill
was already obvious, e.g. at the sealing of the covenant (Exod. 24)
or the dedication of the tabernacle (Num. 7).

b. Other sacrifices

In Bible times meat was a rare luxury for the average man. His diet
was largely vegetarian (2 Sam. 12:3; Prov. 15:17). It was, therefore,
provided that in certain cases the poor could offer meal instead of
animals (Lev. 5:11–13). And whenever a man was wealthy enough to
offer animals in sacrifice, it was expected that he would offer the
staple products of the land as well, grain, oil and wine (Num. 15).
Grain and oil were the main ingredients of the cereal offering (Lev.
2). In this case only a token handful was burnt on the altar: the rest
went to the priests as part of their income. The wine is described as
a drink offering or libation, indicating that it was poured out beside
the altar like the blood of the animal. In offering these other fruits
of the earth to God, the worshipper pictured the offering of his entire life to his creator. For just as sacrificial animals symbolized
Israel's holy men, the priests (cf. Lev. 21:17–23; 22:19–24), so in other
passages loaves of bread represent the twelve tribes (Lev. 24:5–8; see
comment on Num. 8:3) and the vine stands for Israel (Isa. 5:7).

   iv. **Waiving vows (30:1–16 [Hebrew 2 – 17]).** In times of crisis men turn to God in prayer. And their prayers often take the form
of vows: 'If God helps me now, I shall go on pilgrimage, go to
church, etc.' Many examples are found in the Scriptures (e.g. Gen.
28:20–22; Num. 21:2; Judg. 11:30ff.; 1 Sam. 1:11; 14:24; Jon. 1:16; 2:9;
Acts 18:18; 21:23; 23:12ff.). But when the crisis passes and the
prayer is answered, there is a temptation to forget the vow. Ecclesi-
astes warns: 'When you vow a vow to God, do not delay paying it;
for he has no pleasure in fools. Pay what you vow' (5:4; cf. Deut.
23:21–23). This principle, that vows ought to be kept, is fundamental to the laws in the Pentateuch. Vows either took the form of a
promise to give something to God, usually a sacrifice, or a pledge to
abstain from something. But sometimes the vows could not be literally fulfilled: a layman might vow himself to serve God full time,
but only members of the tribe of Levi could do this. Leviticus 27
deals with vows that for one reason or another are unfulfillable and

prescribes what the votary must do instead. Here another problem
is discussed. What should be done if a woman's father or husband
takes exception to her vow? The law states that if they object to a
woman's vow as soon as they hear of it, the woman is released from
her vow without penalty (5, 8, 12), but that if the woman's husband
at first raises no objection and then later protests about it, he, not the
woman, will pay the penalty (15).

Various possible combinations of circumstances are described to
illustrate these principles. They are arranged in two groups of three
cases in a scheme typical of biblical law (cf. Lev. 1 – 7; 13 – 14; Deut.
22:13–29).

2	Men's vows unbreakable	9	Widows' and divorcees' vows unbreakable
3–5	Girl's vows voidable by father	10–12	Wives' vows voidable by husband without penalty
6–8	Girls' vows voidable by fiancé	13–15	Wives' vows voidable with penalty

The second and third laws in each group both fall into two parts,
considering first the case when the woman's husband or father says
nothing, thereby confirming her vow, and second the situation
where he annuls it by objecting to it. Although this looks at first sight
like a comprehensive discussion of the topic, there are certain obvious omissions. For instance, vows by sons bound by parental authority are not discussed, nor those of unmarried older women. Such
omissions are typical of ancient oriental law: the biblical documents
are not comprehensive codes but collections of interesting and important cases.

Finally, one should ask why this group of laws is placed here. The
only answer offered by the few commentators who consider the
question is that vows are a type of offering, the subject-matter of
chapters 28 – 29. This may be so, but the offerings just discussed are
official priestly ones, whereas anyone can make vows. It would
seem to me that there may be other reasons for the insertion of the
laws on vows at this point. First, vows were usually sealed with a

sacrifice; and when the prayer was answered, another sacrifice would
be offered (e.g. Lev. 7:16; Ps. 50:14). This would require the worshipper to go to the sanctuary, and the most convenient time to do
that would be during the annual pilgrimage feasts, the subject of chs.
28 − 29 (cf. 1 Sam. 1). Second, vows were frequent during war
(Num. 21:2; Judg. 11:30–31; 21:1–7), and Israel was about to engage
in a long campaign of conquest (cf. chs. 21, 31 − 32, etc.). During this
war the wives of the Transjordanian warriors would be left on their
own, so the question of vows made in their husbands' absence
might arise (32:26). Third, vows are discussed in the Sinaitic legislation (Lev. 27; Num. 6); the inclusion of the subject here emphasizes
again the parallel between the first law-giving in the wilderness of
Sinai and the second in the plains of Moab. There may be yet a
fourth reason for the inclusion of the law here. Israel had made a
vow that they would annihilate the Canaanites (21:2). The covenant
relationship between God and Israel is likened to that between father and child, or husband and wife (11:12; 25:1ff.). Could it be that
the LORD's silence concerning this vow is understood as confirmation of the programme of conquest?

1–2. The general principle is stated first: men's vows must be kept
(cf. Deut. 23:21–23; Eccl. 5:4–6). Problem cases, such as boys' vows
objected to by parents, or vows that cannot be fulfilled, are not discussed here. The law mentions two kinds of vow: *vows* (*neder*) and
pledges (*'issār*). The former term is the more common, and here at least
means a vow to do something positive such as offering a sacrifice,
whereas *'issār* (used only in this chapter)[48] is a vow of abstinence, a
self-imposed fast (cf. 1 Sam. 14:24; Ps. 132:2–5). The Nazirite vow
is generally supposed to be an example of a pledge of abstinence
(Num. 6), though *neder* is the word used there. But it may simply be
that outside this chapter *neder* covers both positive and negative vows.

3–5. The law now deals with its prime concern: under what circumstances are vows of women valid? The first case concerns
young unmarried girls living at home. They are subject to their
father's authority. If he hears about the vow and says nothing, it is
binding. If he objects or discourages (32:7, 9) her, the vow must not

---

48. RSV translates the cognate Aramaic word *'ĕsār*, 'interdict' in Dan. 6:7–13.

be carried out. *And the LORD will forgive her*, because her *father opposed her* (5). Not to fulfil a vow without such constraint is sin (Deut. 23:21), but the law puts obedience to parents above voluntarily undertaken religious obligations (cf. Mark 7:10–13). In most cases the girls concerned would be quite young, as they generally married in their early teens.

6–8. On marriage a woman passed from her father's control to her husband's. The second case deals with the situation of a girl who made a vow while in her father's house and then married. If her new husband learns of the vow and says nothing, it stands; but if he objects immediately, it is nullified. Only TEV brings out the sense of the Hebrew clearly, 'If an unmarried woman makes a vow … and then marries'. The RSV and NEB confuse this case with those considered in verses 10ff., vows made by married women after marriage.

9. If a woman was widowed or divorced, she would usually return to her father's home, if he were still alive (Lev. 22:13), or be cared for by one of her sons. But in this situation her vows could not be annulled by her son or father.

10–16. Vows entered into by married women after their marriage are the topic of this paragraph. Husbands can veto their wives' vows, as long as they do so immediately they hear about them. But silence indicates consent (10–12). If the husband says nothing for a long time *from day to day*, he has thereby established his wife's vows (14). If he then changes his mind after a period of tacit consent, *after he has heard of them* (15), he (not his wife) *shall bear her iniquity*. In other words, his initial silent approval makes him responsible if he later forces his wife to break her vow. *He shall bear her iniquity* means he will suffer for the broken vow as though it were his (cf. 5:31; Lev. 7:18). To make atonement he would have to offer a sin offering (Lev. 5:4).

The clear implication of these laws about married women's vows is that a wife's duty to submit to her husband is comparable to the child's duty to obey his parents (cf. 3–5). Neither wives nor children may substitute self-imposed religious obligations for God-given duties.

The New Testament church certainly kept up the practice of vows and fasts (Matt. 6:16; Mark 2:20; Acts 13:2; 18:18; 21:23). But Jesus was very caustic about those who used vows to evade their responsibility to their parents (Matt. 15:3–9). The New Testament also expects wives to submit to their husbands (Eph. 5:24; 1 Pet. 3:1–7), but insists that vows of abstinence require mutual consent. In other words, a wife must give way to her husband's desires as well as he to hers (1 Cor. 7:4–5). This is of a piece with the rest of the New Testament teaching on marriage, which introduces full reciprocity between the sexes, as far as rights and obligations of the married couple are concerned,[49] while reasserting the husband's headship of the family.

E. Defeat of Midian and settlement in Transjordan (chapters 31 – 32)

i. Revenge on Midian (31:1–54). This account of a short but fierce campaign against the Midianites is adjudged to be an unhistorical midrash by some commentators: that is, it is a story made up to illustrate the principles of sharing the spoils of victory with the priests and Levites (verses 25–54). In support of this conclusion it is pointed out that not all the Midianites were destroyed in this battle (cf. Judg. 6 – 8), that the date and site of the battle are unrecorded, and that it is improbable that Israel should have inflicted such a defeat without losing a single man.

None of these arguments is conclusive though. The Midianites were a large confederation of tribes, associated with various smaller groups such as the Ishmaelites (Gen. 37:28; Judg. 8:22, 24), the Moabites (Num. 22:4, 7), the Amalekites (Judg. 6:3, 33), and Ephah (Gen. 25:4; Isa. 60:6). They roamed through the arid lands of Sinai, the Negeb and Transjordan. Here it is those Midianites associated with Moab that are picked out for vengeance (8, 16; cf. chapters 22 and 25), not the whole group. The date and site of the battle are fixed with as much precision as most of the other

---

49. The Old Testament allows more latitude to husbands than it does to wives with regard both to polygamy and adultery. The New Testament insists that the man must be faithful to one wife (Luke 16:18, etc.). For fuller discussion see my article, 'May Divorced Christians Remarry?', *Churchman*, 95, 1981, pp. 150–161.

battles described in Numbers (cf. 14:42ff.; 21:1ff., 21ff.). It evidently
took place in the plains of Moab shortly before Moses' death (1, 12).
Finally, there are both biblical and extrabiblical[50] parallels to
battles where the victors suffered negligible loss (1 Sam. 14:6ff.;
Judg. 7).

The number of captured women and animals does seem im-
probably high. A solution may be sought along the lines suggested
earlier for the census lists (see Additional note on the large numbers,
p. 68).

In favour of the antiquity of these traditions may be mentioned
the list[51] of Midianite kings named in verse 8, the annalistic form[52]
of the booty lists in verses 32–46, and the general similarity of the
account of the battle to the wars described in Judges and 1 Samuel.

Nevertheless it is right to say that the narrator is more concerned
with the aftermath of the battle than with the battle itself. The deci-
mation of the Midianites fulfilled the divine command issued in
25:16–18 and reiterated in 31:1ff. But it also looks forward to the conquest of the Canaanites, who were to be treated similarly (cf. 21:2–
4; 32), and the distribution of the spoils on this occasion between
warriors, people, priests and Levites serves as a model for the big
campaign. The percentage of booty allocated to the priests and
Levites anticipates the allocation of special cities to them in chapter 35.

1–12. The campaign is called *the LORD's vengeance on Midian* (3)
because it is seen as punishment for the Midianites' seduction of
Israel from their true husband, the LORD (cf. 25:1–13). Adultery carried the death penalty in the ancient world (e.g. Lev. 20:10; Deut.
22:22), so no doubt the near-extermination of Midian was viewed
as quite appropriate in those days. We, though, are appalled. We
should like to believe such things never happened, or if they did that

---

50. Keil, p. 230, quotes the classical authors Tacitus (*Ann.* xiii.39) and Strabo
    (xvi.1128), who mention that the Romans captured a Parthian castle
    without loss, and a battle in which 1000 Arabs fell but only 2 Romans.
51. Cf. Gray, p. 419.
52. Such lists mention the object before giving the number, e.g. sheep – 5;
    cf. B. A. Levine, *JAOS*, 85, 1965, pp. 314–315.

they were never commanded by God. Attractive as such rational-izations are, they are obviously far removed from the canonical writer's understanding of the situation, and we should, therefore, try to understand it.

A full discussion[53] is out of place here, but certain observations may mitigate our sense of shock. In the books of Exodus and Numbers Israel was several times threatened with extinction in divine judgment for her apostasy and was spared only through Moses' intercession for them (Exod. 32:9ff.; Num. 11; 14:11ff.). Moses, Aaron, Miriam and all the older generation save Joshua and Caleb were sentenced to die in the wilderness for their unbelief. Plague and fire carried off many in spectacular fashion (Exod. 32:35; Lev. 10:2; Num. 11:1; 14:37; 16:31–34, 46–49; 21:6; 25:9). The priests and Levites guarding the tabernacle were expected to slay those who encroached on it illicitly, and twice they are recorded as slaying flagrant covenant breakers (3:10, 38; 25:7–8; Exod. 32:26–28). Thus the same principles governed judgment within Israel and among the nations. All would perish for their sins, but for the grace of God (cf. Gen. 6:7ff.; Amos 1 – 2). But Israel was punished first, then it was the turn of the surrounding peoples. The New Testament endorses these principles. 'There will be tribulation and distress for every human being who does evil, the Jew first and also the Greek' (Rom. 2:9). 1 Peter 4:17–18 points out that under the new covenant the church will be punished first and afterwards unbelievers.

The participation of Phinehas, son of Eleazar the high priest (6), shows that this is a holy war. The priests' duties are described in Deuteronomy 20:2ff. The high priest stayed behind in the camp to avoid contracting any uncleanness through contact with the dead (19, cf. Lev. 21:11; 1 Sam. 4). *With the vessels of the sanctuary.* Commentators cannot decide whether this means 'with the ark' (cf. Josh. 6:6; 1 Sam. 4), or with *the trumpets of alarm* (10:1–10; Josh. 6), or 'wearing priestly garments' (*kĕlî*, 'vessel', means 'garment' in Deut. 22:5). The alternatives are not mutually exclusive.

---

53. See further J. W. Wenham, *The Goodness of God* (IVP, 1974), esp. chapter 8.

Zur (8). His daughter Cozbi had been executed by Phinehas (25:15).

The sacking of cities and the gathering of booty (10–12) was to become standard practice in the conquest of Canaan (cf. Josh. 6; 8; 10 – 11).

13–18. Sparing the women fits their lesser degree of legal responsibility set out in chapter 30, but Moses protests that in this case they are most to blame for Israel's sin[54] (16; cf. ch. 25). Therefore only the sexually inexperienced, who must be innocent of involvement in the sin of Baal-peor, are allowed to survive (cf. Judg. 21:12). They were allowed to marry the Israelite warriors, thereby being incorporated into the elect nation of Israel (18; cf. Deut. 21:10–14).

19–24. Though the Midianite war was a holy war carried out in obedience to the divine command and sanctified by the presence of the priest, those involved became unclean through killing or contact with the dead. They were, therefore, excluded from the camp until they were purified (cf. 5:1–4; 12:14–15). Purification involved sprinkling with the water of impurity (19:11–22) on the third and seventh day after contact. The booty too had to be purified. Metal objects had to be passed through fire and then sprinkled with the water of purification.[55] Other items simply had to be washed (23–24).

The regulations in verses 21–24 and the statement that all the golden objects listed in verse 50 were given to the priests *to make atonement* for the soldiers give a more nuanced picture of holy war than appears at first. All loss of human life, whether natural, wilful murder, accidental manslaughter or executions carried out in response to divine command, may defile (cf. 35:9ff.; Lev. 21:1–9; Deut. 21:1–9, 22–23; 22:8) and require cleansing. Over every war, however glorious its outcome from the victor's point of view, hangs the shadow of death. These purification rules reminded Israel that the death of one's fellow men was a catastrophic disruption of God's

---

54. *On Balaam's departure* (16, NEB). NEB ascribes a rare meaning to the common Hebrew word *dābār*, 'word', 'thing'. The translation of RSV and TEV is preferable.

55. The Hebrew of verse 23 is unclear, RSV insisting on fire and water to purify the metals is to be preferred to NEB and TEV requiring only fire.

creation, even though in some cases it was the Creator himself who demanded the execution of the sinner.

25–30. The booty is shared equally between those who fought in the battle and those who stayed behind (cf. 1 Sam. 30:24–25). The priests, however, receive one five-hundredth of the warriors' share, and the Levites one fiftieth of the congregation's share. This fits in with the 10:1 ratio of the tithes (18:26).

40. The thirty-two girls assigned to the priests either became their slaves or were employed in the sanctuary (Exod. 38:8; 1 Sam. 2:22).

50. The golden earrings collected in Gideon's war against Midian were made into an ephod (Judg. 8:24–27). But here they are used *to make atonement* (*lĕkappēr*), literally 'to pay a ransom'.[56] Ransoms (*kōper*) saved those sentenced to death from that penalty (e.g. 35:31; Exod. 21:30). What prompted their feelings of guilt is unclear. Gispen[57] suggests it was the census (49; cf. Exod. 30:11–16); de Vaulx[58] that it was their participation in the war.

ii. Gad and Reuben settle in Transjordan (32:1–42). To appreciate the significance of this episode it should be noted that Transjordan lay outside Canaan, the land promised to the fathers. Its boundaries are defined in chapter 34, where it is clear that from the sea of Galilee southwards the Jordan marks the eastern frontier of Canaan. That any Israelite tribe should consider settling outside the land promised to Abraham showed a disturbing indifference to the divine word, the word on which Israel's existence entirely depended. The nation stood poised to cross the Jordan and take up its inheritance, when suddenly three of the tribes announced their intention of opting out. It looked like the spy story (chapters 13 – 14) all over again. That time the whole nation except Caleb and Joshua had cold feet, refusing to trust in God's promises. This time the tribes of Gad, Reuben and part of Manasseh declared they were uninterested in settling in the promised land. This led to a heated exchange with Moses in which their attitude is explicitly compared to that of the

---

56. Cf. Lev. 1:4. See Wenham, pp. 27f., 59ff.

57. Gispen, II, p. 236.

58. de Vaulx, p. 359.

earlier generation (6–15), and throughout the story implicit allusions are found to the events some forty years earlier at Kadesh.[59] Gad and Reuben then proposed that their fighting men should accompany the other tribes across the Jordan and return home only when the conquest of Canaan was complete. This proposal satisfied Moses and he therefore allocated them the land they had requested (16–38).

1. Reuben, Jacob's first-born, is here mentioned before Gad in deference to his seniority (Gen. 29:32), but elsewhere in this chapter the Gadites are mentioned first, no doubt because they were the leaders in the drive to settle Transjordan (cf. Deut. 33:21).

The land of Jazer means the area surrounding Jazer (3; cf. 21:32). For a possible location of this and other towns mentioned in this chapter see map on p. 256.

Gilead designates a variety of areas in the Old Testament. Its primary meaning (as here) is the hilly district south of the Jabbok, but it may also refer to the area north of the Jabbok as well (e.g. 39–40) and sometimes it designates the whole of the Transjordanian territory held by Israel (e.g. Josh. 22:9, 13, etc.). These high lands (c. 2500 ft) overlooking the Jordan valley enjoy a good rainfall and are therefore very fertile. G. A. Smith travelling through this area in the late nineteenth century commented on the abundance of its flocks and herds. 'The scenes which throng most our memory of Eastern

---

59. Outside verses 6–15 where the parallels with Num. 13 – 14 are obvious, other terms in chapter 32 apparently alluding to the spy story include 'place' (1; cf. 14:40), 'smite' (4; cf. 14:45), 'pass over' (21, 27, 29, 30; cf. 13:32; 14:7, 41), 'little ones' (16, 17, 24, 26; cf. 14:3, 31), 'inhabitants of the land' (17; cf. 14:14), 'fortified cities' (17, 36; cf. 13:19), 'return' (18, 22; cf. 13:25; 14:36), 'drive out' (21, 39; cf. 14:12, 24), as well as more common terms such as 'land', 'congregation', etc. The pervasiveness of these allusions to the spy story in this chapter argues for its substantial unity, despite the common assertion that it contains several sources. Gray noted 'A strict analysis of the chapter between JE and P cannot be satisfactorily carried through' (p. 426). Though more recent writers continue to postulate multiple sources, they do not agree on their limits or identity and it seems preferable to assume the basic unity of 32:1–32. The closing verses of the chapter may have a different history.

Palestine are … the streams of Gilead in the heat of the day with the cattle standing in them, or the evenings when we sat at the door of our tent near the village well, and would hear the shepherd's pipe far away and the sheep and the goats, and cows with the heavy bells, would break over the edge of the hill and come down the slope to wait their turn at the troughs. Over Jordan we were never long out of the sound of the lowing of cattle or of the shepherd's pipe.'[60]

2–5. These towns are mentioned again in verses 34–38. For possible locations see map, p. 256. They fell within the territory of the Amorites, *the land which the LORD smote*, whose defeat is recorded in 21:21ff. As chapter 21 makes clear, Israel had no plans to conquer Sihon's kingdom, but because he blocked their path to the Jordan, battle was joined. Gad's request not to go on to Canaan represented a major change of policy.

6–15. Moses' condemnation of their proposal is very severe. They will make the rest of the people lose heart, just as the spies did. Last time the nations' unbelief led to the extinction of the adults in the wilderness: this time the whole people could be obliterated. This section[61] is full of references to Numbers 13 – 14.

16–19. The Gadites and Reubenites therefore modify their suggestion, so as to avoid Moses' objections. They will build *sheepfolds*, probably dry-stone walled enclosures are meant, and *cities for our little ones*. In view of the time factor, nothing very substantial can be meant by *city*. This fits in with the archaeological evidence which shows settlement in Transjordan was quite sparse in the Middle and Late Bronze Ages. At some of the sites named nothing of the period of the conquest survives, though this could suggest that they have not been correctly located. The little ones will be left behind in Transjordan, while the fighting men of these tribes *will take up arms, ready to go before the people of Israel. Ready to go* is literally 'hurrying'.[62]

---

60. G. A. Smith, *The Historical Geography of the Holy Land* (Hodder and Stoughton, 1894), pp. 523–524.

61. 7: cf. 13:2; 14:8, 34. 8: cf. 13:18, 26. 9: cf. 13:23ff. 10: cf. 14:10ff. 11ff.: cf. 14:21ff. 13: cf. 14:37ff.

62. *ḥušîm*, passive participle of *ḥûš*, 'to hurry', NEB emends the Hebrew to *ḥamūšîm*, 'armed'.

In other words they suggest that their men should head the column and bear the brunt of the attack. According to 2:16 Gad and Reuben were to be in the second group of tribes on the march. They promise not to return home until all the other tribes have occupied their inheritance.

20–32. Moses is satisfied with their offer, but reiterates the importance of supporting the national effort. The LORD will allow them to live in Gilead, if they keep their promise (22). Otherwise, *Be sure your sin will find you out* (23). This vivid personification of the way the consequences of sin catch up on the sinner has become proverbial in English. Verse 30 makes clear what will happen to the Gadites and Reubenites if they are unfaithful to their promise: they will be driven out of Gilead and forced to settle across the river in Canaan. The book of Joshua records how the Gadites and Reubenites kept their word, spear-heading the campaign in Canaan until the main opposition was subdued and the land distributed among the other tribes (Josh. 4:12f.; 22:1ff.).

33–42. This is the first mention of half the tribe of Manasseh being allocated a share of Transjordanian territory. It is therefore often surmised that the references to Manasseh are from a different source from the material about Gad and Reuben. This may be so, but when the sources are not extant, one cannot be certain. But there is no reason to suppose the references to Manasseh are late: Deuteronomy 3:13 and Joshua 13:29ff.; 17:1ff. both assume the settlement of part of Manasseh in Transjordan, and Numbers 27:1–11 has given a hint that some people in the tribe of Manasseh were already thinking about the problem of girls inheriting land. The same tribe brings up the question again in chapter 36. It could be that the representatives of Manasseh took no part in the negotiations until Moses had approved in principle a settlement in Transjordan.

According to the final distribution of the land (Josh. 13:15ff.) the tribe of Reuben occupied the land immediately east of the Dead Sea, whereas the tribe of Gad settled east of the Jordan between the Dead Sea and the Sea of Galilee. But under the temporary arrangements described here some Gadites rebuilt Dibon and Aroer, which lay in the later tribal territory of Reuben (see map) (34; cf. Josh. 13:16–17), whereas Heshbon, here occupied by Reuben, later

belonged to Gad (37; cf. Josh. 21:39). *Their names to be changed* (38) because Nebo and Baal were both pagan deities. The new names
given to these cities are not recorded, perhaps because their old
names were revived when the Moabites reconquered them (Isa.
15:2; Ezek. 25:9). For possible locations of the cities, see the map,
p. 256.

The apparently independent actions of various Manassite clans,
Machir, Jair and Nobah, resembles the struggles of the west bank
tribes to conquer the territory allotted them, as described in Judges
1. Later passages (e.g. Deut. 3:12ff.; Josh. 13:29–31) state that the half-
tribe of Manasseh was given the northern part of Gilead lying east
of the Sea of Galilee (often called Bashan). The only town mentioned here, Kenath, lies about 50 miles east.

Early Christian commentators[63] likened the tribes of Gad and
Reuben, who preferred material prosperity to living in the promised
land, to those in the gospels who gave similar excuses for ignoring
Christ's call (Luke 14:18–20; 16:10–31). Calvin[64] on the other hand
pointed to the enlargement of the Israelite territory that resulted
from their action as an example of God's providence bringing good
out of human sin.

F. List of camp sites (33:1–49)

This long section lists forty places at which Israel encamped between
their departure from Rameses in Egypt and their arrival in the
plains of Moab. The first part (3–18) not only lists the camps but also
mentions the most important events that occurred at some of them.
It could be described as a summary of the geographical material
from Exodus 12 to Numbers 12. The central section (18–36) simply lists the camp sites and finds no parallel in Numbers, though
verses 31–33 do appear to find an echo in Deuteronomy 10:6–7. The
final part of the list (37–49), like the first, contains historical rem-
iniscence as well as place-names. It parallels the geographical material in Numbers 20 – 22, but not all the place-names are identical.

---

63. de Vaulx, p. 371.
64. Calvin, IV, p. 286.

As can be seen, the list raises a number of tricky geographical and critical questions. These are discussed more fully in the Additional note.

Here we must ask what is the theological purpose of the passage, why it should be inserted at this point in Numbers, and why these particular stops should be mentioned. It leaves out a number of places mentioned elsewhere, e.g. Taberah (11:3), Mattanah, Nahaliel and Bamoth (21:19) and inserts many others mentioned nowhere else (13, 19–29).

Since Moses' great achievements took place at the stations mentioned, this list serves as a sort of obituary for him, and this is an appropriate place in Numbers to insert an obituary. But there is more to the list than this: it summarizes the main themes of the books of Exodus and Numbers. It reminds the reader of the great obstacles that the nation has overcome in escaping from Egypt and crossing the Sinai desert. If God has helped Israel thus far, then he will surely enable them to reach their goal, the land of Canaan. This glance back at history is, therefore, a fitting prelude to the last group of laws in the book (33:50 – 36:13) which deal explicitly with the land. God's past dealings with Israel are a guarantee that they will soon be in a position to implement these laws in the land promised to the patriarchs.

But why should these places be listed, when all that is known about the majority of them is their name? It cannot be that the forty intermediate stations were thought to correspond to the forty years of wanderings, as Exodus is perfectly clear that the first twelve stations to Sinai were covered in about two months. Patristic commentators[65] pointed out that our Lord's genealogy in Matthew consists of $3 \times 14 = 42$ generations, and that here we have a list of 42 stations. But this observation by itself hardly sheds light on the intention of this chapter. It does raise the question whether the number of stopping-places is coincidental.

If these are set out in six columns some interesting features emerge:

---

65. Origen, Ambrose and Jerome, according to de Vaulx, p. 381.

1	Rameses	8	Wilderness of Sin	15	Rithmah
2	Succoth	9	Dophkah	16	Rimmon-perez
3	Etham	10	Alush	17	Libnah
4	Pihahiroth	11	Rephidim	18	Rissah
5	Marah	12	Wilderness of Sinai	19	Kehelathah
6	Elim	13	Kibroth-hattaavah	20	Mount Stepher
7	Red Sea	14	Hazeroth	21	Haradah

22	Makheloth	29	Hor-haggidgad	36	Punon
23	Tahath	30	Jotbathah	37	Oboth
24	Terah	31	Abronah	38	Iyim
25	Mithkah	32	Ezion-geber	39	Dibon-gad
26	Hashmonah	33	Kadesh	40	Almon-diblathaim
27	Moseroth	34	Mount Hor	41	Mountains of Abarim
28	Bene-jaakan	35	Zalmonah	42	Plains of Moab

When the events noted elsewhere in the Pentateuch are added to those mentioned explicitly in Numbers 33, two things emerge from this tabulation of the stations. First, there is a tendency for similar events to recur at the same point in the cycle. Second, some of the events occur at stations whose number may be symbolically significant. The second cycle of seven stations resembles the first quite noticeably.

1/8	Miracle: first-born's death/manna and quails
2–3/9–10	Unknown
4/11	Victory over Egyptians/Amalekites (Exod. 14; 17)
6/13	Abundant water/food (Exod. 15:27//Num. 11)
7/14	Miriam (Exod. 15:20//Num. 12)

In the fourth, fifth and sixth cycles, the sixth station Moseroth

(= Moserah, Deut. 10:6), Mount Hor, mountains of Abarim (before Nebo, Num. 33:47) are the scenes of Aaron and Moses' deaths. Marah, the site of the first water miracle, and Kadesh, site of the last provision, are both fifth in their respective cycles (Exod. 15:25; Num. 20:11).

Within the Bible the numbers 1, 3, 4, 7 and 12 are clearly recognized as specially significant. The way this table falls into 6 (3 × 2) panels with 7 members shows the importance of these numbers. Epoch-making events, the exodus and the manna, are associated with the 1st and the 8th (1 + 7) stations (Exod. 12:2; 16:35). One wonders whether it is just coincidence that after the fourth station the Red Sea was crossed, and that at the twelfth station the law was given. Twelve is the number of election (12 tribes, 12 apostles, 144,000 [12^2 × 1000] saints in heaven, Rev. 14:1), and in the covenant of Sinai Israel's election as God's holy people was sealed (Exod. 19:5–6).

What is the point of this arrangement of the place-names? As I argued above,[66] the use of symbolic numbers does not necessarily mean they are artificial: similarly, symbolism in ritual does not imply the rites never take place. But the use of symbolism enhances the significance of the events and draws attention to them: there is more to such events or rituals than at first appears. The text does not answer our question directly, but, given the incorporation of chapter 33 into Numbers, certain conclusions seem quite plausible.

Experiences on the journeys from Sinai to Kadesh, and Kadesh to the plains of Moab (11 – 12; 20 – 21) echo those on the journey from the Red Sea to Sinai (Exod. 13 – 19). The events and lawgiving in the plains of Moab parallel those at Sinai (Num. 22 – 30; Exod. 19 – Num. 10). The reluctance of the tribes of Reuben and Gad to enter the promised land is compared to the spies discouraging the people at Kadesh (Num. 32; 13 – 14).

This list of stations expresses the typology[67] of divine action more briefly, though more powerfully, in its sixfold repetition of events. By the listing of particular events at appropriate points in the cycle, the reader is reminded of the special importance of the crossing of

---

66. Additional note on the large numbers, pp. 68ff.
67. See Introduction, 2. Structure, pp. 16ff.

the Red Sea and the lawgiving at Sinai, while the unknown places, like those men remembered only for their inclusion in a family tree, receive recognition as sites where God's eternal purposes were worked out. Though from a human point of view nothing memorable may have happened at Dophkah or Alush, these are recorded as places where the hosts of Israel, the LORD's army, marched through on their way to the promised land.

2. *Moses wrote down … their stages.* Though most of the contents of Numbers claims to have been mediated by Moses, this is the only section that he is said to have written down himself. Davies[68] suggests that the earliest form of the list may have simply listed the stopping-places in order. He observes that the present basic formula in the list

'They set out from X and encamped at Y,

they set out from Y and encamped at Z'

corresponds more closely to the style found in Assyrian annals of the ninth century BC than to any other known records of the ancient Near East. The adoption of the formula here is designed to emphasize that the people of Israel marched as an army under the ommand of the LORD, their divine king (cf. Num. 1 – 2). This theological interpretation is no doubt correct, even if the observations about the earliest form of the narrative must remain conjectural.

3–5	cf. Exod. 12:37	17	cf. Num. 11:35
6	cf. Exod. 13:20	31–33	cf. Deut. 10:6–7
7–8	cf. Exod. 14:2ff.	36	cf. Num. 20:1
8	cf. Exod. 15:22ff.	37–39	cf. Num. 20:22–29
9	cf. Exod. 15:27	40	cf. Num. 21:1–3
10–12	cf. Exod. 16:1	41	cf. Num. 21:4
14	cf. Exod. 17:1	43	cf. Num. 21:10
15	cf. Exod. 19:2	44	cf. Num. 21:11
16	cf. Num. 10:33ff.	48	cf. Num. 22:1

68. G. I. Davies, 'The Wilderness Itineraries', *TB*, 25, 1974, pp. 46–81.

Additional note on the route of the Israelites

Numbers 33 presents an apparently straightforward list of the places
at which the Israelites camped on their way from Rameses in Egypt
to Abel-shittim in the plains of Moab. Moreover verse 2 states that
Moses wrote down their starting places, stage by stage, a strong claim to the
antiquity and reliability of this itinerary at least.[69] The ordinary
Bible reader may be forgiven for supposing that there is little difficulty in knowing exactly which route the Israelites followed on their
wanderings. His convictions will be enhanced by the clearly marked
routes and precisely identified town sites found in atlases of the Holy
Land. But in fact the problems of the place of the exodus, the location of Sinai and the subsequent wanderings are some of the most
intractable that are faced by biblical scholars.

There are two principal causes for our predicament. First, place-
names survive only if there is a continuity of settlement at the
places concerned. Even then there may be changes of name for social, political or religious reasons (e.g. 32:38; Gen. 28:19; Judg. 18:29).
And if a name has survived from biblical times to the present, it can
often have become attached to a different place. Old Testament Jericho is now called Tell es-Sultan: the name Jericho survives in the
Arab town (er-Riḥa), not far from the ancient mound. But in the case
of Arad and Heshbon (Num. 21:1, 26) there are no remains of the
conquest period at the modern sites bearing these names, and it looks
as though the biblical sites must have been elsewhere. In the wilderness the problems are compounded. The inhabitants have been
fewer and more mobile and there is very little assurance of the biblical names having been preserved at all, let alone always attached to
the correct site. And there is always the suspicion that when a bib-
lical-sounding name is found, it may not rest on ancient tradition but
have been coined by a local trying to help a pilgrim searching for the
holy sites.

The second major problem in identifying the sites is created by the
critical theories about the composition of the Pentateuch. It is generally held that three main sources, J, E, P, lie behind Genesis to

---

69. For the meaning of this phrase see commentary.

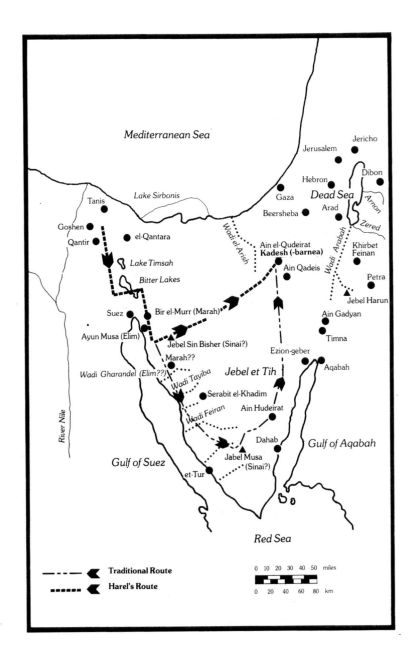

The route of the Israelites from Goshen to Kadesh (Num. 33)

Numbers, and that on many issues including the route of the wilderness wanderings these sources disagree. Thus though Exodus 13:17 (E) says that God did not lead the Israelites along the coast road from Egypt to Canaan, 'the way of the Philistines', several eminent scholars have argued that this was indeed the way another source (P) supposes they went. This is based on identifying Pihahiroth, Migdol and Baal-zephon with places near the north-eastern coast of Egypt, and supposing the Red Sea (Sea of Reeds) to be identical with Lake Sirbonis. When it comes to Numbers 33 it is generally held that it is a very late composition, based on the late P-itinerary notes scattered through Exodus and Numbers and an old pilgrimage route to Sinai. According to Noth and Koenig this route led from the head of the Gulf of Aqabah down into Arabia.[70] This evaluation of Numbers 33 has recently been strongly challenged by Davies,[71] who holds that, when shorn of various later additions, the chapter does represent a genuine itinerary from Egypt to the plains of Moab. However, in attempting to identify the names on the route, Davies too feels compelled to ignore most the stories associated with the places in Exodus and Numbers, because he holds that the narratives did not originally belong with the place-name. For example, Marah, where Moses sweetened the bitter water, cannot be located by looking for bitter wells in the Sinai peninsula, because the story originally had nothing to do with the place named Marah. The Marah story and the place-name come from different sources.

Now the first set of problems caused by the lack of continuous settlement in Sinai cannot be avoided. It will always make any of our identifications at best tentative. However, it seems to me that the problems caused by source criticism have been exaggerated, and that the method of approach practised by Simons[72] is logically superior.

---

70. M. Noth, 'Der Wallfahrtsweg zum Sinai', *Palästinajahrbuch*, 36, 1940, pp. 5–28; Noth, pp. 245–246. J. Koenig, 'La localisation du Sinaï et les traditions des scribes', *Revue d'histoire et de philosophie religieuses*, 43, 1963, pp. 2–31 and 44, 1964, pp. 200–235.

71. G. I. Davies, *The Way of the Wilderness* (CUP, 1979), pp. 56ff.

72. J. Simons, *The Geographical and Topographical Texts of the Old Testament* (Brill, 1959), pp. 234ff.

He argues that since so many of the identifications are tentative, it is more economical to look for one coherent route. Even if the different putative sources did have different views about the route of the exodus, it is reasonable to suppose that the final editor of the material supposed all the data he presented fitted a single coherent route. We should work on the assumption that there was one route, and adopt the hypothesis of multiple routes only if we have irrefragable evidence that the places named cannot fit a single itinerary.

In the discussion that follows I shall, therefore, draw heavily on the work of Simons and Harel,[73] who adopt this method, modifying their conclusions where necessary in the light of the more recent studies of Davies. To make for clarity I shall avoid constantly reminding the reader of the very hypothetical nature of the proposed identifications, but their uncertainty must be borne in mind. We do not know for sure where the Israelites crossed the Red Sea, received the law, or ate the manna. From a theological point of view, this uncertainty is of no greater moment than that surrounding the site of Calvary or the ascension. That these things happened is vital: to know where they occurred may provide food for thought, but is not of the essence of our faith.

The journey from Goshen to the plains of Moab falls into four main sections: Goshen to the Red Sea, the Red Sea to Mount Sinai, Sinai to Kadesh, Kadesh to Moab. The first and last sections of the journey can be traced with some confidence, but the two sections covering the Red Sea to Kadesh are very uncertain. We shall consider each section of the itinerary in turn, pausing to examine in more detail the locations of the Red Sea, Sinai and Kadesh.

a. From Goshen to the Red Sea (3–8)

Goshen (Gen. 47:27; Exod. 8:22), the area of Israelite settlement in Egypt, lay on the eastern edge of the Nile delta. This fits in with their point of departure being Rameses (Exod. 12:37; Num. 33:5), a city in the eastern delta generally identified with Qantir or Tanis (San el-Hajar). From Rameses the Israelites journeyed to Succoth and

---

73. M. Harel, *Masei Sinai* (Tel Aviv: Am Oved, 1968).

Etham (Exod. 12:37; 13:20; Num. 33:5–6), probably situated in Wadi Tumilat between Lake Timsah and the Bitter Lakes. In other words, they travelled southeast from Goshen towards the desert.

They were then told to 'turn back' and encamp in front of Pihahiroth, between Migdol and the sea, in front of Baal-zephon (Exod. 14:2; Num. 33:7). Egyptian texts mention a Migdol and a Baal-zephon close to Wadi Tumilat, but do not allow them to be located more precisely. However, the 'turning back' of the Israelites gives a clue to their route. Instead of continuing east straight toward the desert they altered direction, most probably southwards, as heading north or west would have brought them closer to the Egyptians. This brought them alongside the Bitter Lakes, where the Egyptians caught up with them and trapped them along the lakeside. However, the Israelites were enabled by a heaven-sent east wind to pass through the lake during the night (Exod. 14:21–22; Num. 33:8). Before the Suez canal was dug there was a shallow stretch of water about 2 miles wide that could be forded. It seems most likely that Israel crossed the Red Sea at this point.

In English the Red Sea designates the open sea separating Africa from Arabia. However, the Hebrew words *yam sûp*, traditionally translated Red Sea, could more literally be rendered 'sea of reeds'; this has been appealed to in support of the idea that Israel crossed an inland lake, not part of the Red Sea. However, since in some passages *yam sûp* does unambiguously refer to the Gulf of Aqabah (the north-eastern branch of the Red Sea), this argument is fallacious (e.g. Exod. 23:31; Deut. 1:40). It seems more likely that in ancient times the Bitter Lakes were directly connected with the Red Sea: this would only require a lowering of the land by about 6 feet (2 m). Alternatively, one may suppose the term *yam sûp* was used in a wider sense than our term, Red Sea, and included the inland Bitter Lakes adjacent to it.

b. From the Red Sea to Sinai (8–15)

Opinions differ as to the route followed after the Red Sea crossing. It all depends where Sinai is to be located. As Davies has shown, there is only one ancient tradition and this identifies Jebel Musa (Mount Moses) with Mount Sinai. The earliest certain identification of Jebel Musa with Mount Sinai is found in Christian writings of the late fourth century AD, but Davies[74] thinks that Jews may have already made the equation two centuries earlier.

Assuming that Sinai is to be located in the south of the peninsula, Simons[75] and Davies[76] make the following suggestions about the intermediate stopping-places. Marah (Exod. 15:23; Num. 33:8–9) with Ain Hawarah, Elim (Exod. 15:27; Num. 33:9–10) with Wadi Gharandel, the camp by the Red Sea with the plain of el-Marhah (Simons), or with Wadi Tayiba (Davies). Simons also tries to identify the other places mentioned before the arrival at Sinai with places in the vicinity, but Davies reckons they are quite uncertain.

Since some fifteen hundred years separate the events of Sinai from the traditions locating the mountain in the south of the peninsula, modern scholars have looked for other sites that fit the biblical accounts more satisfactorily. Questions raised by identifying Sinai with Jebel Musa include the following: Why is it described as being only three days' journey from Egypt (Exod. 5:3; 8:27, etc.)? Why did they complain of a lack of fish, when southern Sinai is good for fishing (Num. 11:5)? How could Sinai have supported so many people, even with the miraculous provision of manna, when in 1937 the south of the peninsula supported only 1,400 people? Why journeying south from the Bitter Lakes did the Israelites not stop at Ayun Musa where there is plenty of water, but press on to Ain Hawarah whose sources are much poorer? Why single out one camping site as beside the Red Sea, when according to the southern hypothesis much of the route lay along the coastal plain? For these and other reasons, other sites for Mount Sinai have been proposed. Some have favoured a site in Arabia, believing that Mount Sinai must have been a volcano. Others, that it was near Kadesh. These proposals are incompatible with the clear statements that Sinai is 3 days' distance from Egypt and 11 days from Kadesh-barnea (Exod. 3:18; Deut. 1:2).

The proposal of Harel[77] to identify Sinai with Jebel Sin Bisher,

---

74. Davies, *The Way of the Wilderness*, p. 24.

75. Simons, *Geographical Texts*, pp. 251–253.

76. Davies, *The Way of the Wilderness*, pp. 83–84.

77. Harel, *Masei Sinai*, pp. 224ff.

about 30 miles (50 km) south-west of Suez, has more to commend it. Not only does it meet the objections that the other suggestions face, it lends itself to appropriate identifications for the camps mentioned between the Red Sea and Kadesh. Marah (Exod. 15:23; Num. 33:8) Harel equates with Bir el-Murr, 9 miles (14 km) east of Suez, 25 miles (40 km) from the crossing-point, a place with a salty well. Elim (Exod. 15:27; Num. 33:9) he identifies with Ayun Musa; today it has twelve wells and a palm grove, and would have been a likely place for them to stay a good while (Exod. 16:1). The next point that Harel thinks can be identified is Rephidim (Exod. 17:1; Num. 33:14). There the Israelites suffered from lack of water and fought the Amalekites. The shortage of water resulted from the Israelites leaving the coastal plain and moving inland towards the et-Tih desert. In the north-eastern corner of the et-Tih plateau there is good pasture-land, which would explain its attraction to the Amalekites and why they attacked Israel attempting to move into the area.

Israel's victory at Rephidim enabled them to move into the wilderness of Sinai (Exod. 19:2; Num. 33:15) which Harel identifies with Wadi Sudr, a meeting-point of several important trade routes in northern Sinai well supplied with water and pasturage and even a little arable land. This would have been a suitable place for the tribes to have lived for a year or so (Exod. 19:1; Num. 10:11). There in the middle of the plain stands the isolated peak of Jebel Sin Bisher (1900 ft, 618 m high, 300 m above the plain), whose name could mean 'heralding of the law' or 'the laws of man'.

Davies[78] rejects Harel's identification for the following reasons. First, it is difficult to fit seven stages between Marah and Sinai (Num. 33:9–16), a distance of some 30 miles, even supposing that the Israelites with all their cattle and baggage travelled only a short distance each day. However, it must be said that Davies' estimates of the Israelites' pace of travel are certainly too high. If Marah is located at Ain Hawarah, and Sinai identified with Jebel Musa, the seven stages from Marah to Sinai cover about 85 miles, whereas the three-

78. Davies, *The Way of the Wilderness*, pp. 67–69.

day journey from the Red Sea to Marah is about 70 miles. Bedouin moving camp cover about 6 miles a day.[79]

Secondly, Davies objects to Harel's appeals to the dew mentioned in Exodus 16:13, and to the long time they spent at Sinai as clues to locating these places, holding that these remarks come from the late source P. He admits that the strongest argument in favour of Harel's position is the repeated remark that the mountain of God is close to Egypt (Exod. 3:1; 4:27), apparently just 3 days' march from the border (Exod. 3:18; 8:27). Again Davies supposes that we are dealing with different sources. One source located the mountain of God near the Egyptian border, another placed Sinai in the south of the peninsula.

Davies' objections are not compelling, first, because Exodus 3:1 identifies Horeb with the mountain of God, and Davies accepts the identity of Horeb and Sinai. Secondly, even if it is held that we are dealing with a multiplicity of sources with potentially different views about the location of the various events, the sources have been combined by an editor who thought they made good sense. It may be that he did not have the finesse of a modern geographer, but it appears certain that he identified the mountain of God with Sinai (Exod. 18:5; 24:13; cf. 16; Num. 10:33). Thus, although it may be argued that Harel's scheme does not fit the data of the earliest sources, it can still claim to represent the pentateuchal editor's understanding of the route of the wanderings.

c. From Sinai to Kadesh (16–36)
Numbers 10:33 – 13:25 mentions only three stopping-places between the mountain of the LORD and Kadesh in the wilderness of Paran, Taberah, Kibroth-hattaavah and Hazeroth (11:3, 34–35), whereas Numbers 33:16–36 mentions twenty-two stages beginning with the wilderness of Sinai and ending 'with the wilderness of Zin (that is Kadesh)'. Apart from the points of departure and arrival, the only correspondences between these

---

79. Harel, *Masei Sinai*, p. 111. Harel reckons the three days from Egypt to Sinai and the eleven days from Sinai to Kadesh represent optimal marching times, not actual camp stages.

itineraries are Kibroth-hattaavah and Hazeroth (11:34–35; 33:16–17).

On the traditional southern location of Sinai, Hazeroth can be identified with Ain Hudeirat, north-east of Jebel Musa. Ezion-geber lies at the head of the Gulf of Aqabah (Num. 33:35–36), and Kadesh at or near Ain Qadeis, roughly half-way between Ezion-geber and the Mediterranean. The other camping sites cannot be identified.[80]

If Sinai is identified with Jebel Sin Bisher, there is again only one place between Sinai and Ezion-geber for which a plausible location may be suggested: Rithmah (Num. 33:18) could be Ain Rathmah 13 miles (20 km) east of Jebel Sin Bisher. However, Harel[81] prefers to rely on the more explicit statements of Numbers 11 – 13 and Deuteronomy 1:19 which speak of Israel passing through 'a great and terrible wilderness' between Sinai and Kadesh-barnea. This description suits the area between Sin Bisher and Kadesh, identified by Harel with the desert of Paran, which is covered with gravel and contains little vegetation and scant supplies of water. It would have been natural for Israel to hurry through this area, making as few encampments as possible. The chronological data in Numbers 10:11 and 13:20, 25 would suggest they took about thirty days (of which seven were spent at Hazeroth, 12:15) to cover some 120 miles (200 km).[82] Harel reckons that the other camping stations mentioned in Numbers 33 indicate places the tribes camped at during their thirty-eight years of wandering.

d. From Kadesh To Moab (37–49)

According to the biblical chronology (33:38) nearly forty years elapsed between the Israelites' arrival in Kadesh and their final departure. Numbers 14:25 mentions that they first left Kadesh to

---

80. Davies, pp. 87–89 has rebutted the Noth-Koenig hypothesis which located many of these sites in Arabia.

81. *Masei Sinai*, pp. 277–279.

82. Departure from Sinai on 20th of second month (Num. 10:11) + 30 days' journey (Sinai to Kadesh) + 40 days' spying (Num. 13:25) = beginning of fifth month (time of first grapes at Hebron [Num. 13:20]).

begin their wanderings shortly after the spies' return. However, since Ain Qadeis and Ain Qudeirat have the most abundant springs in the Sinai peninsula, it is generally assumed that the tribes returned there periodically, and that it was on one of their subsequent visits that they set out to go round Edom (20:21; 21:4). Their first encampment after Kadesh was Mount Hor (20:22; 33:37), by old tradition identified with Jebel Harun near Petra. But if Kadesh in the wilderness of Zin is to be identified with Ain Qadeis, as is almost universally done, then a site west of the Arabah must be found for Mount Hor. The other site confidently located is Punon = Feinan, some 30 miles (50 km) south of the Dead Sea. This would imply that Israel travelled more or less due east from Mount Hor[83] till they reached Punon, where they turned north keeping a little to the east of the fertile hills of Edom and Moab.

More precision is impossible. Only the rivers Zered and Arnon which flow into the Dead Sea can be positively identified (21:12–13). Dibon-gad (33:45) is probably modern Diban. 'The mountains of Abarim' (33:47) are the hills overlooking the Dead Sea. The final encampment of Israel was in the Jordan valley opposite Jericho. 33:49 is more specific saying 'they encamped by the Jordan from Beth-jeshimoth as far as Abel-shittim', but it is difficult to be sure which sites in the valley immediately north of the Dead Sea are meant.

G. Laws about land (33:50 – 36:13)

i. **Occupation of the land (33:50–56).** The whole book of Numbers looks forward to Israel's settlement of the promised land. It is, therefore, highly appropriate that it closes with six laws dealing explicitly with the theme of the occupation of Canaan.

33:50–56 demands the extirpation of the Canaanites and their religion.

34:1–15 fixes the boundaries of the promised land.

---

83. If Mount Hor is located at Jebel Harun, Num. 33:36–49 describes an Israelite advance northwards from Ezion-geber at the head of the Gulf of Aqabah along the high ground east of the Arabah and Dead Sea.

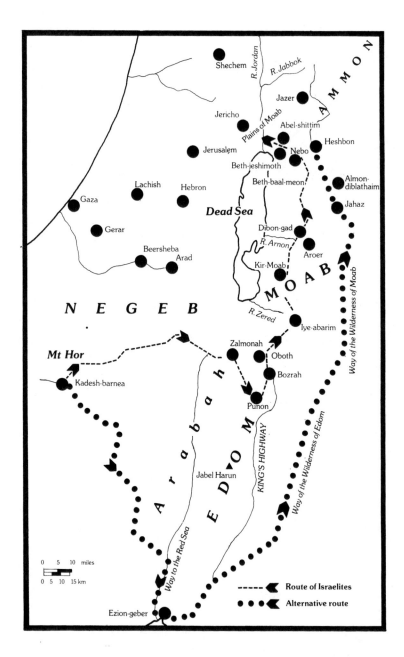

The conquest of Transjordan (Num. 33)

34:16–29 names the men who will distribute it.

35:1–8 appoints cities for the Levites in the land.

35:9–34 shows how the land is to be purified from blood guilt.

36:1–12 rules that the tribal lands must not be transferred between tribes. They are to be held in perpetuity.

These laws, like others in the book, are more than pure legal enactments, they are implicit promises. God is in effect pledging that he will give his people victory over their enemies (ch. 33), a huge land (ch. 34) made holy by the dwelling of the Levites and God himself within it (ch. 35), that they will hold for ever (ch. 36). Its careful arrangement in two groups of three laws,[84] a regular device in pentateuchal law, gives the book a well-rounded conclusion consonant with the importance of its theme.

50–53. In phrases typical of Deuteronomy (cf. ch. 7) the destruction of the natives of Canaan and their religion is commanded. But this theme is found in all the main blocks of pentateuchal law (Exod. 23:23ff.; 34:11ff.; Lev. 20). For a discussion of the theological problems raised by this policy, see commentary on ch. 31. Christian commentators have often drawn parallels between Israel's war against pagan religion and the Christian's call to subdue the vices of the old Adam in himself (cf. Rom. 6; Col. 3).

54. cf. 26:52–56.

55–56. Warnings of the failure to obey God's directions run through the Pentateuch. This is mild compared with many, perhaps drawing attention to the basically promissory nature of these laws (cf. Lev. 26; Deut. 28). *Pricks in your eyes and thorns in your sides*: Joshua alluded to this warning in his farewell speech (Josh. 23:13).

ii. The boundaries of Canaan (34:1–15). Appropriately at this point in the story the limits of the promised land of Canaan are defined. Canaan was a recognized geographical entity from the 15th century BC onwards and is mentioned frequently in texts from

---

84. Note the standard introduction, *The LORD said to Moses*, in 33:50; 34:1, 16; 35:1, 9; cf. 36:6, and the expansion, *in the plains of Moab by the Jordan at Jericho* (33:50; 35:1; 36:13), as title and colophon. On the grouping of laws in multiples of three cf. Lev. 1 – 7 and Deut. 22:13–29 and see G. J. Wenham and J. G. McConville, *VT*, 30, 1980, pp. 248–252.

Egypt of the following centuries, a period it was under nominal Egyptian control. These extra-biblical texts do not spell out the boundaries of Canaan as this chapter does, but they evidently presuppose much the same limits to Canaan as the Bible.[85] As usual, not all the place-names mentioned can be confidently located, but enough are sufficiently probable to allow a map of Canaan's borders to be drawn. See map on p. 260.

1–5. The southern border runs from the Dead Sea, up the ascent of Akrabbim (literally 'scorpions'), possibly Naqb es-Safa, through the wilderness of Zin (cf. 13:21; 20:1; 33:36), south of Kadesh-barnea (Ain el Qudeirat or Ain Qadeis) (32:8). Hazar-addar and Azmon cannot be positively identified, but must lie between Kadesh-barnea and the Brook of Egypt (Wadi el-Arish).

6. The western border was the Mediterranean sea.

7–9. The only points on the northern border that can be positively identified are *Lebo-Hamath* (13:21), probably modern Lebweh, and *Zedad* which can be equated with Sedad. Mount Hor, to be distinguished from the Mount Hor near Kadesh (20:22–27; 33:37–38), must lie somewhere between Lebo-Hamath and the sea, while Ziphron and Hazar-enan must lie east of Zedad, possibly Hawwarin and Qaryatein.

10–15. The eastern border until it reaches the eastern slopes of the sea of Galilee (*the shoulder of the sea of Chinnereth*) is quite problematic: Shepham, Riblah and Ain cannot be located. After that it follows the Jordan valley down to the Dead Sea. The land occupied by the tribes of Gad, Reuben and Manasseh therefore lay outside Canaan (13–15).

Nevertheless Canaan as defined here is a much larger area than ever Israel settled. David controlled most of Canaan and much of Transjordan as well, but the land defined here does not correspond to Israel's actual boundaries at any time in her history. The land described here is therefore an ideal, the territory promised by God to the people of Israel, but never fully occupied by them. But the fact

---

85. Y. Aharoni, *The Land of the Bible* (Burns and Oates, 1966), pp. 61–70; R. de Vaux, 'Le Pays de Canaan', *JAOS*, 88, 1968, pp. 23–30; M. Weippert, *IDBS*, p. 126.

that the land as defined here in Numbers 34 does correspond to the
geographical entity of Canaan as known from Egyptian texts of the
14th–13th centuries BC is a clear sign of the antiquity of this section.[86]

The size of the land and Israel's inability to occupy it all remind
us of God's liberality 'who is able to do far more abundantly than
all that we ask or think' (Eph. 3:20; cf. Rom. 8:32; Jas 1:5).

iii. Distributors of the land appointed (34:16–29). The importance of their task is underlined by their being nominated directly
by God (16; cf. 1:5). Just ten tribal leaders are mentioned here, as Gad
and Reuben had already settled in Transjordan. The names (cf. 1:5–
15) are archaic, but only Caleb (19; cf. 13:6, 30, etc.) is mentioned elsewhere. The tribes are listed in rough order of their settlements, beginning with Judah and Simeon in the south and ending with Asher
and Naphtali in the north (cf. Josh. 14 – 19).

iv. Cities for the Levites (35:1–8). Directions about the Levites
regularly follow directions about the other tribes (cf. 1:47–54 after
1:1–46; 3:1–49 after ch. 2; 26:57–62 after 26:1–56. So here, after the
remarks in chapter 34 about the allocation of land to the other tribes,
the tribe of Levi is dealt with. The importance of the priests and
Levites is repeatedly stressed in Numbers, and the other tribes' ob-
ligation to support them is set out fully in chapter 18. There the laity
were enjoined to give a tithe of all their produce to the Levites
(18:21–24), here they are instructed to set aside a few cities, proportionate to the land holdings of the various tribes (8). Even with
the surrounding pasture-lands for the cattle, the total area assigned
to the Levites came to 15 square miles (40 km²), about 0.1% of the
land of Canaan. In a society where farm-land was wealth, this

---

86. Aharoni, *Land of the Bible*, p. 69, says 'the biblical description matches
perfectly the boundaries of the Egyptian district of Canaan during the
second half of the thirteenth century. This is one of those most
instructive examples of ancient sources being preserved among the
geographical texts of the Bible, because we have here a document that
makes no sense whatever in later periods.' Similarly de Vaux, *JAOS*, 88, p.
29: 'Num. 34:2–12 ... preserves the memory of what Canaan signified for
the Israelites in the period of settlement: it was Canaan of the Egyptians.'

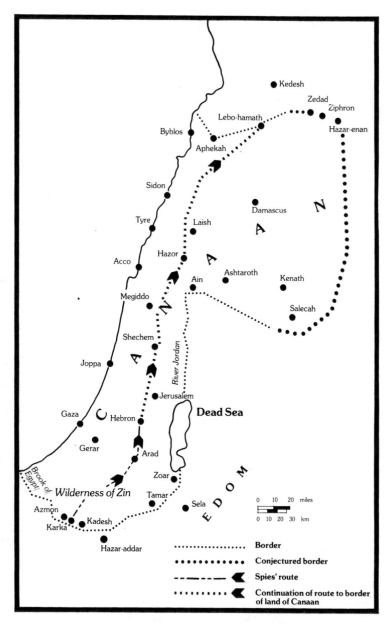

The borders of Canaan and the mission of the spies
(Num. 34:1–12)

minute fraction of the land meant that the Levites would still be dependent on the generosity of the secular tribes among whom they lived. Relative to the other tribes it could still be said of the Levites that they had 'no inheritance in their land' (18:20, 23f.).

1–5. The dimensions of the pasture-lands has exercised the geometrical ingenuity of commentators for centuries. Verse 4 apparently prescribes that the pasture-lands should have a depth of 1000 cubits (500 yards/450 m) from the city wall, whereas the total area of pasture-lands should be a square 2000 × 2000 cubits, according to verse 5. These requirements can be met only if the city is of negligible dimensions.

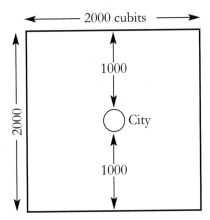

The idea that the city was very small is not so absurd as many commentators suppose. Settlements in biblical times were very small. Large towns such as Jerusalem covered a few acres until late monarchy times. Most of the levitical cities were like hamlets, probably just a few small houses grouped together: only a few of those mentioned in Joshua 21 were major centres.

It is impossible to be sure what was done when the cities grew, but the most probable suggestion is that the city was squared and the thousand cubits then added on, so that the overall dimensions of the pasture-land were a bit more than 2000 cubits square.[87]

---

87. This is M. Greenberg's solution based on tannaitic rules (2nd century
    AD) for determining the distance one could travel from a town on the

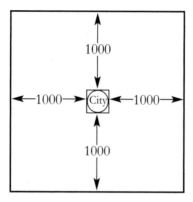

6–8. The forty-eight cities are listed in Joshua 21. Note the symbolic number 48 = 4 × 12. Keil[88] suggests that four symbolizes the kingdom of God, and that the Levites were distributed among Israel to remind them of their calling to be the holy people of God (Exod. 19:5–6; Lev. 10:11; Deut. 33:9–10).

v. The cities of refuge (35:9–34). Canaan is more than the promised land: it is the holy land sanctified by the presence of God living among his people (34; cf. Lev. 26:11–12). It is therefore of the utmost importance to keep this land pure especially from the most potent pollution of shed blood. It is paradoxical that in the right place blood is the most effective purifier, the only means of atonement between God and man, but in the wrong context it has precisely the opposite effect:[89] *for blood pollutes the land* (33; cf. Deut. 19:10; 21:9, 23).

Since the holy God cannot live in a polluted land without judging its inhabitants, Israel must take special care to preserve the purity of the land by dealing with blood guilt whenever it occurs. Blood guilt is singled out for special attention because the pollution it causes is the most serious. In other words this section is placed here

---

sabbath in 'Idealism and Practicality in Num. 35:4–5 and Ezk. 48', *JAOS*, 88, 1968, pp. 59–66. A basically similar solution was offered by Michaelis quoted by Keil, pp. 259–260.

88. Keil, pp. 260–261.

89. See commentary on chapter 19.

not merely because some of the levitical cities were cities of refuge (6), but because homicide could have such a disastrous effect on Israel's tenure of the promised land. The notion that the murderer must be executed because man is made in the image of God runs through all the biblical law (Gen. 9:5–6; Exod. 21:12–14, 28–32; Deut. 19:1–13; 21:1–9), but it is Numbers and Deuteronomy which focus most clearly on the effect on the land if homicide is not atoned for.

This law is concerned with regulating the existing customs for avenging murder to prevent the pollution of the land. When a man was killed, it was the duty of his nearest male relative, *the avenger of blood* (12, 19, 21, 24, 25, 27), to kill the man responsible. In other contexts the Hebrew word *gōʾēl* is translated 'redeemer' or 'kinsman', as he is the one who should 'buy' his relative out of trouble (5:8; Lev. 25:25–26; Ruth 3:12; 4:1, 6, 8; Job 19:25; Isa. 59:20). It is generally supposed that the avenger of blood used to have the right to kill a manslayer, whether or not the killing was deliberate. This law carefully distinguishes between deliberate murder and accidental manslaughter, permitting the execution only in the former case (16–28). Other ancient Near Eastern law permitted composition, that is payment of a ransom in place of the death penalty.[90] However, this law insists that no monetary composition is possible. Murderers must be executed and manslaughterers must dwell in a city of refuge until the death of the high priest (28). This is a good example of a punishment designed to fit the crime. The murderer who took life deliberately is deliberately put to death himself. The manslaughterer who took life by chance (Exod. 21:13) must await the chance of the high priest's death before he can be released from the city of refuge.[91]

The law's prime concern is the provision of cities of refuge for manslaughterers (15), but it moves to consider related issues. First, who qualifies for admission (16–25), then what happens if he leaves the city before the high priest's death (26–28), the evidence required for a conviction of murder (30), and the prohibition of ransom (31–32).

---

90. Hittite Laws 1–5 (*ANET*, p. 189). Composition in place of the death penalty was however permitted in Exod. 21:30. Prov. 6:35 implies adulterers could offer a ransom to save themselves from execution.

91. Saalschütz, p. 535.

9–14. The six cities chosen as cities of refuge are named else-where, Bezer, Ramoth-gilead and Golan in Transjordan, and Hebron, Shechem and Kedesh in Canaan: they were all levitical cities as well (Deut. 4:43; Josh. 20:7–8; 21:13, 21, 27, 32, 36, 38).

15. Like other important rules this law applied to all the inhab-itants of the land, strangers and sojourners, not just to native Israelites (9:14; 15:15; 19:10; Lev. 16:29; 17:8, 15; 18:26; 20:2; 24:16, etc.).

16–21. Various examples defining murder are given. Where there is clear evidence of premeditation,[92] the man is to be convicted of murder and therefore put to death. The type of weapon used is proof of murderous intent, such as an iron tool or a stone or wooden tool with a handle[93] (16–18). The weapon used is, however, irrelevant where the murderer is known to have hated his victim be-forehand: just a punch that leads to death is murder when there is evidence of pre-existing enmity (21).

22–23. If, however, a man is killed accidentally (e.g. Deut. 19:5) or in a sudden brawl, this does not count as murder. Even throwing a potentially lethal stone is not to be construed as murder where the man did not see his victim and was known to be on good terms with him (23).

24–34. Whatever the circumstances of the killing, the man-slayer was expected to flee to the nearest city of refuge, to which

---

92. The stress placed by the texts on evidence of preparation and advance planning and previous hatred (cf. Deut. 19:11) makes it probable that premeditation is the key factor differentiating murder and manslaughter in the biblical texts, rather than the slightly broader principle of intention. In the fury of a sudden brawl the participants may intend to kill each other, but according to Num. 35:22 death would not count as murder unless the fight was part of a long-standing feud. So, B. S. Jackson, *Essays in Jewish and Comparative Legal History* (Brill, 1975), p. 91; cf. Saalschütz, pp. 529–534. For the view that intention not premeditation is the guiding principle see A. Phillips, *JJS*, 28, 1977, p. 114.

93. Literally 'stone of a hand(le)', 'wood of a hand(le)', *yād* means 'hand' or 'handle'. Most commentators and translations suppose *yād* means 'hand' here, but Saalschütz's suggestion, p. 527, n. 650 fits the context better.

he would be admitted if his case seemed plausible to the elders of
the city (Josh. 20:4). However, his trial took place before the *congregation*, a group representing all Israel (cf. above on 10:3; 14:10).
This may well have been held outside the city of refuge, as verse 25
speaks of returning him to his city of refuge. It was the congregation's job to decide whether the killing was premeditated or not, *in
accordance with these ordinances*, by listening to the evidence of the accused, the avenger of blood and the elders of the city where the
death occurred (Deut. 19:12). Following standard oriental practice[94]
one witness was inadequate for conviction: at least two were required
(30; Deut. 19:15). If the man was convicted of murder he was
delivered to the avenger of blood to kill (Deut. 19:12), but if the
court decided it was just manslaughter he was sent back to the city
of refuge to live there until the death of the high priest (25, 28).
The cities of refuge thus had a twofold purpose: to protect uncon-
victed manslaughterers from the avenger of blood and to serve as
places of banishment for convicted manslaughterers. But the
banishment itself was not construed as making atonement for the
dead man's blood. Atonement for manslaughter came through the
death of the high priest. This is shown by the ban on ransom-
ing murderers and manslaughterers. Just as a murderer cannot buy
his life for money (31), so a manslaughterer cannot purchase freedom (32). Both have caused the death of another man, and only the
death of a man can atone for the killing. That it was the high priest's
death, not the exile of the manslaughterer, that atoned is confirmed
by the mishnaic dictate, 'If after the slayer has been sentenced
as an accidental homicide the high priest dies, he need not go into
exile' and the talmudic comment thereon, 'But is it not the exile that
expiates? It is not exile that expiates, but the death of the high
priest.'[95]

   This law reaffirms in judicial fashion the sanctity of human life (cf.
Gen. 9:5–6; Exod. 20:13). The commandment simply says 'Thou shalt

---

94. Note the plural in the laws of Hammurabi 5: 'they shall prove'; cf. laws
    9–11 (*ANET*, p. 166).
95. Makkoth 11b; cf. M. Greenberg. 'The Biblical Conception of Asylum',
    JBL, 78, 1959, pp. 125–132.

not kill'. The Hebrew *rāṣaḥ* 'kill' is used in this law both of murder and manslaughter (16, 25). Both incur blood guilt and pollute the land,[96] and both require atonement: murder by the execution of the murderer and manslaughter through the natural demise of the high priest.

So this law is a reminder of some of the great themes of Numbers. God walks in the midst of his people and they must therefore be preserved from all impurity, particularly that caused by death (cf. 5:1–4; 9:15–23; chs. 16 – 17; 19). In the task of protecting the people from sin and making atonement, the priests and Levites play the central role (cf. chs. 3 – 4; 18; 25). According to chapter 35, it is the Levites who are the permanent inhabitants of the cities of refuge and therefore responsible for admitting manslaughterers, and it is the death of the high priest that atones for manslaughter and allows the guilty man to return home. Thus the high priest of ancient Israel anticipated the ministry of our Lord, not only in his life of offering sacrifice and prayer on behalf of the people, but also in his death (cf. Heb. 4 – 9).

vi. Heiresses to marry within their tribes (36:1–13). In chapter 27 the daughters of Zelophehad raised the problem of their father's name dying out. Since he had no sons, his land would pass to other members of his family. The rules of inheritance were therefore altered to allow daughters to inherit if they had no brothers. But this raised another problem: when they married, the land would pass into their husband's family, and if he belonged to another tribe, out of their own tribe. This would upset the God-given allocations of land announced in 33:50 – 34:29.

1–12. The problem is raised by the heads of the family most closely concerned with the issue (1; cf. 27:1). The matter is referred to God, and Moses mediates the reply (5; cf. 27:5–6; cf. Lev. 24:12–13). The rules of inheritance enunciated earlier need no alteration, but a daughter of Zelophehad, indeed any girl inheriting land, must marry a man from her own tribe (6, 8). This will eliminate land transfers between the tribes and enable *every one of the people of Israel* to *cleave to the inheritance of the tribe of his fathers* (7). The repetition of this principle in verse 9 underlines its importance. The dutiful compliance of

---

96. 33–34. For other sins that pollute the land, cf. Lev. 18:25–28; Deut. 21:23; Isa. 24:5; Jer. 2:7; 3:1, 9, etc.

the daughters of Zelophehad is noted in 10–12. In the year of jubilee (4) land that had been bought returned to its original owner (Lev. 25:25ff.), but this would not apply to land transferred as a result of marriage.

13 (cf. 33:50; 35:1) marks the end of the section beginning in 33:50.

The resolution of the case of Zelophehad's daughters in chapter 27 was immediately followed by the command to Moses to appoint Joshua as his successor and ascend the mountain to die (27:12–21). An unusually brief note records the appointment of Joshua (27:22f.), but there has been no further mention of the death of Moses. A full description of the handover to Joshua, Moses' farewell to the nation, and an account of his death are the subject of Deuteronomy. The reappearance of these daughters of Zelophehad right at the end of Numbers reminds the reader that God's last command to Moses (27:12–13) awaits its fulfilment: obliquely they hint at a sequel to Numbers.

At the same time the story of Zelophehad's daughters does provide a fitting conclusion to the book of Numbers itself. The last group of six laws in Numbers 33:50 – 36:13 has been concerned with the land, its distribution, its extent and its holiness. Indeed, the whole story of Numbers has been one of movement towards the land of promise. The last judgment Moses gave concerns the land and asserts: *every one of the Israelites shall cleave to the inheritance of the tribe of his fathers* (36:7). Formally this is of course a statement of a legal principle forbidding the transfer of land from tribe to tribe, but theologically, like many of the laws in Numbers, it is a promise that the tribes of Israel will always dwell in their God-given land. In the words of Genesis 17:8, 'I will give to you, and to your descendants after you ... all the land of Canaan, for an everlasting possession; and I will be their God.' On this strong note of hope the book closes, inviting the curious to read on to see how God's purposes were worked out in the subsequent history of Israel.